W9-CHD-829

THEY WERE RAGTIME

THEY WERE RAGTIME

BY WARREN FORMA

GROSSET & DUNLAP
Publishers • New York
A FILMWAYS COMPANY

Copyright © 1976 by Forma Art Associates, Ltd.
All rights reserved
Published simultaneously in Canada
Library of Congress catalog card number: 76-23487
ISBN 0-448-12553-6 (hardcover edition)
ISBN 0-448-12569-2 (paperback edition)
First printing
Printed in the United States of America

The publishers are grateful for permission to quote from the following works:

Living My Life by Emma Goldman. 2 vols. New York: Alfred Knopf; Dover edition, 1931.

The Life and Times of Theodore Roosevelt by Stefan Lorant. Garden City, N.Y.: Doubleday and Company, 1959.

Pulitzer by W. A. Swanberg. New York: Charles Scribner's Sons, 1967.

Peary: The Explorer and the Man by John Edward Weems. Boston: Houghton Mifflin Company, 1967.

Ford: Expansion and Challenge by Allan Nevins and Frank Ernest Hill. New York: Charles Scribner's Sons, 1957.

BOOKS BY WARREN FORMA

Five British Sculptors Work and Talk
The Falling Man

TELEVISION DOCUMENTARIES BY WARREN FORMA

Images of Leonard Baskin
The Weapons of Gordon Parks
Shadows of the I.R.A.
Life, Liberty and the Pursuit of Happiness, a Celebration

This book is a work of love by many dedicated people. Harry and Meredith Collins of Brown Brothers in Pennsylvania pored through their seven million photographs to come up with just the picture needed in many a difficult case. P. James Roosevelt steered me to Dr. John Gable of the Theodore Roosevelt Association and on to Mr. Wallace F. Daily, curator of the Theodore Roosevelt Collection at the Harvard College Library in Cambridge, Massachusetts. Mr. Daily skipped lunch with me so that we could have more hours to pore over the thirty-five thousand pictures in the collection. For anyone with the slightest gift of ferocity toward scholarly pursuit, the Harvard Library is your jungle.

Lesser libraries but with major persons guiding one lovingly through their labyrinthian shelves were Larchmont Library, Mamaroneck Public Library and especially the ladies of the New Rochelle Public Library.

I thank New York City and Andrew Carnegie's ghost for the use of the Donnell Library, the Cathedral Branch Library and the Fortieth Street Public Library. The Forty-second Street Library was a special blessing to me, for without its research facilities many facts would have taken years to confirm.

Bernard Owett of the J. Walter Thompson Company was especially helpful in throwing open to me the library facilities of that company which contained books long out of print and unavailable to me from other sources. Also thanks to Trudy Owett for her aid as fashion editor of the *Ladies' Home Journal* in throwing light on the mores of the turn-of-the-century ladies.

ACKNOWLEDGMENTS

Thanks, too, to archivist Kenneth Cramer of the Dartmouth College Library in Hanover, New Hampshire, for his able advice on Saint-Gaudens and his work. Also, thanks to Mr. Cramer, we gained the assistance of the exuberant John Dryfhout, curator of the Saint-Gaudens Historic Site in Cornish, New Hampshire.

Also thanks to Suzanne Forma and Christy Smith for their constructive contributions. Special mention must be made of Donna Freeman who was in at the pre-beginning of the work but was not given an assignment as she was on another assignment when actual work began. However, she continued to send in research materials and suggestions throughout the project as she came upon them. My appreciation to Lorraine Lorber of Lorraine's Antiques of Larchmont for the use of her rare personal collection of books and memorabilia of the period.

A special blessing upon Mr. John Horn, former producer of the Edward R. Murrow show and TV critic of the *Herald Tribune*. His expertise on all aspects of the era was literally carried from his home in Brooklyn and dumped upon me weekly in the form of periodicals, rare articles and two-ton encyclopedias.

Especial thanks are due my chief researcher, Belle Forma, who outdid herself in Boston, Chicago and New Rochelle. Although she is also my wife, I listened to her and this book is the result. If I was unworthy of the task attempted, blame her. She thought I could do it.

I also thank my publisher for believing in me when the book was just a series of enthusiastic ideas on white paper. I never promised them a rose garden; I couldn't. I never knew where my characters would lead me until the close of the book. It was a learning experience for me and I am grateful for it. The project brought me in contact with Claire and Robert White at the old Stanford White estate, Box Hill. Stanford White had two sons but only one, Lawrence, survived childhood. Robert White, an artist/sculptor in the classical sense, is the son of Lawrence White. Claire, Robert's wife, is a fine writer and charming human being. But I also met and received much time and attention from Robert's mother, the widow of Lawrence White. Mrs. White, Laura, was seventeen when Stanford White met his death and remembers vividly that delightful human being. Mrs. White was a sculptor and still has a good eye for minute details in fading photographs in the family albums which my eye could hardly grasp. I talked with her friend who used to play with her on the lawn of Sagamore Hill but has since moved to Washington, D.C. She was charming and spry as I knew she'd be, although she's a few years older than Laura White. She asked me why people are so interested in the past and when I guessed it was because they were unhappy with the present, she pooh-poohed the idea and said with a laugh, "there's nothing wrong with the present." I knew then that Alice Roosevelt Longworth was still enjoying every minute of her life. I hope you are, too.

To my love, Belle.

History is the essence of innumerable biographies.   Thomas Carlyle

New York Journal, November, 10, 1905.

THEY WERE RAGTIME

You are a visual historian. Faintly, through the mist of the distant past, at the edge of our century, you see a cairn, a memorial or marker left from that era. But this cairn is not like those left by Robert Peary on his search for the North Pole, it is not a pile of cold rocks but a pyramid of human beings. From this distant view in time, it appears the pyramid has a fault running through it; it shakes. But you must remember, it's only human.

And so, tenderly, you begin to examine the parts of the form so that you may better understand the form itself, and in turn yourself and your society. The aim of your examination of their lives is to aid this and future generations in their pursuit of civilization.

Drift, float, eyes firmly shut, past two World Wars into a dimension of the past known as the turn-of-the-century. Quietly, a sleigh pulled by prancing black stallions glides through the snow-blanketed silence of Central Park. Through the swirling flakes, images of upturned faces, eyes wide, mouths agape, stare silently from the packed deck of a small steamer passing Bedloe's Island. Behind a misty tenement window, a twenty-three-year-old woman watches passively while her lover fuses a bundle of dynamite sticks. Stiff-backed men on horseback, in formal attire, are having dinner while another abandoned infant is found dead, in a refuse heap. The famous architect who brought so much beauty to his fellow man sits happily on the open-air roof garden atop the building he designed, and is shot three times in the head. Behind the dusty windows of an unventilated mill, an eight-year-old child labors ten hours a day, seven days a week, for two dollars, while a full-dress ball is given for a guest of honor who is a well-mannered monkey.

A bulbous-nosed aristocrat considered *nouveau riche* acquires a thousand million dollars, while a fifteen-year-old artist's model is lured into a velvet-dark studio and enticed to sit on a swing, billowing her ankle-length skirt. And the society to aid women announces that thirty percent of fallen women are bike riders. A Viennese Jew with a Vandyke beard arrives for a visit on these alien shores and announces there are two driving factors in life, the alleviation of pain and the pursuit of happiness.

According to Sigmund Freud, the purpose of life is simply the program of the pleasure principle. But, he continues, the regulations of the universe run counter to man's desire for happiness. When a situation desired by the pleasure principle is continued over a protracted period, it leads to mere contentment, or even ennui. Perhaps unhappiness is less difficult to achieve. There are three directions from which unhappiness threatens us. From within, our own body, doomed to decay. From without, the external world of nature raging against us. Last and far from least, our relations with other persons. Using these Freudian keys, we fall back in time, focusing our concern on the human relationships of the habitants who aided the birth of the twentieth century.

*April 5, 1892, the head of the financial committee for
the Washington Memorial Arch stands poised to
drive home the final block of marble. Directly behind
the mallet, Stanford White.*

caught by the copper nude atop the Spanish tower. The weather vane was over eighteen feet tall, too tall for the proportion of the tower. At his own expense White commissioned Saint-Gaudens to sculpt another Diana. Saint-Gaudens jumped at the chance. A workman had put a rod through her heel and he wanted her to stand on her toes, and

The thirteen-foot Diana, on her toes in the workshop before replacing her eighteen-foot clumsier sister who was being shipped to the World Columbian Exposition in Chicago.

In April of 1892 twenty men climbed to the top of the nearly completed Washington Arch. William Rhinelander Stewart carried a round wooden mallet. He wore striped trousers and formal jacket. A gold watch chain hung across his vest. All of the men wore hats, Stewart a top hat or tile. The man standing beside him raised his derby and rubbed his close-cropped reddish hair. He was the architect who had designed the arch. Behind them on the south side of Washington Square was Judson Memorial Church, by the same architect. Looking north, they could not help but see the Spanish tower of the Madison Square Garden. The *New York Sun* described it as the most beautiful building in New York. The architect, again, was the man with the reddish close-cropped hair. As Stewart hammered home the last block of marble, White's gaze was

slight changes in her attitude would add grace. Although the original weighed two thousand pounds, it took the pressure of half a pound of wind to move her. In her new size, she would be half the weight and thirteen feet high. New York was Victorian and there had been vociferous complaints about the suitability of a nude Diana overlooking a public park. In the northeast corner of the park was the Farragut memorial, also by Saint-Gaudens, with a delicate, flowing art nouveau base by White. One New York correspondent had written about the

New York's most beautiful pedestal, Madison Square Garden, for its best-loved statue, Diana. Facing both, the Jennie Jerome mansion.

CREATED BY
ST. GAUDENS
PURIFIED BY
ST. ANTHONY
COMSTOCK

DIANA'S DOOM—IF OUR ST. ANTHONY IS ALLOWED TO HAVE HIS WAY

DRAWN BY E. W. KEMBLE

Anthony Comstock, president of the Society for the Suppression of Vice and agent for the Post Office. George Bernard Shaw coined the term Comstockery.

nudity complaints, and White: *As a matter of fact, all this fuss and fury is simply further evidence of the love of the architect for his work, for all the expenses of removing the old statue and replacing it with a smaller model is being borne by Stanford White. This, however, is only a minor feat for Mr. White who, with his white stone and yellow brick, is transforming New York from one of the dullest, brownest, most monotonous cities on earth to one of the most interesting and beautiful....*

White was only following in his father's footsteps. Less than ten years before, Richard Grant White had attacked in *Century* magazine the maze of telephone and telegraph wires strangling the architecture of the city. In 1884, the year following the article, New York passed a law prohibiting wires and poles on the city streets. At the time of his father's death, White invited his mother to live with his family and she accepted. His father had been a famous Shakespearean scholar and critic. He had also been described in the *New York Tribune* as: *an epicure, a dilettante, a gallant, a critic, almost a coxcomb.* When Richard Grant White praised Lydia Thompson and her burlesque troupe, he shocked not only the public but his peers. Stanford's mother had shared her husband's interest in literature and had published a book of *Little Folks' Songs.* Part of one Stanford loved to listen to in the comfort of his mother's lap:

> Where is Stannie? Where can he be?
> Where is he hiding away from me?
> I've looked in the closet and out on the stair,
> Under the table, behind the big chair.
> Where is the scallawag? Where has he gone?
> Leaving his poor mamma all forlorn?
> I must send the crier all over town.

But here he is, tucked under grand-mamma's gown!
Now I've got him, the rogue, I must give him a shake,
Twenty good kisses . . . and a slice of plum cake!

Stanford White.

The 1889 temporary Washington Centennial Arch by White. The funding, like its permanent counterpart, was by private subscription.

The largest stockholder of Madison Square Garden with two thousand shares was J. Pierpont Morgan. Stanford White owned five hundred shares. He also kept a suite in the tower and often stayed there entertaining friends after an entertainment in the Garden. Originally they had left space for a fine restaurant on the garden roof, but neither Sherry nor Delmonico would accept the concession. It was offered to them rent free. Still they would not accept. After a horse show, people would want oysters and champagne. After the Barnum and Bailey Circus, hot dogs and moxie. No restaurateur could cater to the divergent tastes demanded by the flexible facilities.

They entertained themselves. Mrs. Stanford White as Brünnhilde.

Stanford White entertained in his apartment in the Madison Square Tower and could lead one to the very top to touch Diana's foot.

Although the Diana would be replaced, she would not be wasted. The overscale model would be shipped to Chicago for the World's Columbian Exposition, which would be held in 1893, one year late. New York had bid five million dollars for the Fair, but Chicago had then upped her own bid to ten million. McKim, Mead and White was the firm chosen to design the Agricultural Building, and Diana would be fine on top, though Mrs. Potter Palmer wanted it for the Woman's Building.

"Is Augustus Saint-Gaudens the greatest of our portrait sculptors? Ans. Saint-Gaudens is certainly regarded as the greatest of our sculptors—portrait or otherwise." —Ladies' Home Journal, *1904.*

Saint-Gaudens was busy now on the plaster model of the smaller Diana. The finished piece would again be in beaten copper. At the same time, he had just completed a delicate medallion profile of a pretty three-year-old boy with turned-up nose, hair almost concealing his forehead and right ear. It was not a commission. It was a gift to his lovely slender model, Davida. Augusta, Saint-Gaudens' wife, had never met her, or the little boy. The man who made the medallion had also fathered the little boy.

Bas-relief of Novy by his father, Saint-Gaudens. Novy's mother was Davida, the model for Diana's head.

Another of the original shareholders of Madison Square Garden was the steel man from Pittsburg. (In Cleveland's first administration, the Post Office ordered the "h" dropped from Pittsburg*h* as superfluous. It was officially restored in 1908.) He and Morgan had admired each other and gone into the original plans for the Garden together. Then a young musician, Walter Damrosch, had persuaded the steel man that now that Steinway Hall was closing, New York must have a fine concert hall. Carnegie's Hall opened May 9, 1891, with Tchaikovsky conducting some of his own compositions. The acoustics were magnificent. Paderewski played there the same year. (Twenty-eight years later he would be the first Prime Minister of the Republic of Poland.)

But now, in 1892, Andrew Carnegie was not thinking of music. There was trouble at his largest steel mill, Homestead, near Pittsburg. Henry Clay Frick was in charge there, and Carnegie left for the peace and quiet of his castle in Scotland. Frick had decided that when the contract with the steelworkers expired, he would lower wages. To do this, he would first have to break the union.

Three young comrades, all in their early twenties, ran an ice-cream parlor in Worcester, Massachusetts. In May of 1892 they read about the Homestead steel strike. Fedya and Sasha were fired with enthusiasm for the American worker, as was their artic-

MISS GOLDMAN AT HER FAVORITE OCCUPATION OF ADDRESSING OPEN-AIR MEETINGS.

The steel man from Pittsburg, Andrew Carnegie, ran his company like a fiefdom. In Scotland he takes the whip to give the local clan a ride.

ulate companion Emma Goldman: *To us it sounded the awakening of the American worker, the long awaited day of his resurrection . . . our hearts were fired with admiration for the men of Homestead. Entire nights were spent in discussion of the possibilities of this struggle between labor and capital.*

One day Emma Goldman came rushing back to the flat the three shared, a newspaper clutched in her fist:

LATEST DEVELOPMENTS IN HOMESTEAD—FAMILIES OF STRIKERS EVICTED FROM THE COMPANY HOUSES—WOMAN IN CONFINEMENT CARRIED OUT INTO STREET BY SHERIFFS.

In the morning, after settling with their landlord, the trio left by train for New York. They would write a manifesto for the workers and take it to Pittsburg. In New York they were taken in by the family of Mollock the baker. He worked nights and his wife said the trio could share the small flat with her two children until they left for Pittsburg.

In Pittsburg Frick had a ten-foot fence with barbed wire erected around the mill. He then hired several hundred armed Pinkerton men to be towed up the Monongahela had been locked out, called the mill Fort Frick. They patrolled all sides of the walled encampment, including the waterside.

The strikers of Homestead steel mill firing back at the Pinkertons.

encampment, including the waterside.

The following day the headlines cried of the fruit of the ironmaster's resolve to crush his men . . . twelve dead, twice as many wounded. There was a picture, under the headline, of Henry Clay Frick.

We sat down, Sasha between us, holding our hands. In a quiet and even tone he began to unfold to us his plan: I will kill Frick. Of course I shall be condemned to death. I will die proudly in the assurance that I gave my life for the people.

Sasha, Alexander Berkman, was ten years old when his beloved uncle had been sentenced to death. On the assassination of the Czar, the Nihilists had been rounded up, including his uncle Maxim. The peasants detested their would-be liberators and feared a trick. They had believed Czar Alexander II favored them and had regarded him as their liberator. Now Sasha would do something for the oppressed workers of America. He would strike down the man responsible for the crimes at Homestead. His act, too, would be thought a trick.

Sasha had never made bombs before, but anarchist Johann Most's *Science of Revolu-*

Henry Clay Frick, often called the "perfected business man," opposed Carnegie's concepts and stood instead for a corporate system of interlocking noncompetitive industries—socialism at the top.

tionary Warfare was to be his textbook. He would procure dynamite from a comrade on Staten Island, then proceed to Homestead.

We will go with you, Fedya and I cried together. But Sasha would not listen. He insisted it was criminal to waste three lives on one man.

And so he convinced Fedya and Emma they must stay behind and articulate to the workers the meaning of his "deed." Frick was a symbol of wealth and power, of the injustice and wrong of the capitalistic class, as well as personally responsible for the shedding of workers' blood. The act was directed against Frick not as a man but as an enemy of labor.

Sasha's experiments (with dynamite) took place at night when everybody was asleep but Emma Goldman! *While he worked, I kept watch, in dread every moment, for Sasha, for our friends in the flat, the children, and the rest of the tenants. What if anything should go wrong? But then, did not the end justify the means?*

Using most of their money, Sasha completed the fusing of two bombs. He took one of them to Staten Island and tested it. The bomb failed to go off. Either the formula was wrong or the dynamite was damp. The other bomb being identical, it, too, would fail. Taking their total fortune of fifteen dollars, Alexander Berkman entrained for Pittsburg. Emma was left with the problem of raising twenty more dollars for the purchase of a suit and a gun. But that much money was not easy to come by on such short notice. Emma Goldman had worked as a skilled seamstress at two dollars and fifty cents a week. The most she had ever earned was four dollars a week. *I woke up with a very*

At the age of twenty-one Alexander Berkman decided to kill Frick for the workers of Homestead.

clear idea of how I could raise the money for Sasha. I would go on the street. I recollected Dostoyevsky's Crime and Punishment *which had made such a profound impression on me, especially the character of Sonya. She had become a prostitute in order to support her little brothers and sisters and to relieve her consumptive stepmother of worry. My cause was greater than hers. It was Sasha . . . his great deed . . . the people. But could I be able to do it, to go with strange men for money? The thought revolted me. It took several hours to gain control of myself. When I got out of bed my mind was made up.*

At this same time, Havelock Ellis was compiling papers from around the civilized world for his monumental work, *Studies in the Psychology of Sex.* From the *American Gynaecological and Obstetric Journal*, an article, "The Economics of Prostitution," informed him that a handsome or attractive-looking prostitute was a rarity. The article stated: "Whatever other evils the fatal power

Havelock Ellis . . . his major work was banned on obscenity charges.

of beauty may be responsible for, it has nothing to do with prostitution." Ellis concluded that beautiful, agreeable and harmoniously formed faces are rare rather than common among prostitutes and that minute

examination would reveal a large number of physical abnormalities. He continued with the results of an important study of the physical investigations of prostitutes in Russia by Dr. Pauline Tarnowsky. She examined and compared fifty inmates in a brothel in St. Petersburg with fifty peasant women of similar age and mental development. Skull measurements showed the prostitutes had shorter anterior-posterior and transverse diameters. Also, a proportion equal to eighty-four percent showed various signs of physical degeneration (asymmetry of face, anomalies of palate, teeth, etc.). Four-fifths of the prostitutes had parents who were habitual drunkards.

Emma Goldman would find much competition when she walked the streets in 1892. Port Said, Marseilles and the Casbah could

EMMA GOLDMAN IN 1892

15

Woman-beater Professor Reid/woman-protector Harry Thaw.

not touch New York's per-mile ratio of prostitutes. There were over twenty-five thousand girls in the trade, mostly confined to the Tenderloin and the Bowery. If Emma Goldman stayed on the street for more than one night, she would be straightened out by a policeman or a pimp. There was a slave system, and she could fit into it, but there was no freelancing and the police received a polite cut for every trick turned. Houses catered to every taste. One of the largest, a dance hall called the Haymarket, had private rooms for the five hundred girls entertaining on the premises. Strict rules forbade robbing clients on the turf. There were houses for voyeurs, masochists, homosexuals and, of course, sadists. One young man from Pittsburg spent over forty thousand dollars in an establishment catering to unorthodox tastes. Using the name Professor Reid, he advertised the training of young girls, ages fifteen to seventeen, for stage careers. Using a whip, he raised welts on their naked bodies and paid handsomely for giving the lessons.

A Mrs. Reid was paid seven hundred dollars for her "training." Evelyn Nesbit would be surprised when her Pittsburg millionaire husband gave her lessons in their honeymoon castle high in the Austrian Tyrol.

At this time, Assistant District Attorney William Travers Jerome was forced to resign his office. He had convicted one of the Tammany bosses in an assault case. Himself an appointee of Tammany, he suddenly rebelled and honestly prosecuted the huge ruffian James Barker for beating a smaller, weaker man named Herman to such an extent that he was hospitalized for eight months and never fully recovered from his injuries. Barker was sentenced to a year's imprisonment, and Jerome established the beginning of a reputation for integrity. However, as soon as Jerome was replaced in office, Barker's bail was reduced and sentence stayed. Now, in 1892, Jerome watched hopefully as another reformer attacked Tammany and prostitution. The man was Dr. Charles Parkhurst, minister of the Madison Square

Fiery reformer the Reverend
Dr. Parkhurst. His church was
on Madison Square.

Presbyterian Church. The frail Parkhurst was laughed at by the bosses, who demanded indignantly that he shut up or put up. The reverend decided to put up. In disguise with two companions he made the rounds, securing evidence of the sex packages openly available. The political tides ran out for Tammany, as Parkhurst remained steadfast and implacable and the two madams he testified against were found guilty.

Emma Goldman was drawn to try street-walking for economic reasons. Havelock Ellis states: *Writers on prostitution frequently assert that economic conditions lie at the root of prostitution and that its chief cause is poverty.* Prostitutes themselves often declare that the difficulty of earning a livelihood in other ways was a main cause in inducing them to adopt this career. A survey on prostitution in Paris concurred with this opinion: *Of all the causes of prostitution, particularly in Paris, and probably in all large cities, none is more active than lack of work and the misery which is the inevitable result of insufficient wages.* Other papers, such as one from England, state: *morals fluctuate with trade.* From Berlin: registered prostitutes increase during bad years. From Japan: the cause of causes is poverty. A similar report came from America. However, as Ellis continued his investigations, he found a considerable number of prostitutes came from the servant class. They had the least monetary worries, usually living under almost similar conditions as their mistresses without their financial worries. Degradation was the major cause. Self-hatred another, with the concomitant aid of alcohol.

Emma Goldman never had a low regard for herself. That night she tramped up and down Fourteenth Street in the heart of the Tenderloin, but each time a man approached, her footsteps quickened in the opposite direction. A man in his sixties took her by the arm and led her to a bar. He bought her a glass of red wine, gave her ten dollars and advised her to return home. She had proved a failure at prostitution and now borrowed the rest of the money from her sister and sent it on to Sasha in Pittsburg. The "deed" was scheduled for the following Saturday, July 23. Sasha would use the gun, a knife with poison on the blade and a capsule of fulminate of mercury concealed in his mouth if all else failed.

Emma Goldman had left Russia when she was sixteen. She and her sister Helena had sailed on the small, crowded steamer *Elbe* for the promised land. Steerage class cost ten dollars. Emma escaped her father's brutality by threatening to throw herself in the Neva if he refused to let her accompany her sister to the New World: *I left without regrets. Since my earliest recollection, home had been stifling. My father's presence terrifying. My mother, while less violent with the children, never showed much warmth . . . many blows intended for my brother and me were given Helena. Now we were completely together, nobody would separate us. The last day of our journey everybody was on deck. Helena and I stood pressed to each other, enraptured by the sight of the mist. Ah, there she was, the symbol of hope, of freedom, of opportunity. She held her torch high to light the way to the free country, the asylum for the oppressed of all lands. Our spirits were high, our eyes filled with tears.*

In Rochester Emma secured work in a corset factory, ten and a half hours a day for

EMMA GOLDMAN
AT THE AGE OF SEVENTEEN, IN 1886

two-fifty a week. The following year conditions in St. Petersburg became intolerable for Jews. Her parents and two younger brothers set sail for New York, and then went on to Rochester to share a home together. As they could not meet their bills, they took in a boarder who worked in the factory with Emma. At eighteen, Emma Goldman married the boarder, Jacob Kershner.

At about the time Emma Goldman married, a young doctor in Germany was striving for instant fame. His reason was a compelling one. He had been engaged for over four years, three of which he had been separated from his love. His greatest desire was to earn enough money to marry the recipient of his nine hundred love letters during their three-year separation. Instant fame would ensure him patients if he went into private practice. But he had not been lucky. After a small unsuccessful operation on a famous actor, he felt compelled to return the fee to his patient. A few years before, he had found the drug cocaine beneficent for all manner of illnesses. Since it had no addictive effect upon himself, he published a paper supporting its safe, beneficial use. One of his best friends, a fellow doctor who was a morphine addict, was weaned to cocaine. After many years of absolute horror, he died a cocaine addict with delirium tremens. Dr. Freud quickly wrote his fiancée warning her not to use too much of his recommended drug.

He had also lectured on hypnotism, being impressed with results achieved through that medium. Then he advocated a technique of rubbing the forehead vigorously while having the patient concentrate in hope of recalling incidents of his past life that might clue the origin of his ailment.

But now, years later, he was a happily married man and the father of six children, at work developing a technique for the treatment of neurosis. His theory that the mind, not the brain or nervous system, was the root of the body's malfunction was closer to the thoughts of Mary Baker Eddy than the beliefs of his professional colleagues. The new technique required listening to and interpreting the meanderings of the patient. Dr. Freud would have his patient lie comfortably on a couch while he sat concealed from view behind the head of the couch. He would call his technique free association.

The first erotic sensation I remember had come to me when I was about six. Father kept an inn. Among the stable help was a young peasant, Petrushka. Often he would take me with him to the meadows and I would listen to the sweet tones of his flute. In the evening he would play horse-run as fast as his legs could carry him, then suddenly throw me up in the air, catch me in his arms and press me to him. It used to give me a peculiar sensation, fill me with exultation, followed by blissful release.

After an altercation with Emma Goldman's father, the peasant boy was sent away. It was a great loss to the little girl, who now dreamed of Petrushka, the meadows, the music and the ecstasy of their play.
One morning I felt myself torn out of my sleep. Mother was bending over me, tightly holding my right hand. In an angry voice she cried: If I ever find your hand again like that, I'll whip you, you naughty child.

When she was fifteen, Emma's father spotted her in a summer garden, in the evening, with a group of girls and some boy students. When she reached home he pounded her with his fists, screaming he would not have a loose daughter. A few months later, in St. Petersburg, a boy asked her if she would like to see some of the luxurious rooms in the hotel he clerked in. She had never been inside a hotel before.

The boy led me through a side entrance, along a thickly carpeted corridor, into a large room. It was brightly illuminated and beautifully furnished. A table near the sofa held flowers and a tea-tray. We sat down. The young man poured out a golden-coloured liquid and asked me to clink glasses to our friendship. I put the wine to my lips. Suddenly I found myself in his arms, my waist torn open. His passionate kisses covered my face, neck and breasts. Not until after the violent contact of our bodies and the excruciating pain he caused me did I come to my senses. I screamed savagely beating against the man's chest with my fists. After that I always felt between two fires in the presence of men. In February, 1887, aged eighteen, Emma Goldman became the wife of Jacob Kershner: *My feverish excitement of that day, my suspense and ardent anticipation gave way at night to a feeling of utter bewilderment. Jacob Kershner lay trembling near me. He was impotent.*

Now, at twenty-three, she had decided no man would ever own her again. She was free and so would her love be free. It would be days before she would have word of her beloved Sasha in Pittsburg.

One Sunday (when I was seventeen) it was announced that a famous socialist speaker from New York would lecture (in Rochester) on the Haymarket case being tried in Chicago. Johanna Greie told of the labor strikes that broke out throughout the country in 1886 for an eight-hour day. The center of the movement was Chicago and there the struggle between the toilers and their bosses became intense and bitter. A meeting of the striking employees of the McCormick Harvester Company in that city was attacked by the police. Men and women were beaten and several persons killed. To protest the outrage, a mass meeting was called in Haymarket Square. The response was gratifying. There were many speakers, among them Albert Parsons, August Spies and Adolph

Fisher. The mayor attended. He was content the meeting was peaceful and departed with a nod to his officers that all was well. After he left, the police decided to speed up the closing of the meeting with their nightsticks while someone was still speaking. A bomb was thrown, killing seven policemen. No one knew where the bomb had come from. Eight anarchists were rounded up, including the speakers, and placed on trial for murder. *At the end of Johanna Greie's speech I knew what I had expected all along; the Chicago men were innocent. They were put to death for their ideal, but what was their ideal? Greie spoke of Parsons, Spies, Lingg and the others as socialists, but I was ignorant of the real meaning of socialism. On the other hand the papers called these men anarchists, bomb-throwers. What was anarchism? I walked home in a dream. Sister Helena was already asleep, but I had to share my experience with her. I woke her up and recited to her the whole story, giving almost a verbatim account of the speech. I must have been very dramatic, because Helena exclaimed: The next thing I'll hear about my little sister is that she too is a dangerous anarchist.*

The industrialists justified their actions by recourse to "social Darwinism," a concept of Herbert Spencer, Andrew Carnegie's favorite philosopher. If in nature it was survival of the fittest, then in human relations and industry the same must follow.

The growth of a large business is merely a survival of the fittest . . . a law of nature and of God.   John D. Rockefeller

Niggers are lazy, ignorant and unprogressive; railroad traffic is created only by industrious, intelligent and ambitious people.   J. P. Morgan

When John D. Rockefeller had a distant industrial chimney camouflaged, a college removed and a mountainside transferred, all to perfect his Pocantico estate, it was whispered these were the things God would have done had He been rich.

The most beautiful sight we see is the child at labor; as early as he may get at labor the more beautiful, the more useful does his life become.
                                    Asa Candler
                                    Founder of Coca-Cola

I can hire one half the working class to kill the other half.   Jay Gould

Emma Goldman's idol and teacher, Prince Peter Kropotkin, shook his head sadly at the believers in "social Darwinism." The gentle Russian philosophical anarchist proclaimed softly: *There is cooperation in nature.*

In the early afternoon of Saturday, July 23, Fedya rushed into my room with a newspaper proclaiming in large black letters: **YOUNG MAN BY THE NAME OF ALEXANDER BERGMAN SHOOTS FRICK—ASSASSIN OVER-POWERED BY WORKING MEN AFTER DESPERATE STRUGGLE.**

Working-men overpowering Sasha? The

paper was lying. He did the act for the working-men. They would never attack him. And they spelled his name wrong.

Berkman gained entrance to Frick's private office under the pretense of being from a New York employment service. At close quarters, he shot Frick three times, was beaten to the floor by Frick's assistant, pulled a knife and stabbed the fallen Frick in the ankle and thigh. The explosive found between his teeth failed to explode. Before collapsing, Frick asked to see the face of his assailant, whispered: *let him live.*

Johann Most was the fiery editor of the anarchist paper *Die Freiheit.* While still in Rochester, Emma Goldman had begun reading his vitriolic literature denouncing the powers that were at that time preparing the outcome of the Haymarket trial.

I devoured every line on anarchism I could get, every word about the men, their work, their heroic stand while on trial. I saw a new world opening for me. Then the terrible thing everyone feared yet hoped would not happen, actually occurred. Extra editions of the Rochester papers carried the news: **THE CHICAGO ANARCHISTS HUNG.***

Emma Goldman made up her mind to go

*Three were hanged, one blew himself up with a capsule of fulminate of mercury concealed in his mouth. Three others received life sentences.

21

*Proponent of violence,
anarchist Johann Most. Emma
Goldman found him hungering
for affection and fed him.*

to New York, to look up Johann Most. He would help her prepare for her new work.

My first impression of Most was one of revulsion. He was of medium height, with a large head crowned with greyish bushy hair: but his face was twisted out of form by an apparent dislocation of the left jaw. Only his eyes were soothing; they were blue and sympathetic.

A relationship sprang up between the two. Most decided Emma should become a speaker for the movement. There were too few women speaking for the workers.

Most took me to the Grand Central in a cab. On the way he moved close to me. Conflicting thoughts and emotions possessed me; the speeches I was going to make, Sasha, Fedya, my passion for the one, my budding love for the other. Something mysterious stirred me . . . it was infinite tenderness for the great man-child at my side. As he sat there, he suggested a rugged tree bent by winds and storm, making one supreme last effort to stretch itself toward the sun. All for the cause, Sasha had so often said. The fighter next to me had already given all for the cause. But who had given all for him? He was hungry for affection, for understanding. I would give him both.

The week after Frick was shot, Most's *Die Freiheit* came out and denounced the "deed," suggesting the gun had been a toy. It was all a trick by Frick to win support and sympathy.

Hardly a week passed without some slur in the Freiheit *against Sasha or myself. It was painful enough to be called vile names by the man who had once loved me, but it was beyond endurance to have Sasha slandered and*

maligned. Most, whom I had heard scores of times call for acts of violence, who had gone to prison in England for his glorification of tyrannicide . . . Most, the incarnation of defiance and revolt, now deliberately repudiated the deed. The steel strikers were beaten, sympathy had turned against them with the shooting of Henry Frick. The maximum sentence Berkman could receive since Frick had survived was seven years. Had there been a show of strength in the courtroom, they never would have given Sasha fourteen years. The basis of the additional seven years was the false accusation that he had meant to kill Frick's assistant as well.

Emma Goldman blamed Most for the lack of support Berkman had received: *Only the naked fact remained that Most had betrayed his ideal, had betrayed us. I bought a horsewhip. At Most's next lecture I sat in the first row, close to the platform. My hand was on the whip under my long grey cloak. When he got up and faced the audience, I rose and declared in a loud voice: I've come to demand proof of your insinuations against Alexander Berkman. There was instant silence, then Most mumbled something about 'hysterical woman,' but nothing else. I then pulled out my whip and leaped towards him. Repeatedly I lashed him across the face and neck, then broke the whip over my knee and threw the pieces at him. It was all done so quickly that no one had time to interfere.*

When Emma Goldman was ten years old, everyone used to whisper about the flogging of peasants. *One day I came upon a half-naked human body being lashed with the knout: the bleeding body, the piercing shrieks, the distorted faces of the gendarmes, the knouts whistling in the air and coming down with a sharp hissing upon the half-naked man, threw me into hysterics.*

As Most lectured, Emma sat quietly listening, but concealed beneath her calm exterior was a horse whip.

The original Diana was daintily lowered from her perch atop the Spanish tower and replaced by her slighter, more graceful counterpart. Opinions change in New York. The *Tribune* proudly announced: "Our new Diana will rise at dawn today, weather permitting, to delight the eye with all her glistening beauty as well as tell New Yorkers which way the wind blows."

The old Diana's arrival in Chicago for the quadricentennial of Columbus' discovery was given a jaundiced reception by the *Chicago Tribune*. Thousands blushed. *What! a statue without a stitch of clothing on top of the Woman's Building!* (She ended up atop the Agricultural Building.)

Richard Morris Hunt, architect for the Vanderbilts, set the style for the Fair with his centrally situated Administration Building. It was a whipped-cream concoction to

be followed in spirit by the architects and sculptors commissioned by Daniel Burnham to whip up physical structures. Burnham and John Root, leading practitioners of the architectural trade in Chicago, were given supervisory command of the Fair, but Root died and Burnham went it alone. Frederick Law Olmsted, designer of New York's Central Park, had taken a marsh, a wasteland along the lake front, and transformed it miraculously into order and beauty. But it was all a glistening pile of plaster-of-paris with statuary for icing. Saint-Gaudens and millions of others were carried away by it. Without a blush, Saint-Gaudens, in charge of sculpture, looked another artist in the eye and stated: *this is the greatest meeting of artists since the fifteenth century!* The century he chose was apt: the Fair looked like it. It was nicknamed the White City and the Park of Palaces. It gave sanctity to the sand castles of Newport and Fifth Avenue and

At the end of the lagoon, Richard Morris Hunt's whipped-cream Administration Building. ON THE LEFT: *Diana, twisting in Chicago's wind atop the Agricultural Building.*

drove further home the wedge between the super-rich and the super-poor. McKim, Mead and White built the Agricultural Building. They had been chosen not for their tasteful work in colonial residences, but for the castlelike quality of their churches and public buildings. An architect named Louis Sullivan shook his head when Hunt built William K. Vanderbilt's home at Fifty-second Street and Fifth Avenue and asked: *Must I show you this French château, this little Château de Blois on this street corner, here in New York, and still you do not laugh? Have you no sense of humor, no sense of pathos?* He went on to complain that a man might inhabit the house, but he couldn't live in it morally, mentally or spiritually, *that the man and his home were a contradiction, a New York absurdity.* One of Sullivan's assistants was Frank Lloyd Wright. Looking at the constructions and pretensions of art at the Columbian Exposition, Sullivan feared it would set architecture into a mold that would retard American native creativity for the next half-century. A few wondered seriously if this breach of continuity of historical sequence was reality or illusion.

Hunt's "Château de Blois" for the Vanderbilts on Fifth Avenue. "The process of selective adaption of designs to the end of conspicuous waste, and the substitution of pecuniary beauty for aesthetic beauty, has been especially effective in the development of architecture." —Thorstein Veblen.

A nineteen-year-old boy rushed to the Fair from the sidewalks of Coney Island in the hopes of capitalizing on illusion. He changed his name from Weiss to Houdini, and was soon set up on the Midway Plaisance. Near him on the Midway was an Eskimo Village, a South Seas Village and

Inspired by the French conjuror, Erich Weiss changed his name.

Little Egypt, a belly dancer. Anthony Comstock, America's official protector of morals, was enraged. Farther down the Midway could be heard the syncopated African drums of the Dahomean Village. For Chicagoans, the beat seemed vaguely familiar. Rinky-tink piano players in the Tenderloin and Red Light district had the same rhythm. Chicago was comparatively free of prejudice and brown-skinned pianists could move about in entertainment circles, with a better chance for a livelihood. Among the hundreds of itinerant musicians who were swept in on the wave of sporting-life types was a serious piano player from Texarkana. When he was seven, his parents had scraped up enough money to buy him a decrepit square grand. By the time he reached eleven, there was talk about his natural abilities; his harmonic sense and rhythm seemed extraordinary, even for a Negro. An aging German music professor had the boy play for him, then decided to give him free lessons in harmony and technique. They spent hours together, the professor telling the boy about the European masters and composers of operas. But now the boy was a man, listening to the syncopated African drums at the Dahomean Village. African music, like a bifurcated tree, bent in two directions. One could choose between the lament and the jubilant. The beat from the West African village was jubilant, joyous, a syncopated rhythm that would give to this decade the sobriquet Gay Nineties. After the closing of the White City, Scott Joplin left for Sedalia where he found work playing piano in the Maple Leaf Club. But millions of visitors left the Fair humming the song John Philip Sousa had featured, "After the Ball." It became America's first pop tune to sell over a million copies.

Hard on its heels was "Daisy Bell," the song about a bicycle built for two. When pneumatic tires were added to the safety bike, cycling became the craze of the forty-four states. Cobblestone streets were swiftly macadamized as one in every seven Americans became the owner of a bicycle. Sunday, the only day off, became a paradise of two-wheelers. Walking across the street became a menace. A cyclist could strike you straight on, you could become mired in horse droppings underfoot, or covered with soot and ashes from overhead dropped by the elevated railway.

One of the memories that stayed in the dreams of visitors to the Columbian Exposition was the display set up for the jeweler Charles L. Tiffany. The man, of course, was known for his great taste. Nine years before, Stanford White had completed the famous residence for Tiffany on Seventy-second Street. Joseph Pulitzer's *New York World* described it as the largest private residence in the city, a bold departure from all stereotyped forms, a great success. Sir Edmund Gosse returned to Europe and wrote: *The Tiffany House on Madison Avenue is the one that pleased me most in America.* He went on to rave about sculptor Augustus Saint-Gaudens, artist John La Farge and architect Stanford White, who had all worked together. But for his exhibition in Chicago, Charles Tiffany the jeweler let his son Louis Comfort Tiffany create the display. In multi-colored iridescent glass Tiffany made a mo-

In 1900 the new home of Louis Comfort Tiffany called by the Ladies' Home Journal *"The most artistic house in New York City." The architects were McKim, Mead and White.*

Dr. Parkhurst successfully frequented the brothels for his evidence.

William Travers Jerome, formidable cousin of Jennie Jerome. His mother put their name on a New York avenue.

saic of blue vines and peacocks that dazzled the viewers. It was a Byzantine chapel. The formula Louis Comfort Tiffany devised with the aid of a German chemist enabled him to create the most exquisite objects in iridescent glass, which he called Favrile. President Chester A. Arthur had him make a towering screen of this opalescent glass for the White House. Arthur had been Vice President and became President when a disappointed office seeker assassinated President Garfield.

When Dr. Parkhurst raided the brothels, he was accompanied by a private detective named Charles Gardner. Gardner later acted as one of the witnesses at the trial. Dr. Parkhurst had gone at reform in an unusual manner. Instead of stating prostitution was evil, he said it was against the law. Since the police refused to take action, the police were being corrupted by an illegal profession just as they were by the all-night saloons. He did not base his attack on the contention that packs of *cadets* were paid to *recruit* young comely girls for local brothels. There was a simple method of recruitment: kidnapping. Young girls were grabbed, drugged and beaten into submission. There was no way out, as in the case of a rabbi's daughter whose story was published in the newspapers but without hope of freeing her.

The police, seeking to break Parkhurst's campaign against their corrupt practices, arrested Charles Gardner on the charge that he had tried to shake down the madam of one of the brothels Dr. Parkhurst had investigated. Through the testimony of the madam, Lillie Clifton, Gardner was convicted and sentenced to two years' imprisonment. His defender, chosen by Dr. Parkhurst and the reform committee, was William Travers Jerome. It was a stunning defeat. However, Jerome refused to give up. He kept after

Madam Clifton after the trial and brought an appeal before the state Supreme Court, where the conviction was reversed. Lillie Clifton confessed she had perjured herself under police pressure. Now the higher-ups in the police department were implicated. Although neither party wanted it, the state legislature was forced to form an investigative committee to look into police corruption. This was done under Senator Lexow as chairman. Dr. Parkhurst and William Travers Jerome would be the mainstays of the committee. Two police reporters who had been following the reformers' every action were Lincoln Steffens and Jacob Riis.

Jerome began the investigation by bargaining with witnesses. He could keep them out of prison, or in, as he chose, and he was willing to compromise. Lincoln Steffens said he watched him fight the devil with fire. Finally, the break came. He cracked the notorious collector for the Tenderloin district, tall, handsome Captain Max Schmittberger. This was a tough man, a fighter, and there he was on the stand, telling everything there was to know about police graft, precincts, names, prices, customs, the whole system.

The frail Dr. Parkhurst had beaten the entire Tammany family of crooks. Byrnes, the chief of police, resigned. Reform would win, but Boss Croker told reporter Steffens, *the people who vote Tammany out can't stand the police corruption; by next election they won't be able to stand reform either.* Steffens listened to newly elected reform Mayor Strong, who was making political promises he couldn't keep. Confused, he talked to his reporter friend Riis. The main bone of contention was the position of police commissioner. Riis told him: *Theodore Roosevelt is the man for president of the police board, and God will*

A Thompson Street dive photographed by Riis.

The Short Tail Gang photographed under a Jackson Street pier by Riis.

"I don't care who the other commissioners are. T.R. is enough." —Police reporter Jacob Riis.

attend to his appointment. *That's all I want to know. I don't care who the other commissioners are. T.R. is enough.*

T.R. got the appointment, and the day they got the news Riis and Steffens saw the four-man police board coming down the street; one was running, the others were trying to keep up. T.R. called: *Hello, Jake,* to Riis as he ran past, up the stairs to his office to get started.

In the back of the new police commissioner's mind was the idea to fire Schmittberger, the key to the old corrupt police system and star witness for the Lexow Committee. Schmittberger was a young German apprentice pastry cook in New York when he caught the eye of some Tammany leaders. They joked about his height and good looks and how well he'd look in a police uniform. *Won't cost you a cent, either,* one of them told the tall youth. At that time there was a fixed fee for an appointment to the force. Schmittberger studied for the police examination, not actually believing he'd be called, but he was. He was pushed through and found himself immediately popular for his simplicity and naive attitude with the higher-ups. They used him decoratively, putting him on posts where he would show off to best advantage. Although there was no traffic squad, he was put in the middle of Broadway and Thirty-fourth Street where he met many people who put in a good word for him with the captain. On the night beat, he did nothing about the many houses of prostitution. He had no instructions to do anything and did not even know they were against the law. One day a girl dashed downstairs from a brothel and pressed a tenner in his hand. A veteran cop explained the captain must like him to put him on that post. What was the tenner for? Schmittberger wondered. "To fatten you up." Schmittberger then tried to give the money to his captain, who blew up, insulted at the chicken feed. The captain gradually realized the innocence of the recruit. Eventually he became a ward man, trusted enough to collect the department payoffs from prostitutes, gamblers and all the other lawbreakers under the protection of the law.

The summer after the Lexow investigations, Lincoln Steffens moved to Riverside-on-the-Hudson. That was a bicycle commute to the city. To the police it was known as Goatville, and that's where Steffens saw the now notorious Captain Schmittberger, on horseback, constantly on the job. When Schmittberger saw Steffens, he tried to avoid him, but Steffens eventually drew him out in conversation. He found out that Schmittberger had one year to pay on his home but would never own it now. Steffens pressed him about getting a little on the side just to make his payments and saw horror on his face: *Never again, never again. Say, you don't know what I've been through. You never had your kids sit silent at dinner, nudge one another on, and so pass the buck to the big boy you always kind of . . . wanted the respect of, and then had him swallow a lump and blurt out, I say, Pop, is it true this stuff they are saying? It's all lies, ain't it?*

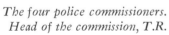

The four police commissioners. Head of the commission, T.R.

T.R. listened to police reporters Lincoln Steffens and Jacob Riis. Schmittberger remained on the force.

Steffens watched Schmittberger's district and could see not one saloon open off hours, not a law broken. In the *Evening Post* it had been Steffens who had pounded away at "get Schmittberger" until the captain had "talked" to the Lexow Committee. Now Steffens argued with Dr. Parkhurst that they could not afford to penalize a man for coming over to their side. Between him and Riis, T.R. was finally convinced that although Tammany wanted Schmittberger out, there was no reason why the reformers should. A few weeks later, Schmittberger was transferred to the precinct below, and immediately two pool parlors were closed down and the precinct swept clean. Soon they had a test for Captain Schmittberger. Two wiretappers who were getting racing news and holding it up till their confederates could get their bets down were arrested. They were given marked money and told that if they could buy off Schmittberger they could run their little swindle. There was no police record on

the two men and they were not seen for several days. When they approached Schmittberger with their idea, he leaped upon them, knocked them down and threw them out the door and down the steps. Then he sent for an ambulance to cart them away. T.R. yelled: "Atta boy," and thereafter Schmittberger was known as "the broom" to Parkhurst and as "my big stick" to T.R.

Schmittberger later became New York's chief of police and served with distinction for many years. Upon his death his family heard the highest praise from reform commissioners Roosevelt, Colonel Arthur Woods and General S. V. Greene, among many others.

On Emma Goldman's first visit to Sasha, the official who gave out the passes warned her Berkman would never get out of prison alive. Emma then sprang upon the hapless man and threatened his life should anything

The Cornelius Vanderbilt
citadel at Fifth Avenue and
Fifty-eighth Street.

evil befall Alexander Berkman. When she discovered she was in the early stages of tuberculosis, Emma was forced to return to her sister in Rochester for a two-month rest. Her doctor made plans for her to enter a sanatorium for the winter. But the recent depression had thrown thousands out of work in New York and Emma felt she must help them. A few days later, she was the last speaker at a mass demonstration in Union Square: *I saw a dense mass before me, their pale, pinched faces upturned to me. My heart beat, my temples throbbed, and my knees shook: Men and women, do you realize that the State is the worst enemy you have? It is a machine that crushes you in order to sustain the ruling class, your masters.*

The "other half" was really,
ninety percent or more.
Carnegie razed their shacks
and built his citadel here at
Fifth Avenue and Ninety-first
Street.

Do you not see the stupidity of asking relief from Albany with immense wealth within a stone's throw from here? Fifth Avenue is laid in gold, every mansion is a citadel of money and power. Yet there you stand, a giant, starved and fettered, shorn of strength. Cardinal Manning long ago proclaimed that 'necessity knows no law' and that 'the starving man has a right to a share of his neighbour's bread.' Emma ended her fiery speech with: Well, then, demonstrate before the palaces of the rich; demand work. Demand bread. If they deny you both, take bread. It is your sacred right!

When the Astoria joined the Waldorf and became the Waldorf-Astoria, people said, "Meet me at the hyphen," which meant Peacock Alley in between.

For inciting to riot, Emma Goldman was sentenced to one year in prison. When she refused to appeal her sentence, she was shipped to Blackwell's Island Penitentiary. A month later she fell ill and was sent to the prison hospital. Medical attendance was from a nearby charity hospital. When the doctor read on her card that she had been imprisoned for inciting to riot, he laughed and told her she could not hurt a fly. Would she, after she recovered, stay and care for the other patients? *But I know nothing about nursing,* she replied. He assured her neither did anyone else in prison. He would teach her to take the pulse and temperature and perform similar services.

Emma Goldman stayed on: *We received a large influx of women prisoners. They were nearly all prostitutes rounded up during recent raids. The city had been blessed by a new vice crusade.... The Lexow Committee, with the Reverend Dr. Parkhurst at its head, wielded the broom which was to sweep New York clean of the fearful scourge. The men found in the public houses were allowed to go free, but the women were arrested and sentenced to Blackwell's Island. Most of the unfortunates came in a deplorable condition. They were suddenly cut off from the narcotics which almost all of them had been habitually using. The sight of their suffering was heart-breaking. With the strength of giants the frail creatures would shake the iron bars, curse and scream for dope and cigarettes.*

Havelock Ellis in examining the causes of prostitution finds defenders of that profession going back thousands of years. He tells of Cato expressing satisfaction on seeing a friend emerge from a brothel, *for otherwise he might have gone to lie with his neighbor's wife.* Lord Morley wrote: *The purity of the family, so lovely and dear as it is, has still only been secured hitherto by retaining a vast and dolorous host of female outcasts.* Balzac in his *Physiologie du Mariag* said of prostitutes: *they sacrifice themselves for the republic and make of their bodies a rampart for the protection of respectable families.* Quoting other writers, Havelock Ellis writes: *The immoral guardian of publi morality, the prostitute fulfils a social mission. She is the guardian of virginal modesty the channel to carry off adulterous desire, tl protector of matrons who fear late maternity; it is her part to act as the shield of the family.* Another writer described the prostitute as: *ultimately the most efficient guard ian of virtue.* Colette's husband stated simpl the French concept: *Adultery is the founaation of society: by making marriage bearable it ensures the survival of the family* Havelock Ellis sums up: *The history of the rise and development of prostitution enable us to see that prostitution is not an accident of our marriage system, but an essential con stituent which appears concurrently with it other essential constituents.*

After serving her prison sentence, Emma Goldman decided to continue her work in nursing. For the sum of sixteen dollars she booked passage to Europe and made her wa from England to Austria, where she studiec at the Allgemeines Krankenhaus. To Emm this was a city in itself with thousands of patients, doctors, nurses and caretakers. Th instructors were renowned physicians. Gynecologist Professor Braun, a lovable teacher, explained the high birth rate of November–December by the irresistible carnival when girls are so fertile all a man has to do is look at them. After his male stu dents examined a female patient and not on would venture a diagnosis, he made a caref examination and gave his opinion: *Gentle-*

men, it is a case most of you have already had, or you have it now, or you will have it in the future. Very few can resist the charm of its origin, the pain of its development, or the price of its cure. It happens to be syphilis. She also managed to hear the lectures of Sigmund Freud: *His simplicity and earnestness and the brilliance of his mind combined to give one the feeling of being led out of a dark cellar into broad daylight. For the first time I grasped the full significance of sex repression and its effect on human thought and action. He helped me to understand myself, my own needs; and I also realized that only people of depraved minds could impugn the motives or find 'impure' so great and fine a personality as Freud.*

The citadel of Blackwell's Island Penitentiary housed Emma Goldman when she refused to appeal her case. Heating system is to the right, solitary cell doors to the left.

In Newport, Hunt was hard at work for his steady clients, the Vanderbilts. The cottage he was readying this time was called The Breakers. Stanford White was completing work with McKim on the Brooklyn Museum, with its monumental flight of steps leading to the graceful Ionic columns of the entranceway. In Boston, Mary Baker Eddy was following the construction of what she called the Mother Church. Years before, she had been miraculously healed of invalidism by a man named Quimby. He had used mesmerism, laid his palm across her forehead until she felt electricity. Like Freud, she began to seek the healing power in mesmerism and hypnotism and the rubbing of the forehead. And just as Freud was to do more than a decade later, she denounced hypnotism and mesmerism. She also abandoned belief in the need for rubbing foreheads or any other physical contact. In the age of materiality she boldly announced: *there was no life, truth or intelligence in matter.* Healing was not concerned with the brain or nervous system, but with right thinking through Divine Mind.

RIGHT: *Mary Baker Eddy, seeking something other than drugs.*

BELOW: *Readying The Breakers for the coming Newport season cost three million dollars. Richard Morris Hunt died on the job.*

When John P. Altgeld was elected governor of Illinois one of his first actions was to set in motion a study of the Haymarket trial. On June 26, 1893, he pardoned the three surviving men. He also released an eighteen-thousand-word document announcing that those hung could now be presumed innocent of the bomb throwing they had been executed for. The trial judge had admitted there was no evidence to connect the accused with the crime. They had been executed for advocating violence to large numbers of persons, leaving time and place up to the individual.

RIGHT: *Lincoln's funeral car. One man's loss . . . Pullman's gain.*

In 1894 Governor Altgeld was himself faced with labor strife. Nine miles from Chicago, in the town of Pullman, a general rail strike had been called. Colonel Mann, a veteran of the Civil War, had sold the

Colonel Mann sold his boudoir car to George Pullman, then published Town Topics.

patents on his Mann Boudoir car to George Pullman. This was the first railroad sleeping car. Pullman built his Palace Car and called it the Pioneer. The car was too big for the narrow station platforms and too high to pass under the overhead bridges. It had been set aside to rust on a siding when President Lincoln was assassinated. George Pullman became one of the few to benefit from the passing of Lincoln. When the funeral managers of the martyred

President cast about for a railroad car suitable for the transportation of the Great Emancipator, only Pullman's Pioneer seemed magnificent enough. Platforms were widened, bridges raised and George Pullman became a millionaire. He built the town of Pullman and constructed homes for the workers. When he announced wage reductions of twenty-five to thirty-three percent without lowering the rent of the company houses, the workers demanded arbitration. Pullman refused. A general strike began. The leader of the strike was a tall, thin young man named Eugene Debs. In describing a labor meeting, Emma Goldman said: *The most striking figure at the convention was Eugene Debs. Very tall, very lean, he stood out above his comrades in more than a physical sense. What struck me most about him was his naive unawareness of the intrigues going on around him.*

As the strike spread, workers began detaching Pullman cars and stopping trains that included them. The part of the rail system that used Pullman's cars was paralyzed. The shocked owners felt they could not handle the hundred-fifty-thousand-member American Railway Union. The Chicago Managers' Association said softly: *We cannot handle Debs. We have got to wipe him out.*

They secured an injunction making it illegal for the leaders of the strike to write, speak or telegraph support for the strike. The grounds for the injunction were that the strike interfered with delivery of the mail. Debs' union offered to run the mail trains, insisting they were only stopping Pullmans that did not carry mail. President Cleveland announced that if it took every dollar and every soldier to deliver a postal card to Chicago, that postal card would be delivered. Debs pleaded for nonviolence. But fourteen thousand local, state and federal troops turned the area into an Armageddon. The hero-butcher of Wounded Knee, General Nelson Miles, assumed command. Debs pleaded with Samuel Gompers of the A.F. of L. to intercede with the Pullman managers. He declined. On July 10 Debs was jailed. Nine days later twenty-five persons lay dead, and the strike was broken. A Chicago lawyer defended Debs against the conspiracy charge. *Conspiracy*, Clarence Darrow said, *from the days of tyranny in England down to the day the General Managers' Association used it as a club, has been the favorite weapon of every tyrant. It is an effort to punish the crime of thought.*

The conspiracy charge could not be proved. But Debs was sent to prison for six months. Years before, he had denounced the Great Rail Strike of 1877 and had received

Eugene Debs. Clarence Darrow called the conspiracy charges against Debs "an effort to punish the crime of thought." But Debs went to prison for six months and converted to socialism.

warm praise from at least one rail president. Now his union had been decimated, the leaders imprisoned, the treasury wiped out, the membership on a blacklist. Governor Altgeld had pleaded with President Cleveland not to send in federal troops and marshals, insisting he could avoid violence and maintain order with the state militia. Altgeld was defeated in the following election. In Woodstock prison Debs changed his mind. He now rejected the American ruling class. He intended to combat the syndicates, trusts, monopolies and huge corporations. He would help promote a new way of life abolishing social classes: *When the bread and butter problem is solved and all men and women and children the world around are rendered secure from the dread of war and fear of want, then the mind and soul will be free to develop as they never were before.*

Debs converting others.

Pullman's own strength lay in his perception of himself: *I have always held that people are greatly influenced by their physical surroundings. The more artistic and refined the external surroundings,* he said, referring to his Pullman Palace Cars, *the better and more refined the man.* But Edward Bok, editor of the *Ladies' Home Journal,* considered the current ornate frippery in architecture and interior design to be the direct result of travel in Pullman's overplush Palace Cars.

Pullman, "good taste" or "ornate frippery."

Bok hated the wretched architecture most Americans called home. He believed people were wasting their money on useless turrets and filigree nonsense. In 1895 he approached leading domestic architects to draw plans the average American could build from. He argued that the average man could not afford an architect. He simply used a builder. These plans, which Bok would publish in the *Ladies' Home Journal,* would improve the choices available to him. Stanford White was one of the many to turn Bok down. However, architects who would draw plans, elevations and estimates for small homes were found. Their plans were published and the homes built by both speculators and individuals. The estimates proved accurate, since they were published only after intensive research of costs throughout the country. The architects who thought Bok's idea would cheapen their profession changed their minds a few years after Bok began publishing his plans for houses that could be built for fifteen

Stanford White refused to help Bok, left, then admitted he was wrong.

hundred to five thousand dollars. Stanford White wrote: *I firmly believe that Edward Bok has more completely influenced American domestic architecture for the better than any man in this generation. When he began, I was short-sighted enough to discourage him, and refused to cooperate with him. If Bok came to me now, I would not only make plans for him, but I would waive any fee for them in retribution for my early mistake.*

But it was still the grandiose château on Fifth Avenue built by Richard Morris Hunt that influenced the firm of McKim, Mead and White. The residence Hunt built for William K. Vanderbilt at Fifty-second Street pulled McKim out onto Fifth Avenue late at night because he slept better after feasting his eyes on the little "Château de Blois" that Sullivan had laughed at.

Emma Goldman, too, had walked up Fifth Avenue, but with her artist-lover Fedya. Berkman used to make her feel guilty about her love of flowers, music, the theater and beauty. Sasha argued it was inconsistent for an anarchist to enjoy luxuries when the people lived in poverty. Emma had argued back that beautiful things were not luxuries but necessities. *The next day Fedya took me to Central Park. Along Fifth Avenue he pointed out the various mansions, naming their owners. I had read about those wealthy men, their affluence and extravagance, while the masses lived in poverty. I expressed my indignation at the contrast between those splendid palaces and the miserable tenements of the East Side. Fedya agreed: Yes, it is a crime that the few should have all, the many nothing. My main objection is that they have such bad taste. Those buildings are ugly.*

One of the palaces Fedya referred to was built by Hunt for John Jacob Astor IV, also the owner of some of the miserable tenements Emma Goldman complained of on the Lower East Side. Between Avenue A and First Avenue, an Astor-owned block, over five hundred families were packed into firetraps with a death rate matching that of Calcutta, twenty-three per thousand. The original John Jacob Astor had gone into fur trapping when the trade was mainly with the Indians. He plied them with liquor (although it was illegal) and reaped a fortune. His post in Oregon was called Fort Astoria.

From the tower of Madison Square Garden, Stanford White could look east and see a portion of Long Island that also belonged to Astor, also called Astoria. Now John Jacob Astor IV had inherited properties, lands and buildings that gave him an income of over three million dollars. Colonel Mann, the inventor who sold his Boudoir Car to George Pullman, was now the publisher of *Town Topics*. It referred to John Jacob Astor as one of the richest catches of the day. In an era of great beauties, Ava Willing was the queen. She became Mrs. Astor. The marriage was a miserable one. John enjoyed working with his hands. He invented a bicycle brake, a marine engine, and took first prize at the Chicago Fair with his Pneumatic Road Improver. It blew dirt off roads. Ava liked playing bridge. John liked the new player pianos he had installed throughout their house. But whenever he played one of them, the butler was hastily sent by Ava to have him desist.

Walking through this period but not seeming to be of it, an American by birth, a stranger by inclination, was the apparition called Thorstein Veblen. His wide-apart eyes seemed to see not the civilization presented to them but a predatory culture of some dark, distant, savage society. Approximating his forebears, he looked every bit the Norwegian farmer. A safety pin held his watch to his vest, while two more held his socks to his pants legs. He wore his hair flat, parted in the middle. His lips were concealed behind a scraggly moustache, while a short beard pointed his chin. In 1884 he graduated from Yale with a Ph.D. This was followed by seven lean years in which his sole occupation was reading. Now he presented himself at Cornell with the pronouncement: *I am Thorstein Veblen.* J. Laurence Laughlin,

Inventor of a marine engine and bicycle brake and winner of first prize at the World Columbian Exposition for his pneumatic road improver, John Jacob Astor IV.

head of the conservative Economics Department, regarded this oddity in coonskin cap and rough corduroy trousers and hired him. A year later, when John D. Rockefeller opened the University of Chicago, Laughlin headed the Economics Department and brought Veblen to Chicago at a salary of five hundred and twenty dollars a year. This act would secure Laughlin's memory in the history of economics. Veblen was at work on his book, *The Theory of the Leisure Class* which would reveal his odd thoughts on architecture: *It comes that most objects alleged to be beautiful, and doing duty as such, show considerable ingenuity of design and are calculated to puzzle the beholder— to bewilder him with irrelevant suggestions and hints of the improbable—at the same time that they give evidence of an expenditure of labour in excess of what would give them their fullest efficiency for their ostensible economic end. The canons of beauty,*

Columbia University refused to take journalism or two million dollars seriously but Joseph Pulitzer persisted.

in that it results in making the physiognomy of our objects of taste a congeries of idiosyncrasies, are under the selective surveillance of the canon of expensiveness . . . the substitution of pecuniary beauty for aesthetic beauty, has been especially effective in the development of architecture.

Castle construction continued on Fifth Avenue, in Newport, Lenox, Bar Harbor and points west. Joseph Pulitzer, publisher of the *New York World*, suffered from insomnia and nervous disorders. Almost totally blind, he had a granite tower of silence built on his Bar Harbor château, Chatwold. He could not tolerate noise, yet could not bear to be alone. Eight male secretaries read to him, informed him, talked to him until he fell asleep. His brother Albert also suffered from insomnia and could not tolerate changes of light. He sold his *New York Journal* to John McLean, wealthy owner of the *Cincinnati Enquirer*. A year later, McLean would unload the *Journal*, for which he had paid Albert one million dollars, for a hundred and eighty thousand. He had made the mistake of doubling the price of the paper

to two cents a copy, and this had driven down its circulation with a resultant loss of advertising. The new owner, a young California publisher named William Randolph Hearst, would drop the cost back to a penny and start a circulation war.

But for the present, the future looked good to the near-blind publisher, Joseph Pulitzer. Dedicated to social reform, his *New York World* had backed the fusion campaign of William L. Strong. The campaign manager was the articulate former assistant D.A., William Travers Jerome. He had joined forces with another fighter of political corruption, Reverend Parkhurst. Jerome, a graduate of Columbia Law School, had a fine reputation and questionable forebears. One of his brothers had died of alcoholism at twenty-three, another had run off to disappear in the West. His father, Leonard, and uncle, Lawrence Jerome, were dedicated to dissipation, gambling and horses. Leonard married Clara Hall; Lawrence, her sister Catherine. The girls' father was of English descent, their mother half Iroquois. The Jerome brothers were friends of Tammany boss William Marcy Tweed and Commodore Vanderbilt. The latter, while building his financial complex, the New York Central, gave them market tips that enriched them both. They built many tracks to race their horses, among them Jerome Park. An assemblyman named Murphy put his name on the street leading to the park. In the middle of the night Catherine Jerome hired some workmen to replace Murphy's signs with her own. (The street is still known as Jerome Avenue.) Her husband at a later date, having lost his financial footing, was forced to negotiate for seven months before uniting their daughter with a British son-in-law. The settlement to the groom was ten

N. G. Lorillard party at Jerome Park. *"The utility
of the fast horse lies largely in his efficiency as a
means of emulation; it gratifies its owner's sense of
aggression."* —Thorstein Veblen.

thousand dollars a year, and their Jennie
then settled in at Blenheim Castle.
Jennie's husband, years later, believed
their son Winston was slightly "off" and
sent him to the safety of a military school.
Jennie lost her husband, Lord Randolph,
when he perished of the pox at the age of
forty-six, the same pox that killed the hero
of Fracastoro's sixteenth-century poem,
Syphilis.

With the election of reform Mayor
Strong, William Travers Jerome was ap-

ABOVE: *Thinking their son "slightly off," Jennie's
husband, Lord Randolph Churchill, shipped Winston
to Sandhurst Military School.*

*Jennie Jerome left Madison Square for Blenheim
Castle.*

43

pointed to the Court of Special Sessions. Jerome had been a sickly youth and had gone into the north woods to build himself up. Another sickly youth with a similar childhood was now selected by Mayor Strong to head the four-man police commission. The young man, often described as a four-eyed cowboy, was Theodore Roosevelt. He was raised in New York City, in one of the oldest, wealthiest families. At the age of twelve, before touring the Nile with his family, a doctor suggested eyeglasses for the awkward youth. He then discovered the world was beautiful and it remained so for the rest of his life. During his Harvard years he was considered "odd." He neither drank nor smoked and taught Sunday school in the Episcopal Church. He was a Presbyterian. He lost his teaching position when the rector found out. Roosevelt felt this unfair, as he had been teaching class for over three years. Enthralled with hunting and guns, he wrote from the Maine woods: *By jove it sometimes seems as if I were having too happy a time to have it last. I enjoy every moment I live.* On one hunting trip in Minnesota with his brother Elliott, Roosevelt killed over two hundred animals. (Elliott named his daughter Eleanor.) Theodore loved the West, and with a partner started the Maltese Cross Ranch on the Little Missouri River. T.R. had married Alice Hathaway Lee at the age of twenty-two and had run successfully for New York assemblyman at twenty-three. Alice gave birth to a daughter while he was in Albany, and on learning she was dying, he rushed to her bedside. A double tragedy struck him. At three a.m. his mother died, at two p.m. his wife.

A year later, he traveled west again, abandoned his first ranch and started a second with a large investment in cattle. Ridiculed at first as a four-eyed tenderfoot, he

T.R. and Elliott. *"The ground of an addiction to sports is an archaic spiritual constitution—the possession of the predatory emulative propensity in a relatively high potency."—Veblen.*

No. 1. The Roosevelt Bears at Home
" Two Roosevelt Bears had a home out West
In a big ravine near a mountain crest."

ABOVE: *". . . the boy's predilection for exploit and for isolation of his own interest is to be taken as a transient reversion to the human nature that is normal to the early barbarian culture—the predatory culture proper."—Veblen.*

T.R. in his buckskins. "The cases are by no means rare in which the transition from the boyish to the adult temperament is not made." —Veblen.

traveled fifty miles by horseback in one day to pick up a buckskin suit made to order for him in the Bad Lands. He wrote his first of many books, *Ranch Life and the Hunting Trail*, and had it illustrated by Frederic Remington. Later, Hearst would send Remington to Cuba to help the *Journal* start a war. Roosevelt would back him up.

The Haymarket strike occurred while Roosevelt was in the Bad Lands. His reactions, recorded in a letter to his sister, were similar to those of many other propertied men of the country: *My men here are hardworking, labouring men who work longer hours for no greater wages than many of the strikers; but they are Americans through and through. I believe nothing would give them greater pleasure than a chance with their rifles at one of the mobs. . . . I wish I had them with me and a fair show at ten times our number of rioters.* Teddy himself was a fearless man of action. His friend, Senator Cabot Lodge, appraised the opinions in Washington of Teddy: *the only thing I can hear adverse is that there is a fear that you will want to fight somebody at once.* President McKinley said: *I want peace and I am told that your friend Theodore . . . is always getting into rows with everybody. I am afraid he is too pugnacious.* Teddy Roosevelt's father had been of the correct age during the Civil War, but he did not join the fray. Instead he paid for a substitute.

Now, as a crusading police commissioner, Teddy Roosevelt had the support of the city's largest-circulation newspaper, Joseph Pulitzer's *World*. Pulitzer, almost totally blind now, incapacitated by his insomnia and nerves, traveled from one artificial world of his own making to the next. Total insulation from noise, whether in his château

Chatwold or on his yacht *Liberty*, accompanied the invalid in his dash from himself. On the *Liberty* the crew of sixty-five stayed clear of their master while his eight male secretaries kept up a brilliant stream of words at just the correct audible level and tone (a skill for which they had been hired). He knew Roosevelt, had been invited to dinner by him. Soon he would be locked in a bitter court fight with him. But now, a dedicated reformer himself, he backed the commissioner of police with his editorials. T.R. had stopped the sale of police promotions and was demanding the merit system.

A few years before, a police reporter had written a shocking book on tenements, crime and poverty called *How the Other Half*

Lives. Now the author, Jacob Riis, together with the police commissioner, prowled the Tenderloin and tenement districts in search of negligent police officers. Sometimes they walked for nine hours at a clip, with Roosevelt collaring any officer found tilting a glass of beer or dozing on the beat.

One night in February of 1897, with the mercury dropping fast and the wind blustering through the costumes of the super-rich, Police Commissioner Roosevelt stood outside the Waldorf Hotel. At any other private ball he certainly would have been one of the invited guests. But this time there had been threatening letters, bomb scares and other warnings. This was Society's first ma-

THE BATTLE WITH THE SLUM

Illustrated by scores of original Stereopticon pictures of New York City life.

Jacob A. Riis
LECTURER

Tabernacle
WEDNESDAY, MARCH 22, 1905

J. B. Pond Lyceum Bureau

.. TICKETS AT ..
Fisher's Book Store and
Review & Herald Retail Store

jor ball to be held in a public building, the Waldorf Hotel. Ever since Henry Frick had been attacked by an anarchist, threats were taken seriously. Commissioner Roosevelt had his own city police ringing the grounds of the hotel, and there was also a contingent of private detectives, Pinkerton men.

Yet, in the heart of the ball's sponsor lay the idea of charity. Mrs. Bradley Martin, a plump little lady with icy blue eyes and multimillions in the bank, had learned that there was a depression on. Informed that it was caused by people not spending enough money, resulting in unemployment and lower wages, she decided to take action in her own way. She would have a magnificent ball, but send the invitations out too late for her friends to send to Paris for costumes. Everything would have to be made here.

Photo of Bandits' Roost by Riis. "With the growth of industry comes the possibility of a predatory life; and if the savages crowd one another in the struggle for subsistence, there is a provocation to hostilities, and a predatory habit of life ensues." —Veblen.

Carnegie retired on a pension of forty-four thousand dollars, not bad for his day. The forty-four thousand was not per year, but per day.

John D. Rockefeller at eighteen. Thirty-five million dollars in oil dividends before the advent of the gasoline-addicted automobile.

Her design was to force those who could best afford it to increase their spending. One of the Belmonts immediately contacted a local costumer and ordered a gold-inlaid suit of armor at a cost of ten thousand dollars. But J. Pierpont Morgan's daughter came simply dressed, as Pocahontas. When Anne Morgan was very young and someone at her father's dinner table asked her what she was going to be when she grew up, she answered directly: *not a rich fool.* But most of the guests dressed lavishly, according to the invitation. Mrs. Bradley wanted the Four Hundred to spend their money, so she ordered her guests to dress for presentation at the Court of Louis XV.

At that very moment, a mild-mannered, middle-class, middle-sized Englishman from the Midlands was introducing his economic ideas to London. His name was Hobson and his idea was that thrift savings led to unemployment. Eyebrows went up at this. But he went on saying that *great wealth could not be consumed as fast as it accumulated.* The rich would always get richer while the poor got children. A horrible dilemma, the poor couldn't consume enough because their incomes were too small, while the wealthy couldn't consume enough because their incomes were too high. Hobson soon lost his invitations to lecture but plodded on. He soon found the wealthy could not invest any longer in their own countries because there weren't enough consumers. If the home marketplace was already gutted, what could the wealthy do with their enormous savings, constantly growing upon themselves? His answer was shocking. *The automatic accumulation of savings would be invested overseas. This would lead to—imperialism.*

Between the years 1892 and 1899 John D. Rockefeller's personal dividends from Standard Oil amounted to thirty-five million dollars. In one year Andrew Carnegie received twenty-three million dollars in income from his steel companies. On retirement, his pension was forty-four thousand dollars . . . *per day*.

Next, T.R. discovered a traditional source of police corruption, the Sunday side-door saloons. These were owned mostly by the great brewers, who paid the party bosses to keep the grand saloons open on the Sabbath. Independent saloon keepers paid the beat-cop directly. The only way to stop the subversion of his police force was to enforce the blue laws. On Sunday, the 23rd of June, he began the enforcement.

This time, Pulitzer sided with the party hacks and the liquor interests. Andes thought Glutinous ruinous. Roosevelt had received that code name from Pulitzer and as such had been entered in Andes' code book. This would prevent the opposition from intercepting and understanding Pulitzer's frequent cables from disparate parts of the globe. The Republican party was "Malaria," the Democratic party "Gosling," McKinley "Guinea" and J. Pierpont Morgan "Gadroon." Pulitzer's nerves skated a razor's edge. Between fits of prodigious profanity, ruthlessness and rage, he demanded understanding, loyalty and Shakespeare. Depression, exhaustion and insomnia contrasted with wild flights of brilliant insight and rhetoric. He understood that Roosevelt's zeal could strike the death knell for reform. He abandoned the thirty-seven-year-old police commissioner because of the damage he could do to Mayor Strong and the entire reform movement. T.R. was alienating the huge German population, not to mention the Irish. The Sabbath laws were not democratic. The wealthy could still have liquor with their meals in clubs and hotels, while the rest of the population lost the re-sources of their neighborhood watering hole. This played into the machine politicians' hands by making reform odious.

The German societies organized an anti-blue-law parade and jestingly invited the police commissioner to attend. All smiles and joviality, he did. The *World*, as well as the Germans, admitted his courage and had to smile back at the face full of teeth.

Both Pulitzer and Roosevelt lost interest in the Sabbath laws when the judicious decision was reached that saloons that served food and had "rooms" could remain open. The pretzel became king, prostitution gained rooms. Now, in 1895, the publisher and the policeman turned to thoughts of war, with England. The boundary line between British Guiana and Venezuela was in dispute, and the discovery of gold within the disputed area added sufficient fuel to interest all parties.

President Crespo of Venezuela, citing the Monroe Doctrine, appealed to President Cleveland for protection from British aggression. The new Secretary of State, Richard Olney, who had banned his own daughter from his home after her marriage, wrote the diplomatic note to our English cousins. Invoking the Monroe Doctrine, he demanded England agree to arbitration and told them why: *Today, the United States is practically sovereign on this continent and its fiat is law. It is because, in addition to all other grounds, its infinite resources combined with its isolated position render it master of the situation and practically invulnerable as against any or all other powers.*

President Cleveland denounced the English as a threat to the "peace and safety" of our country. In a fighting mood, he added:

In making these recommendations I am fully alive to the responsibility incurred and keenly realize all the consequences that may follow. The *New York Sun* praised the fighting words, called those opposed aliens or traitors and thirsted for naval battles in the Irish Sea and English Channel. The *Tribune* applauded the jingo tone: *The message will not be welcome to the peace-at-any-price cuckoos....* One headline commented: **ROOSEVELT TALKS WAR. BETTER, HE SAYS, THAN PEACE WITH LOSS OF NATIONAL SELF-RESPECT.** In the article Roosevelt congratulated President Cleveland and Secretary of State Olney on their admirable message. Halfway through the article he allayed the fears of the public: *And I would like to say right here that the talk of British fleets ransoming American cities is too foolish to me for serious consideration. American cities may possibly be bombarded, but no ransom will be paid for them. It is infinitely better to see the cities laid level than to see a dollar paid to any foreign foe to buy their safety.*

Roosevelt then went on to explain how we would march on Canada and conquer it, and: *once wrested from England, it would never be restored.* He wrote a friend: *If there is a muss I shall try to have a hand in it myself!* Joyfully he contemplated the annexation of conquered Canada.

Against all this, in the midst of the Christmas season, Pulitzer sent over a hundred cablegrams to British leaders requesting them to state their peaceful views by return collect cable. The Christmas issue, under the capital headline **PEACE AND GOODWILL** ran the text of the replies from England: *The Prince of Wales and the Duke of York ... earnestly trust and cannot but believe the present crisis will be arranged in a manner satisfactory to* both countries, and will be succeeded by the same warm feeling of friendship which has existed between them for so many years. Gladstone, Lord Salisbury, Cardinal Vaughan, the Bishop of Manchester, as well as the Archbishops of Wales, Dublin and Armagh, all wished blessings of peace between the two countries. Newspapers throughout the nation picked up the Pulitzer peace page. A new feeling swept the country: perhaps the British weren't as unreasonable as Americans had thought. Referring to the editors of the *World*, T.R. wrote to Cabot Lodge: *It would give me great pleasure to have them put in prison the minute hostilities began.* However, there were no hostilities, Canada was not annexed and Teddy did not get into uniform against the English.

In the same year American men were trying for war with Britain, American women were trying for something else with the English. Their struggle in some ways very much resembled the tactics of warfare. Kidnappings, imprisonments and ransoms were involved. The prisoner in one case was the seventeen-year-old wistful beauty Consuelo Vanderbilt. She had been incarcerated on her mother's orders in one of the family stone prisons. To the admiring eye of an outsider, Marble House, on Newport's fabulous Goldcoast, was an eleven-million-dollar dream palace. To young Consuelo, unable to send word to her heart's desire, Winthrop Rutherford, it was a dungeon. In the winter, when the family wasn't abroad, they lived in the "Château de Blois" Hunt had built for them on Fifth Avenue. It was this architecture of Hunt's that had attracted so much attention to the Vanderbilts and had gotten them admitted to "the" Mrs. Astor's Four Hundred.

Caroline Schermerhorn was a plump, un-
attractive, dull twenty-two-year-old when
she married William Backhouse Astor, Jr.
She had two qualities, however, that led
to her leadership of New York and Newport society: dignity and determination. It
was she who led the Astors in their move
uptown to Thirty-fourth Street and Fifth
Avenue. (Her son, John Jacob Astor IV,
would eventually tear down their fortress
mansion to build the Astoria Hotel. He
would also inherit Ferncliff and send for
Stanford White.) Since her husband had
not been the oldest son, his father had ignored
him. He, in turn, ignored his son and daughters. But Caroline showered her children
with tenderness, warmth and sacrifice. In
Society her wish was edict. Four hundred
was the number of guests who could fit
comfortably into her ballroom. The assault
of the Vanderbilts on Mrs. Astor's Newport,
first with the seventy-room "cottage," The
Breakers, then Marble House, had left them
unnoticed by Mrs. Astor. But Alva Vanderbilt announced the opening of her new Fifth
Avenue château with a magnificent ball for
fifteen hundred dinner guests. Young Carrie
Astor and her girlfriends began to practice a
star formation they would execute together
in a quadrille. She did not know Alva Vanderbilt was holding up her invitation because
Mrs. Astor had not called on her. Word soon
went out to her friends that they'd best find
a substitute for young Carrie Astor. Mrs.
Astor watched the tears stream down her
daughter's cheeks, then resolutely changed
into a Worth gown and sent for her carriage.
She then muttered her immortal dictum: "I
think the time for the Vanderbilts has come."
The following day, Pulitzer's *World* described the gala and estimated its cost at two
hundred and fifty thousand dollars. Carrie
Astor was radiant in the star quadrille. The

*Mrs. William K. Vanderbilt, Alva. Marble House,
"Château de Blois" and Belcourt too. She always
knew women were smarter than men.*

Consuelo Vanderbilt with handkerchief. Alva became America's most hated mother.

agreed upon was the twenty-four-year-old Charles Spencer-Churchill. With his newly inherited title, ninth Duke of Marlborough, the impoverished young man became the sole owner of Blenheim Castle. He was invited to Marble House. He came, asked Consuelo to marry him. In tears, the young girl rushed to her mother for protection. The following day, the papers announced the engagement. Her mother had started the betrayal that would take Consuelo from the young man she loved into Blenheim Castle. The following days were a siege. Alva feigned a heart attack. She also announced she would shoot any suitor other than the Duke, and then she would be executed by hanging for that act and her death would be on Consuelo's conscience. Guilt, guilt, guilt was forced upon the seventeen-year-old until, in tears, she was dragged to the altar of St. Thomas' Episcopal Church. Walter Damrosch's sixty-piece orchestra drowned out her sobs. Envious women lined the streets to watch the magnificent procession, which included the British Ambassador. Some said the twenty-minute delay was caused by a breakdown in negotiations, but in truth, the terms of the marriage had all been agreed upon beforehand: one hundred thousand dollars a year each to Consuelo and the Duke, with an additional two and a half million in rail stock to the groom. Eventually the couple impoverished America and enriched England by over ten million dollars. When the public learned of the forced marriage and financial settlement, Society dropped in public esteem and Alva became America's most hated mother. Two months after Consuelo's wedding, after almost a year of secret planning, Alva married O. H. P. Belmont. The arrangements had been difficult, as no Protestant clergyman could be found to officiate at the marriage of a divorced woman. They had to

Vanderbilts had arrived. Alva was triumphant.

But now Consuelo was locked in the confines of Marble House in combat with that same Alva, her mother. Only a few months before, Alva had convinced her husband to give her a divorce. The only basis for such a decree in New York was adultery. Her gallant husband had permitted himself to be trapped in that act and Alva was now single. Marble House was part of the settlement. She had dashed to England after the divorce and sought the advice of Lady Randolph Churchill (Jennie Jerome) and other ex-Americans on an alliance for Consuelo. The candidate

Waiting for the "carriage trade" inside the Waldorf-Astoria.

settle for Mayor Strong. Consuelo did not attend her mother's marriage. After her wedding, Alva Vanderbilt Belmont found herself the possessor of two Newport "cottages," Marble House and Belcourt. She remodeled both, built two estates on Long Island and held onto her Fifth Avenue château. The American Institute of Architects made her their first woman member.

Although Andes, Gush and Glutinous would soon be shouting together for war, Gush and Andes first had at one another. Gush, Andes' code name for Hearst, staged a raid. Among the many innovations at the *World* made by Morrill Goddard, which had helped double the circulation, was the introduction of the "funnies." Richard Felton Outcault's "Yellow Kid," the doings of a street urchin in a long yellow nightdress, won a huge following. Hearst hired Goddard, Outcault and most of the staff away from Pulitzer in one fell swoop. The next day, Andes (Pulitzer) hired them all back. But Gush retaliated the following day and they all left the *World* for good. Both the *Journal* and the *New York World* ran "The Yellow Kid."

Hearst had backed William Jennings

Bryan, and although Bryan lost, Hearst's politics had gained him a huge circulation jump. The day Bryan lost to McKinley, Hearst could brag that his circulation in the morning edition was near a million, and the *Evening Journal*'s near half a million. Sensationalism, money and populism had gained him the readership of the downtrodden and momentarily cost him many of his advertisers. He had taken a gamble and achieved a miracle: the circulation of the older established *Herald* was only one hundred fifty thousand; the *Sun*, seventy-five thousand; the *Tribune*, sixteen thousand; and the *Times*, nine thousand. Hearst was closing in on the frontrunner, Pulitzer's *World*. Andes had to take it when Gush proclaimed in an editorial: *No other journal in the United States includes in its staff a tenth of the number of writers of reputation and talent. It is the* Journal's *policy to engage brains as well as to get the news, for the public is even more fond of entertainment than it is of information....*

Ava and John Jacob Astor IV sent for Stanford White to design the play area for Ferncliff. It would consist of a sixty-five-foot marble swimming pool, squash courts, tennis courts, bowling alley, billiard room and rifle range. While Ava played bridge, her husband played gentleman farmer, as his father had before him. Sundays, John attended church while Ava played bridge at home. With his great love of science and engineering, the frustrated Astor wrote *A Journey in Other Worlds*. In it rain became a science, space travel a reality, the horse and its droppings replaced by clean electricity. The heroine was a passionless socialite. One of the problems John Astor had solved to his great satisfaction was his competition with his cousin William Waldorf. William had inherited the lion's share of John Jacob Astor

III's estate, and in 1893 opened the Waldorf Hotel on Thirty-fourth Street and Fifth Avenue, next door to John's mansion. Infuriated by the hotel traffic, John threatened to build stables where his mansion sat, but decided to outdo his cousin by building an even greater hotel adjacent to the Waldorf. The two cousins then decided to connect the hotels, but cautiously inserted in their contract a clause permitting the sealing off of the two buildings should family relations deteriorate. John called his hotel the Astoria, and when it was completed, the two hotels were joined as the Waldorf-Astoria. It was then referred to as the "hyphen."

The election of 1897 proved a disaster for reform. Boss Croker, forced to depart for foreign shores when Strong was elected, returned before the election confident that the reformers were through. Police Commissioner Roosevelt ducked out of office before the deluge when McKinley granted his request for the position of Assistant Secretary of the Navy. The keynote of the campaign was set by Tammany's candidate for district attorney, Asa Gardner. To cheering crowds he shouted from the platform: *To hell with reform!* Once again, vice was organized, with the Tammany commission collecting over three million dollars a month in graft.

In May of 1897 Saint-Gaudens went to Boston for the unveiling of his Shaw Memorial. Commissioned years before, his original plans had been rejected by the Shaw family. The commission had been for a memorial for the young Bostonian colonel, Robert Gould Shaw, who died at the head of the Negro regiment he had recruited. Saint-Gaudens wanted to do an equestrian statue, and his sketches showed the hatless officer astride his pawing steed, sword in hand. The family complained that type of statue was for a great commander or officer of the highest rank, while Shaw was only a young colonel. Saint-Gaudens could have done a simple panel, as the Shaw family had expected, but the idea of the colonel and his recruits gained in his imagination till the commission became a labor of love. During the ceremonies, Saint-Gaudens sat with William James, one of the orators for the occasion. There was a parade with the veterans of the 54th Massachusetts Regiment, which had fought under Shaw in the Civil War, many of the men crippled and white-haired, some of them bearing flowers for the memorial. Booker T. Washington gave a noble address and caused a sensation. When the monument was unveiled, it received one of Boston's most appreciative ovations. The whole city was excited by the new Shaw memorial.

Booker T. Washington, cheered in Boston.

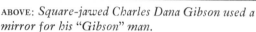

ABOVE: *Square-jawed Charles Dana Gibson used a mirror for his "Gibson" man.*

LEFT: *"The Eternal Question" by Gibson.*

BELOW: *Evelyn Nesbit, model for "The Eternal Question."*

Nannie Langhorne went to Newport to visit her sister Irene and her husband. They introduced her to the wealthy, handsome, wild Robert Gould Shaw, son of the late Colonel Shaw. His family hoped an alliance with someone like Nannie would stop his drinking and quiet him down. Nannie herself was charged with energy. Four years before, at fourteen, she had made a lasting mark for herself at the Chicago World's Fair. When the band struck up "Marching Through Georgia," this slight Southern belle stood and shouted: *Three Cheers for Robert E. Lee.* The crowd, much to the surprise of her family, echoed back: *Hurrah for Robert E. Lee.* The husband of her sister Irene had made a false start when he was thirteen. He had been brought to the sculpture studio of Saint-Gaudens as a potential student-apprentice. He did clever silhouettes and impressed the sculptor, who hired him on the spot. However, when he was bringing back some sketches of Stanford White's, he forgot what he was about and crumpled them into an illegible ball. He was fired. Now he did illustrations for leading newspapers and journals. Having neither moustache nor beard, he used himself as his clean-cut male model. For his female, he used mainly his wife Irene, who had an uplifted chin, piled-up casual hairdo and aristocratic features. Men admired the male image portrayed in his work and shaved off their beards and moustaches. Women piled their hair atop their heads and tilted their chins up ever so slightly to resemble a "Gibson girl." In a few years Charles Dana Gibson would have Stanford White build a showplace residence for him on Seventy-third Street. One of the illustrations that would add to his fame was a profile of a beautiful girl with her dark hair spilling over one shoulder in such a way as to suggest a question mark. His model would be a fifteen-year-old Pittsburg girl new to modeling in New York, Evelyn Nesbit.

Nannie Langhorne married Robert Shaw in October of 1897. On her wedding day, she had poison ivy. On her wedding night, regrets. Two nights later, she ran away, feeling sex was regrettable. Later, she would again visit her sister Irene and Charles Dana Gibson, this time in England. She would marry an Astor, be the first woman elected to Parliament and discover Mary Baker Eddy.

At this time, in Pittsburg, Mrs. Winifield Nesbit was finding it impossible to support herself and her twelve-year-old daughter Evelyn. The money left from her late husband's law practice had run out, and taking in boarders proved insufficient to meet bread and board bills. She would have to move. Another widow, also in Pittsburg, had dissimilar money problems. Her late husband, William Thaw, a rail and coke magnate, left an estate of over forty million dollars. After Mrs. William Thaw settled ten thousand dollars a year on the English Earl of Yarmouth, her daughter Alice married him and became a Countess. It was not immediately known that the effeminate Earl abandoned her on their wedding night. Her sister married George Carnegie, nephew of Andrew Carnegie. Each of the girls had inherited five million dollars. However, there were special stipulations in their father's will concerning his eldest child, his scion, Harry Thaw. The will specified he was to receive no more than twenty five hundred dollars a year. These specific instructions, sadly given by a disappointed father, were not carried out by the loving, guilt-ridden mother. She upped Harry to eighty thousand. In New York's Tenderloin district he used the name Professor Reid and advertised for young girls aspiring to the stage.

The circulation war between Andes and Gush was becoming unbearably costly. Both needed a circulation boost. A small war would do just that. Assistant Secretary of the Navy Theodore Roosevelt also needed a small war to test the new fleet. Another reason had to do with the planned Isthmian Canal. Bases would be necessary to protect it. Since the Cubans already were at war, in revolt against their Spanish overlords, Hearst decided Cuba was the issue he needed. He sent reporters and artists to the country to report on the war. One of them, Frederic Remington, the artist who had illustrated Roosevelt's first book, asked to return home because there was no action or war. Hearst shot back: *You furnish the pictures, I'll furnish the war.* Gush now manufactured atrocity tales for his front pages and circulation leaped. However, to the distaste of Gush, Andes, Lodge and Roosevelt, General Wey-

This little Thaw married the Earl of Yarmouth; her sister married George Carnegie; her brother became the sadist Professor Reid.

ler had almost restored peace to Cuba, having all but quelled the insurrectors. Weyler had been sent to Cuba by the Spanish Premier Canovas, who was now serving his fifth term in that post. Canovas always dressed in black, wore no jewels, lived in a castle in Madrid and collected rare coins, paintings and old china. His poetry was widely read and he had written a ten-volume history of Spain. In 1896 a bomb had been thrown at a religious procession led by the Bishop of Barcelona. Eleven were killed, forty wounded. Canovas had four hundred persons, mostly anarchists, rounded up and imprisoned. There were rumors of torture in his dungeons. While on summer holiday in August of 1897, the Premier took breakfast with his wife on the terrace outside their hotel room. It was hot. While Señora Canovas fanned herself, her husband read the morning paper. Suddenly, an Italian, Michel Angiollilo, appeared before them. He drew a pistol from his pocket, stepped nearer to the Premier and fired three shots, dispatching Canovas to another world. Señora Canovas attacked the stranger with her fan screaming: *Murderer! Assassin!* He backed up: *I am not an assassin. . . . I am the Avenger of my Anarchist comrades. I have nothing to do with you, madame.* He was soon executed by garrote, in the Spanish tradition.

At first, Pulitzer's *World* tried to be factual about affairs in Cuba. The editors printed the reports as received from correspondent Willam Bowen and his temporary aide, twenty-year-old Winston Churchill. They reported not all Cubans heroic nor all Spaniards cutthroats. However, Hearst was gaining readers, so the *World* started continuous thrillers of atrocity stories. General Weyler was called ferocious, bloody, fiendish. Weyler was the same Spanish officer who had

accompanied General Sherman as an observer during our Civil War. The *World* also started a series called "The Hideous History of Spain," and updated it with illustrated accounts of men and women being massacred on the streets by roving bands of armed Spanish soldiers. In the midst of all this a Bower dispatch calling General Weyler a good soldier *of extraordinary energy and great intelligence* somehow slipped into the *World*. James Creelman was immediately sent to Cuba to do more "colorful" reporting. The improvement was considerable: *American citizens are imprisoned or slain without cause. . . . Blood on the roadside, blood in the fields, blood on the doorsteps, blood, blood, blood!* Gradually, Andes came to equal Gush in gory descriptions of old men and children cut up and fed to wild dogs, Cuban food and water poisoned, assaults on Cuban women. A Baptist minister urged immediate American intervention on the former peace-page of the *World*. At the conclusion of one of his orations, Assistant Secretary of the Navy Roosevelt stated: *No national life is worth having if the nation is not willing, when the need shall arise, to stake everything*

Newspaperman Winston Churchill.

Portrait of Alice Roosevelt by T.R.

flying squadron should attack the coast of Spain. Roosevelt admitted in a dispatch to one of the naval commanders that he wanted hostilities with Spain not alone for humanitarian reasons, but also for *the benefit done to our people by giving them something to think about which isn't material gain, and especially the benefit done our military forces by trying both the Army and Navy in actual practice.*

The conciliatory General Ramon Blanco replaced General Weyler and Spain announced it would give self-government to the Cubans. But on the night of February 15, 1898, the battleship *Maine* blew up in Havana harbor. Spanish sailors of the cruiser *Alfonso XII* bravely joined the perilous rescue work as ammunition aboard the sinking ship continued to explode. General Blanco cried when he was informed of the disaster. Captain Sigsbee of the *Maine* wired Secretary Long that: *Public opinion should be suspended until further report. . . . Many Spanish officers including representatives of General Blanco now with me to express sympathy.* Hearst printed Captain Sigsbee's request, with one additional sentence: *Captain Sigsbee, of the* Maine, *and Consul-General Lee both urge that public opinion be suspended until they have completed their investigation. They are taking the course of tactful men who are convinced that there has been treachery.*

The byline for the article in the *Journal* read: *by Captain E. L. Zalinski, U.S.A.* In parenthesis beneath his name: *Captain Zalinski is the inventor of the famous dynamite gun, which would be the principal factor in our coast defense in case of war.*

On February 17 the *World* and the *Jour-*

on the supreme arbitrament of war, and to pour out its blood, its treasures, its tears like water rather than to submit to the loss of honor and renown.* The critical comment on this speech by the *Washington Post: Well done, nobly spoken! Theodore Roosevelt, you have found your proper place at last—all hail!*

After the death of Premier Canovas, alarmed by the bellicose attitude of the Americans, Spain recalled General Weyler and proposed home rule to the Cubans. McKinley's hopes for peace were revived and he asked that Spain be given a reasonable chance. Theodore Roosevelt said President McKinley had *the backbone of an éclair.* He also suggested to Secretary of the Navy John D. Long, who wanted peace (as did the President and the rest of the Cabinet), that in the event of hostilities, an American

"If this country had a fleet of
twenty battle-ships their
existence would make it all
the more likely that we
should not have war."
—Assistant Secretary of the
Navy T.R. in public. In private he wrote of his desire
for war with Spain:
"... especially the benefit
done our military forces by
trying both the Army and
Navy in actual practise."

the *World: Nothing so disgraceful as the
behavior of these two newspapers in the past
week has ever been known in the history of
journalism.* He went on to attack their
*gross misrepresentation of facts, deliberate
invention of tales calculated to excite the
public ... no one, absolutely no one, supposed a yellow journal cares five cents about
the Cubans, the* Maine *victims, or anyone
else.* On his masthead he put: *All the news
that's fit to print.* In Boston Mary Baker
Eddy also worried about the newspapers
people read.

Hearst's *Journal* circulation leaped to a
million. An "extra" put out on February 18
declared: *Whole Country Thrills with the
War Fever, Yet the President Says, "It was
an Accident."* Pulitzer's war with Gush
caused him to raise salaries and expenses.
During the week of the *Maine* disaster, five
million copies of the *World* had been sold,
the highest circulation the paper had ever
achieved. Yet for the year the *World* showed
a loss. Andes asked his staff to cut expenses and
sent an auditor to cut his wife's seventy-two-
thousand-dollar-a-year household budget.
The auditor found the stable of thirty-five
horses cost fifteen thousand dollars a year.
The average number of persons fed at Chatwold per day was fifty-three. The bill for
food and drink for August alone was three
thousand dollars. No cuts could be made.

nal published a "suppressed" cable from Captain Sigsbee to Secretary Long declaring the
explosion was not accidental. The cable was
discovered to be an outright fake. When the
Spanish ship *Vizcaya* visited New York with
her flags at half-mast in honor of the American dead, the *New York World* warned:
*While lying off the Battery her shells will
explode on the Harlem River and in the sub-
urbs of Brooklyn.*

The ailing *New York Times* had been
taken over by young Adolph Ochs. He was
outraged by the reporting of the *Journal* and

In a private letter to America's most vociferous advocate of sea power, Captain Alfred
T. Mahan, Roosevelt wrote ... *I suppose I
need not tell you that as regards Hawaii I
take your views absolutely, as indeed I do on
foreign policy generally. If I had my way we
would annex those islands tomorrow. If that
is impossible I would establish a protectorate
over them. I believe we should build the*

Nicaraguan Canal at once, and in the meantime that we should build a dozen new battle ships, half of them on the Pacific Coast; and these battle ships should have large coal capacity and a consequent increased radius of action. . . . The Secretary also believes in building the Nicaraguan Canal as a military measure, although I don't know that he is as decided on this point as you and I are.

The president of Harvard, Charles William Eliot, felt the building of a large army and fleet of battleships was the policy of England and France. It was the abandonment of what is characteristically American policy, which was reliance upon strength in peace. The jingoes were a creation of the combativeness that is in man. He referred to Lodge and Roosevelt as jingoes and called them: *degenerated sons of Harvard.*

The day after the *Maine* disaster, Roosevelt wrote to his friend Cabot Lodge: *Being a Jingo, I will say, to relieve my feelings, that I would give anything if President McKinley would order the fleet to Havana tomorrow.*

But while Lodge and Roosevelt urged war, McKinley and his Cabinet still hoped for peace. There was no evidence that the explosion of the *Maine* was internal sabotage, Spanish- or rebel-inspired or accidental. There was no motive for the Spanish, who were making every concession toward peace, to have provoked an incident. Pulitzer and Hearst continued their circulation battle under an old English journalist's edict: *the best stimulant for circulation is war.*

The American Geographical Society awarded its Gold Medal to Robert Peary in 1897 for his explorations of Greenland and its northernmost coastlines and of the Inglefield Gulf area. A year later the Royal Geographical Society of London awarded Peary its Patron's Gold Medal. Now, with America on the verge of war with Spain, Peary was having difficulty getting a leave of absence from the Navy Department for another go at reaching the North Pole. He had requested a five-year leave and received a negative reply. Before departing for the West Coast as ordered, he met a prominent New Yorker, Charles Moore, a Republican who had aided in the election of President McKinley. He told Peary he would see what he could do for him. On Peary's last exploration his wife Jo had accompanied him on their small ship into Eskimo territory. She had lived with him in a tent for a while, and then returned to the ship when Peary struck out for another unsuccessful attempt to reach the Pole. During her stay she was taken aback by the Eskimo women's custom of stripping to the waist, along with their men, when their snowhouses or tents became overheated. She was more shocked to notice visiting Eskimos switch *koonahs* (wives). She wrote: *If he*

Portrait of Alice.

Robert Peary forced to join the dogs.

brings his own, they trade for the time being

Robert Peary had learned much from the Eskimos, listening to their speech patterns, watching them build their snowhouses and work their dogs with only a whip as guide. On one expedition he had broken his leg. The doctor on the trip, Frederick Cook, had set it and then made Peary rest before going off again. A few months later, Peary and his party started off with twenty dogs and four men. The dogs would haul the sledges, and if food became scarce, some would be used to feed the others, and the men, too, if necessary. On that trip conditions got so bad the dogs refused to go on. The men then changed places with them and pulled both sledges and dogs. From Peary's diary: *Dogs*

*Matthew Henson, still by his side since canal days
in Nicaragua.*

would not pull sledge this morning in the deep soft snow, so Astrup and I got in the traces with them. The two men were alone at this point, the others having returned to base because of injury and sickness. Peary and Astrup built a cairn, leaving data on their sitings, and set off for home base. The return was as difficult as the original journey. They were plagued by rough ice, blizzards, crevasses and, of course, dying dogs barely able to travel on. Later attempts would be worse.

When Robert Peary was two years old, his father was taken ill. His symptoms were those of pneumonia, but the family lived eighty miles from medical assistance and had to write for professional advice. A doctor's letter regretted he was not improving and recommended more hot footbaths and brandy, salt and lemon juice. He died a week later. His mother took on the rearing of the blue-eyed youngster, protecting his fair complexion by having him wear a bonnet. Without realizing it, she was bringing up her son as a girl. As he had a slight lisp, he had to fight off taunts of "sissy." He tried to frighten little girls and once tripped his aged grandfather to watch him fall. Mary made him attend Sunday school, of which the only memento is a clipping from the Sunday school paper. It describes life among the Eskimos and pictures four boys playing ball with walrus ribs for sticks. It described how they lived away up north among the ice mountains. Peary was six years old at the time. When he was a high school student he wrote in his diary: *About nine o'clock as mother got up to go to bed she suddenly became very weak and cold on her left side so she could not walk. It scared me very much, but she laid on my bed and I chafed her hands and feet till she recovered.*

When he finished high school, his mother enrolled Peary at Bowdoin College. After finally gaining the approval of his high-school peers, he again felt like an outsider on entering college. After describing the physical layout at Bowdoin in his diary, he wrote: *. . . but for all that it is so lonesome, oh so lonesome here that I don't know what to do with myself. All the faces are strange and I seem to be in a distant country.*

After his mother had another bout of illness that worried him, Peary wrote: *Oh, you who have always had a father and a mother can but faintly imagine what it will be. No one to go to in trouble. No home. Nothing but strangers. In a word, to be alone in its deepest, dullest sense of agony.* Living off campus in his senior year, when his mother was enjoying good health and his studies were coming easier, he wrote happily in his diary: *I've got my room fitted up. Mother and I have been two weeks making the curtains and lamerquins and one or two little things. Just think of that. But the result fully repays the labor, I think. The curtains are of a soft glossy buff-tinted material just having enough to fall in graceful folds any way you can arrange it. . . .* When he was twenty-one, on his birthday, he wrote to a girlfriend: *Today as I think of what the world is and that I have my life before me, nothing seems impossible. I wish that as in the story books some fairy might place the mirror of my life before me and tell me to look at whatever scene I wished. Yet, if I could do so, I could hardly say but I should close my eyes and refuse to look. How many have wished and wondered about the mysterious future as I do, and yet if the curtain were permitted to be drawn aside, I would shrink from doing it for fear of gazing upon rugged rocks and yawning graves in place of the velvety paths they wish for.* In his early twenties he began an experiment: *I am testing my ability to*

HARRY

HOUDINI

THE

WORLD'S GREATEST

MYSTIFIER

AND

King of Hand-cuffs

Assisted by

Mme. BEATRICE HOUDINI

❋

PRONOUNCED
by American Managers the
Greatest Drawing Card.

Eight Weeks a Headliner on
the Keith's Circuit. Re-Engaged
and Re-Engaged.

Return Engagement on the
Orpheum Circuit.

Now Playing En-route as a
Special Feature.

WALTER & WALTER PRINTERS, 335 FIFTH AVENUE, CHICAGO, ILL.

make myself agreeable . . . as I should like to gain that attractive personality that when I was with a person, they would always have to like me whether they wanted to or not. (Hugh J. Lee, a member of the 1893–1895 expedition, said: *Peary was a very determined man; he was absolutely ruthless, so far as punishing his own flesh was concerned. It was not his way to say: Do this or that, but rather, Please help me do this. He was gentle and kind and . . . understanding which is true greatness. . . .*)

When he was twenty-four Peary explained in a letter to his mother: *I don't want to live and die without accomplishing anything or without being known beyond a narrow cir-* *cle of friends. I would like to acquire a name which would be an "open sesame" to circles of culture and refinement anywhere, a name which would make my mother proud and which would make me feel that I was the peer of anyone I might meet.*

Charles Moore called on the Secretary of the Navy and told him Peary needed a leave of absence for another try at the Pole. Had he called on the Assistant Secretary, he might have received a positive reply. Instead he got a shouted: *Anything, but that!* Moore then went over the Secretary's head to President McKinley and reminded him of a promise he had made: *Come to me if you ever want anything.* He requested the five-year leave for Peary and got it. Elated, Peary made preparations for the journey to Greenland. It would be his sixth expedition, separating him from his wife and child for a period of four years.

At this time, Houdini and his wife Bess were touring uneventfully with small circuses. Houdini was going through his horizontal-bar period. The marriage papers showed that Wilhelmina Rahner had married Harry Houdini, formerly Ehrich Weiss in July of 1894. They were probably married a number of times, once by civil ceremony, then either by a rabbi for him or by a priest for her. Bess went under the name of Beatrice Raymond, and in the theater her act with her sister was billed as "The Floral Sisters." A discouraged trouper gave Houdini the key to success: *publicity.*

The Houdinis decided to have one more go at show business. Chicago had always been friendly to magicians; the Houdinis would get a two-week booking there and try for publicity. They arrived in Chicago without

POSITIVELY

The only Conjuror in the World that Escapes out of all Handcuffs, Leg Shackles, Insane Belts and Straight Jacket after being

STRIPPED STARK NAKED

Mouth Sealed and thoroughly searched from Head to Feet, Proving he carries no Keys, Springs Wires or concealed accessories.

Police Captains, Sheriffs, Detectives, Etc., Stand Powerless and non-plussed at his marvelous and inexplicable escape from all handcuffs.

BRINGING OUT ALL THE CUFFS, INTERLOCKED, PROVING HE DOES NOT SLIP HIS HANDS OR FEET.

TO SAIL FOR EUROPE SOON

DEFIES THE POLICE OF ALL NATIONS

DIRECTION:
Mr. MARTIN BECK,
609 Ashland Block,   CHICAGO, ILL

a booking and went straight to the police department. While Bess talked to the chief, Harry looked over the cells and locks. They returned a few days later with as many press men as they could assemble and challenged the police chief to lock Houdini in and handcuff him. When he broke out, the chief and press men were laughing. The chief had explained that Houdini had checked out the locks a few days ago. Houdini, who had made wire keys for the locks, challenged them to strip him naked and repeat the lockup and handcuffing: *Go ahead, get a doctor to search me if you think this is a cheap trick.* Bess left the room. He was stripped and searched and locked up. He escaped in shorter time than before and flash powder photographs were taken of him behind bars in cuffs. Houdini rushed to the newsstands as soon as the papers appeared and sent clippings to theater managers and agents in Chicago. Because there was a death in an act at the Hopkins Theatre, the manager phoned the Houdinis and they ended up with star billing at one hundred dollars for the week. Seven days later, they were again out of work.

Assistant Secretary of the Navy Roosevelt informed Commodore George Dewey, a naval officer who had served under Admiral Farragut in the Civil War, that the choice for commander of the Asiatic squadron had been narrowed down to him and Commodore Howell. Roosevelt was for Dewey. Senator Proctor of Dewey's home state of Vermont, at Dewey's request, called on President McKinley, who promised the appointment to the Vermonter. Many others wanted the appointment to go to their favorite sons, and when a delegation read their objections concerning Commodore Dewey to Assistant Secretary Roosevelt, he shot back: *Gentle-*

men, I can't agree with you. We have looked up his record. We have looked him straight in the eyes. He is a fighter. We'll not change now. Pleased to have met you. Good day, gentlemen.

On October 21, 1897, Commodore Dewey received orders to sail for Nagasaki, Japan, on December 7 to take command of the Asiatic fleet. On February 16, in Hong Kong, he learned of the destruction of the *Maine*. He immediately made preparations for war, drilling his men, purchasing coal, provisions and fresh stores of ammunition. He made secret arrangements with a Chinese merchant to supply him with provisions in neutral territory should war break out.

Nine days later, on the afternoon of February 25, 1898, Teddy Roosevelt was the Acting Secretary of the Navy. Secretary Long had gone off for the rest of the day and Roosevelt was left in charge for that short period. He acted almost immediately and sent a cable to Commodore Dewey: *Order the Squadron except Monocacy to Hong Kong. Keep full of coal. In the event of declaration war Spain, your duty will be to see that the Spanish squadron does not leave the Asiatic coast and then offensive operations in Philippine Islands. Keep Olympia until further orders.*

The following day, after learning of Roosevelt's actions, Secretary Long wrote in his diary: *... during my short absence I find that Roosevelt, in his precipitate way, has come very near causing more of an explosion than happened to the Maine.... He means to be thoroughly loyal, but the very devil seemed to possess him yesterday afternoon. Having the authority for that time of Acting Secretary, he immediately began to launch peremptory orders, distributing ships, order-*

ing ammunition, which there is no means to move to places where there is no place to store it; sending for Captain Barker to come on about the guns of the Vesuvius, *which is a matter that might have been perfectly arranged by correspondence; sending messages to Congress for immediate legislation, authorizing the enlistment of an unlimited number of seamen and ordering guns from the Navy Yard at Washington to New York, with a view to arming auxiliary cruisers which are now in peaceful commercial pursuit.... He has gone at things like a bull in a china shop....*

In April, two months after Roosevelt had cabled Commodore Dewey to "coal" up, McKinley left the war-or-peace decision up to Congress and we were at war. *While I think I could face death with dignity, I have no desire before my time has come to go out in the everlasting darkness.* Roosevelt wrote this in a letter in March, explaining that he was not a "parlor jingo" and therefore would fight because *I cannot afford to disregard the fact that my power for good, whatever it may be, would be gone if I didn't try to live up to the doctrines I have tried to preach.*

In April he sent the following order to Brooks Brothers in New York: *Can you make me so I shall have it here by next Saturday a blue cravennet regular lieutenant-colonel's uniform without yellow on collar, and with leggings? If so, make it. Charge Theodore Roosevelt.*

Roosevelt had volunteered and been given the rank of lieutenant colonel under his friend, Army surgeon Leonard Wood. Their volunteer cavalry regiment would come to be known as the "Rough Riders." Secretary Long advised against Roosevelt's resignation and warned him about leaving his position,

T.R. and the Rough Riders.

wife and family. In his diary Long wrote:
*. . . His heart is right, and he means well,
but it is one of those cases of aberration-
desertion-vain-glory; of which he is utterly
unaware. He thinks he is following his highest ideal, whereas, in fact, as without exception every one of his friends advises him, he
is acting like a fool. And, yet, how absurd
all this will sound if, by some turn of fortune,
he should accomplish some great thing and
strike a very high mark.*

This little war to free Cuba from the
black hand of Spain had the enthusiastic backing of the freedom-loving American public.
It was with a feeling of idealism that they
volunteered for the coming crusade on this
nearby island. War was declared on April
25, but on May 6 the American public received a great shock. When Dewey attacked
the Spanish fleet in Manila harbor, he broke
the fight at one point with the laconic order:
Draw off for breakfast. The reason, dis-

covered years later, was his misconception that he was down to fifteen rounds for his five-inch guns. The Spanish command at Manila cabled the home government that the Americans had drawn back and Spain had won. This message reached America and there was fear for our fleet. Then the historic dispatch of the complete American victory (one of the great newspaper scoops) was sent by Ed Harden of the *New York World*. He was on his brother-in-law's revenue cutter in Singapore when the vessel was ordered to Manila to be put under the command of Commodore Dewey. When his cable reached the *New York World*, thirty thousand copies were called back and an extra got out to every subscriber. The editor then telephoned President McKinley and Secretary of the Navy Long, got them out of bed and read them the dispatch.

America learned of Dewey's order: *You may fire when ready, Gridley*. Without the loss of a single man or ship, Dewey had sunk or destroyed ten Spanish men-of-war. The public hung on every word and Dewey was promoted to Admiral. Newspapers headlined: **GREATEST NAVAL ENGAGEMENT OF MODERN TIMES.** Four days after the victory, Commodore Schley, on board the flagship *Brooklyn*, stated: *Admiral Dewey's victory at Manila must deservedly take its place side by side with the greatest naval victories of the world's history*. The public went wild and dozens of songs were written about Dewey, including "Hymn to Dewey" and "The Fight Is Made and Won" by the popular composer Victor Herbert. New York would give him a parade and build an arch to honor his victory.

In the meantime, Admiral Dewey blockaded Manila harbor and settled down to await the troops. The public now demanded maps to learn where these unheard of Philippine Islands were. From Texas, Lieutenant Colonel Roosevelt wrote to Lodge: *As to Cuba, I am in no sort of hurry. . . . Porto Rico is not forgotten and we mean to have it. Unless I am utterly and profoundly mistaken the Administration is now fully committed to the large policy that we both desire*. The larger view Roosevelt had in mind came from the brilliant book on naval expansion, *The Influence of Sea Power upon History, 1660–1783*. When it was published in 1890, Roosevelt, an avid reader, had discovered it and immediately communicated to the author, Captain Alfred Mahan, his appreciation of the work. In Germany the Kaiser had also read the book and felt exactly as Roosevelt did.

As yet, no troops had reached Cuba. There were no summer uniforms and pestilence attacked the newly formed regiments at port of embarkation in Florida. Food was wretched, men were herded about like cattle and there was no room on the ships for the cavalry's horses. Roosevelt complained to Lodge to do something. Lodge wrote back: *I am devoting all my strength to get the annexation of Hawaii . . .* He added there was no longer any doubt but that the United States must have Puerto Rico and the Philippines.

Although Tampa was packed with *Journal* artists and reporters waiting to move on Cuba with the troops, Hearst himself chartered the steamer *Sylvia* and prepared to sail with Creelman and additional photographers.

At last, on June 22, Roosevelt and his Rough Riders landed in Cuba, though their horses had been left behind. With Roosevelt was the handsome *Journal* reporter, Richard Harding Davis. It had been a coup for Hearst to sign up this popular author of romantic fiction. The contract was for one month's reporting on the Spanish conflict for the sum of three thousand dollars. Davis, a friend of and model for Charles Dana Gibson, represented all that was clean-cut in the Gibson male and the American ideal in both looks and fiction. A brief skirmish with some Spanish troops Davis described as: *the hottest, hastiest fight I ever imagined!* With Davis writing his exploits and Remington painting them, Teddy Roosevelt's future was secured. On San Juan Hill over sixty-five hundred men took part in the charge. Less than five hundred were Roosevelt's Rough Riders. Of all the regiments taking part, Roosevelt's had the most casualties, perhaps because the Rough Riders had to go it on foot.

At home, the public read *Journal* correspondent Richard Harding Davis' account of the Rough Riders: *[they] had not glittering bayonets, they were not massed in regular*

Charles Dana Gibson's most famous male model, Richard Harding Davis, now at work for Hearst.

array. There were a few men in advance, bunched together and creeping up a steep, sunny hill, the top of which roared and flashed with flame. . . . It was more wonderful than any swinging charge could have been. Roosevelt's Rough Riders were of the same mettle as Teddy and they sang together:

Rough, rough, we're the stuff,
We want to fight, and can't get enough,
Whoo-pee!

By the time of the surrender of Santiago, mid-July, yellow fever was taking a heavy toll of the troops. For every man who died from Spanish bullets, thirteen died of disease. The War Department did not want these diseased and contagious troops returned to the States. Roosevelt fought for their return to a healthier, northern climate. When they were finally permitted to come back, T.R. was given credit and hailed as a hero when he himself landed.

Roosevelt, thrilled with his glorious adventure, wrote to Lodge: *I do not want to*

T.R. with Davis who caught the "whoo-pee" of the Rough Riders for Journal *readers.*

"My regiment will be mustered out in a few days and then I shall be footloose."

be vain but I do not think anyone else could have handled this regiment quite as I have.

The Battle of San Juan Hill made Teddy famous and one of the most popular men in the country. The humorists then suggested titles for a book by him: *Alone in Cubia . . . Th' Biography iv a Hero Be Wan who Knows . . . Th' Darin' Exploits iv a Brave Man be an Actual Eye-Witness.* Those three were attributed to Finley Peter Dunne's character Mr. Dooley.

Teddy and his Rough Riders arrived at the detention camp at Montauk Point. As they awaited their return to civil life, T.R. wrote to his sister: *My regiment will be mustered out in a few days and then I shall be footloose. Just at the moment there is a vociferous popular demand to have me nominated for Governor, but I very gravely question whether it materializes.*

What Roosevelt said was true. What he did not know was that at that moment Chauncey Depew, president of the New York Central,

was in a smoke-filled room with Republic[a] boss Thomas Platt. Depew explained that i[f] they renominated Governor Frank Black, and during a meeting a heckler interrupted and asked about a stolen million concernin[g] the state canal, he would have trouble. But [if] the same question were asked with Colonel Roosevelt as candidate, he could reply wit[h] indignation: *We have nominated for gove[r-] nor a man who has demonstrated in public office and on the battlefield that he is a figh[t] for the right and is always victorious. If he [is] elected you know and we all know from h[is] demonstrated characteristics—courage an[d] ability—that every thief will be caught an[d] punished, and every dollar that can be foun[d] will be restored to the public treasury. The[n] I will follow the colonel leading his Rough Riders up San Juan Hill and ask the band t[o] play "The Star-Spangled Banner."*

Platt then sent an emissary to Colonel Roosevelt's tent on Montauk Point to ask if [he] would accept the Republican gubernatoria[l] nomination. *Would I? I would be delighte[d.]* The emissary told him he could rely on Se[n-] ator Platt's support and asked T.R. to com[e] to the Fifth Avenue Hotel to see him.

Boss Platt sent word to inquire if T.R. would like the Republican gubernatorial nomination. "Would I?" came his reply.

On the day the Rough Riders and Colonel Roosevelt were to be mustered out, a delegation of men called Teddy to where his men were assembled. Concealed under a blanket was a bronze bronco buster by Frederic Remington. They presented it to Roosevelt: *as a very slight token of admiration, love and esteem in which you are held by the officers and men of your regiment.* Teddy responded: *I am proud of this regiment beyond measure, I am proud of it because it is a typical American regiment. The foundation of the regiment was the cow puncher, and we have got him here in bronze.* He continued his speech, then noticed the colored troops of the Ninth and Tenth Cavalry standing behind his men listening. Roosevelt complimented them on their heroism and added: *The Spanish called them "smoked Yankees" but we found them to be an excellent breed of Yankee.* He then asked to shake the hand of each man, stating: *Outside of my own family . . . I shall never show as strong ties as I do toward you.*

The reform element was disappointed by Roosevelt's acceptance of Platt's offer. They had expected him to be their leader in the fight for good government. In his meeting with Boss Platt, T.R. promised to consult him on all appointments and policy matters and was given the nomination.

Pulitzer urged the Democrats to nominate popular, honest Judge William Gaynor. Tammany Boss Croker, tired of reformers, rejected the suggestion and the nod went to Judge Van Wyck. During the campaign Roosevelt denounced the reformers, calling Reverend Parkhurst *that silly goose.* He lampooned Carl Schurz and other advocates of Good Government as *the idiot variety of "Goo-goo."* With the backing of the financial interests, and managed by Boss Platt and

Hearst's artist in Cuba, Frederic Remington, created this Bronco Buster which the Rough Riders presented to T.R.

T.R. thanks his men for the Bronco Buster.

the Republican machine, T.R. crept into office with a slight margin. But he had tricked them all. Before his term was half over, Platt and the machine would seek to get him out of New York. In desperation they kicked him up onto the dead-end shelf of the vice presidency.

At home, Dewey was already famous and so was his order: *You may fire when ready, Gridley.* Maps of the Philippines were printed in all the papers and the American public began to sympathize with the Philippine insurgents led by Aguinaldo against their Spanish overlords. The war officially ended on April 11, 1899, and peace negotiations began in late July. The US asked for the cession of Puerto Rico, one of the Ladrone Islands as indemnity and the occupation of Manila and Manila Bay. Spain signed this protocol on August 12. But McKinley still had no plan for the Philippines. He then turned to prayer: *I went down on my knees and prayed Almighty God for light and guidance more than one night, and one night later it came to me this way—I don't know how it was, but it came: (1) that we could not give them back to Spain—that would be cowardly and dishonorable; (2) that we could not turn them over to France or Germany—*

our commercial rivals in the Orient—that would be bad business and discreditable; (3) that we could not leave them to themselves— they were unfit for self-government—and they would soon have anarchy and misrule over there worse than Spain's was; and (4) that there was nothing left for us to do but to take them all and to educate the Filipinos, and uplift and civilize and Christianize them, and by God's grace do the very best we could by them as our fellowmen for whom Christ also died.

McKinley had heard the righteous plea of Rudyard Kipling's poem:

> Take up the White Man's burden
> Send forth the best ye breed,
> Go bind your sons to exile
> To serve your captives' need;
> To wait in heavy harness
> On fluttered folk and wild,
> Your new-caught sullen peoples,
> Half-devil and half-child . . .
> Take up the White Man's burden
> The savage wars of peace,
> Fill full the mouth of Famine
> And bid the sickness cease . . .
> Ye dare not stoop to less—

There was some misconception of the Filipinos in President McKinley's mental picture of them. Out of a population of seven million, over six million were already Christianized (Catholic) intelligent individuals with ideals in the Western tradition. When the Spanish flag came down and Old Glory was raised, these Christians of over three centuries believed one foreign tyranny was being replaced by another. To many Americans, firing on these Filipinos, after their long fight for independence, was the end of a dream. Professor Charles Eliot Norton of Harvard

sadly proclaimed America had lost her position as a leader of civilization and taken her place as simply one more *of the grasping and selfish nations of the present day.* William James wrote: *We are now openly engaged in crushing out the sacredest thing in this great human world—the attempt of a people long enslaved . . . to attain their freedom and control of their affairs.*

Emma Goldman had been involved befor the start of hostilities: *America had declared war with Spain, the news was not unexpecte For several months preceding, press and pul pit were filled with the call to arms in defence of the victims of Spanish atrocities in Cuba. I was profoundly in sympathy with the Cuban and Philippine rebels who were striving to throw off the Spanish yoke. In fact I had worked with some of the member of the Junta engaged in underground activities to secure freedom for the Philippine Islands. But I had no faith whatever in the patriotic protestations of America as a disinterested and noble agency to help the Cubans. It did not require much political wisdom to see that America's concern was a matter of sugar and had nothing to do with humanitarian feelings. Of course, there were plenty of credulous people, not only in the country at large, but even in liberal ranks, who believed in America's claims. I could no join them. I was sure that no one, be it individual or government, engaged in enslaving and exploiting at home, could have the integ rity or the desire to free people in other lands. Thenceforth my most important lecture, and the best-attended, was on Patriotis and War.*

Emma Goldman traveled the West, givin antiwar lectures. In New Mexico she was introduced to Mr. V., a wealthy businessman

"I knew that everyone offered the same excuses for vile deeds, the policeman as well as the judge, the soldier as well as the warlord; everybody who lives off the labor and degradation of others."
—Emma Goldman.

who had attended a number of her lectures. He was impressed, wanted to help. *Could he manage some of the lectures for her?* Mr. V. left New Mexico for Los Angeles, where he set up Emma Goldman's next lecture. When Emma arrived, he met her at the station with roses. She complained when she found he had booked her into a luxury hotel: *The luxury room he had reserved for me, filled with flowers, was another surprise. Then I discovered a black velvet dress prepared for me. . . . Is this going to be a lecture or a wedding? Both*, he replied promptly, *though the lecture is to come first.*

The next few days the papers reported Emma Goldman was under the management of a wealthy man from New Mexico. To avoid the reporters, he took her to the Mexican section of town, to cafés and restaurants and for long walks. After one lecture: *Late that evening, in a little Spanish restaurant, away from the crowds, Mr. V. asked me to marry him. Under ordinary circumstances I should have considered such an offer an insult, but everything the man had done was in such good taste that I could not be angry with him. I and Marriage! I exclaimed. You didn't ask whether I love you. Besides, have you so little faith in love that you must put a lock and key on it? Well, he replied, I don't believe in your free-love stuff. I should want you to continue your lectures; I'd be happy to help you and secure you so that you will be able to do more and better work. But I couldn't share you with anyone else. The old refrain! How often had I heard it since I had become a free human being. Radical or conservative, every male wants to bind the woman to himself. I told him flatly, No! I assured him there was no chance of my marrying him: I did not propose to forge chains for myself. I had done it once before; it should not happen again. I wanted only 'that free-love stuff'; no other 'stuff' had any meaning to me.*

Years before, Emma Goldman had discovered she suffered from an inverted womb. Without an operation, she could never bear children. She had decided to dedicate her life to the wretched of the earth and not to bring another child into the world as she saw it. On her return from school in Vienna, she had turned to the modest profession of midwife: *While my work held out no hope of worldly riches, it furnished an excellent field for experience. It brought me face to face with the living conditions of the workers, about which, until then, I had talked and written mostly from theory. Their squalid surroundings, the*

Anarchist Johann Most.

dull and inert submission to their lot, made me realize the colossal work yet to be done to bring about the change our movement was struggling to achieve. Most of them lived in continual dread of conception; the great mass of the married women submitted helplessly, and when they found themselves pregnant, their alarm and worry would result in the determination to get rid of their expected offspring. It was incredible what fantastic methods despair could invent: jumping off tables, rolling on the floor, nauseating concoctions, blunt instruments. These and similar methods were being tried, generally with great injury. It was harrowing but it was understandable.

Many women called on her to perform abortions, some went down on their knees begging: *for the sake of the little ones already here. I would relate the case of a woman killed by such an operation, and her children left motherless. But they preferred to die, the city was then sure to take care of their orphans. . . .* Her Vienna professor had many times shown Emma the terrible results of abortion, and even when the operation had been successful, the patient's health had been undermined. *I would not undertake the task. It was not any moral consideration for the* *sanctity of life; a life unwanted and forced into abject poverty did not seem sacred to me. But my interests embraced the entire social problem, not merely a single aspect of it, and I would not jeopardize my freedom for that one part of the human struggle. I refused to perform abortions and I knew no methods to prevent conception.*

Later, on a case recommended by a doctor she discovered her patient's secret profession. *She burst into hysterical sobbing, begging me not to go away . . . she admitted being the keeper of a "house." Prostitution was not of her making, she argued, and since it existed it did not matter who was "in charge." She did not think keeping girls was any worse than underpaying them in factories; at least she was always kind to them. Mrs. Spenser's reasons did not influence me. I knew that everyone offered the same excuse for vile deeds, the policeman as well as the judge, the soldier as well as the warlord; everybody who lives off the labour and degradation of others. I felt that in my capacity as nurse I could not concern myself with the particular trade or occupation of my patients. I had to minister to their physical needs. Besides, I was not only a nurse, I was also an anarchist who knew the social factors behind human action. As such, even more than as a nurse I could not refuse her my services.*

Emma Goldman was an avid reader. She was greatly influenced by the anarchist writings of Johann Most and at one point took to the street inspired by her reading of Dostoevski's *Crime and Punishment.* Teddy Roosevelt, as a sickly boy of eight, was also an avid reader. His fancy was caught by books of natural history. At that early age he and two cousins started what they called "The Roosevelt Museum of Natural History" with a seal's skull and some old bones.

When she was a very young girl, Henrietta Robinson's father and grandfather lost their eyesight and were unable to read newsprint. As soon as she could read, the little girl was forced to read to them the financial pages of the daily papers. By the turn of the century, the child, now Hetty Green, was the richest woman in the world and known as "the witch of Wall Street." In a two-page article in the *Ladies' Home Journal* about Hetty Green, the reporter stated: *In the pursuit of wealth she has given up everything that other people enjoy in life. She says repeatedly that her financial success is only "a blessing of God." Her sole idea now seems to be to add to the millions she has, every cent she can.*

When, at the age of six, Sunday school pupil Robert Peary was reading about Eskimo life and the frozen reaches of the north, a boy of sixteen was counting out pennies for a dime novel that caught his fancy at a book stall. He concealed it under his jacket, read it by gaslight beneath the thundering Third Avenue Elevated Railroad. At home, he hid it under his bed. The boy had been peddling papers on the street but was admonished by his father that the son of a rabbi and a scholar should seek a higher occupation. He became a lining cutter in a necktie factory. But this dime novel, *The Memoirs of Robert-Houdin, Ambassador, Author and Conjuror*, changed his life. In tribute to its author, the boy changed his name.

Dime novels, half-dime novels and penny dreadfuls were never read in the open. Zane Grey hid his in a secret cave with some neighbor boys' half-dimes. No one was allowed to read one except as a reward for a deed of valor. Inspired by them, Grey wrote his very first story in that secret cave. Reporter-author Irvin S. Cobb got paddled more than once when his parents discovered half-dimes har-

Hetty Green, "The Witch of Wall Street."

The enforcer of the anti-obscenity law, Anthony Comstock. Anything not uplifting was objectionable.

bored behind pantry closets or concealed in the dark recesses of a back shelf. One reason librarians sneered, parents spanked and crusaders burned against dime novels and half-dimes was that they were lies. But the major outcry against them, although heroines even in jungle distress wore skirts to the ground, was that they were immoral. They were cheap-looking, crude in every way, and not a child could resist them. One man collected mountains of them, tons of them, and burned them all. He was the authorized leader of a one-man army against objectionable material. Anything not uplifting he considered objectionable. Anthony Comstock had lobbied for the passage of the federal antiobscenity law and became its major enforcer as special agent for the Post Office Department. He felt his work was done for children and commissioned by God. It has been a complaint of the ages that children have been deteriorating since their first conception. Few are chosen to protect them. Comstock felt the calling, and unflinchingly responded for over four decades. Raised in religious, socially conserv-

ative Connecticut, he served in the Civil War too late for combat duty. Mustered out he came to New York to seek his fortune. H married a woman ten years his senior and upon her father's death took her invalid sister in to live with them. In his diary he wrote: *I am determined to act the part of a good citizen and wherever a man breaks the laws I will make him satisfy the laws' demands if in my power.* At least ten years before Roosevelt became a crusading police commissioner Comstock ran around New York trying to get the police to enforce the Sunday laws and close the saloons. At that time, with a reporter and police captain in attendance, he bought books from two stationery stores, declared them obscene and had six employees, including a thirteen-year-old and an eleven-year-old boy, arrested. Three of the adults were convicted and sent to prison for terms of three months to one year.

The president of the Young Men's Christian Association, Morris Jesup, was impressed by Comstock's account of the dangers of obscenity to the morals of young men. He promoted within the organization a Committee for the Suppression of Vice. Prominent New Yorkers, Peter Cooper and William Dodge among them, made financial contributions and Comstock received an expense account and a salary that soon reached three thousand dollars a year. Within two years he had seized over one hundred and thirty thousand pounds of objectionable books and more than one hundred and ninety thousand drawings and photographs, as well as sixty thousand rubber articles.

The YMCA, which had originally sponsored Comstock's work, dissolved the committee, and the independent New York Society for the Suppression of Vice commenced

"I must say, Hoboken is one of the cheapest places to live in that I know." Hetty Green, richest woman in the world.

secured at the sacrifice of these higher attributes. All the nobler qualities of the mind, the developments of the intellect, the nobility of character, the unlimited possibilities of the future, and the salvation of the soul are jeopardized when parents are indifferent as to what their children read. Comstock had become a famous figure because of his arrest of the notorious abortionist Madame Restell. After her arrest, she committed suicide. Stanford White would be followed for two years by Anthony Comstock at the insistence of Harry Thaw.

When Hetty Green was still a young girl, her father died an unnatural death. Hetty, bewildered by the responsibility of her inheritance, was frightened that someone might do her harm in trying to get part of it. *I was almost afraid to go out, I offered one floor of my house to a friend and his wife and they accepted it. After a while, I never went out. My friends came to see me and I received them in my rooms, but at night I went up to the fourth floor and slipped into a storeroom. There, under a bed, on top of which was piled furniture and rugs, I slept. For days I did not leave my room and lived on crackers and raw eggs. And all the time those schemers were trying to get my money, and they succeeded for the time because I never have gotten all of my father's fortune. That's why I hate lawyers.*

under the sponsorship of Jesup again, but now including J. P. Morgan. From this organization, and as special agent for the Post Office, Anthony Comstock attacked free love, literature, art, theater, lotteries, infidels, newspapers and half-dime novels. Comstock wrote: *Parents, ask yourselves which is of more importance, the moral purity, spiritual welfare, and the cultivated intellect of the boy or girl, or their temporary amusement,*

If in 1900 you wished to find Hetty Green, you would take the ferry to Hoboken, find a modest row of brick flats and ring the bell marked "C. Dewey." This was where she lived and Dewey was the name of her pet dog. The shabbily dressed woman on the seven o'clock ferry every morning, with soft low voice and deep-sunk steel blue eyes, was Hetty on her way to her office room in the

Chemical National Bank Building. Her secret was the same as horse trading. When offered a number of shares, she would buy one. She then sent out to find what it would bring. If it was a good advance, she bought. She did not buy anything to hold onto. Everything was for sale at a price. And she tried to steer clear of Wall Street. Hetty Green was worth well over sixty million dollars at that time, yet she rose early and walked in all kinds of weather to the seven o'clock ferry. *You see, I escape the crowds that otherwise would stare at me, when I get such an early start, and anyway I always have enough business on hand to occupy every hour of the day. And I always like the ride on the water. That's one reason why I live in Hoboken. Rents are much cheaper there too, and it's quieter. And I must say Hoboken is one of the cheapest places to live in that I know.*

On December 20, 1898, using the Arctic moonlight, Robert Peary traveled across snow and ice in search of Fort Conger. He was accompanied by Matthew Henson, Dr. Dedrick and four Eskimo volunteers. In temperatures of fifty below zero they had pushed across the frozen wastes for nine days and were only halfway to the deserted fort. In two days the moonlight would fail and they would have to travel in the total darkness of perpetual Arctic night. To save one Eskimo overcome by the cold and biting wind, they had to stop and dig him a burrow and leave another Eskimo and nine dogs with him. Seventeen years before, in 1881, Lieutenant Greely and twenty-five men had been sent with a three-year food supply to set up Fort Conger. If their supply vessel failed to appear in two years, the men were to start back, using cached foodstuffs left by supply ships on the way. The vessel returning for them

was crushed by ice and sank. Very few supplies were left on the way for them. Washington frantically sent Commander Schley on a relief mission. By the time he reached them only seven of the twenty-five were alive and Greely, unable to move, was pinned under his fallen tent. He was too weak to move, having gone without food for two days in fifty-below-zero weather. When Schley picked up some of the other men, they begged him not to shoot them. Greely had been forced to execute a man for stealing rations. The bodies of some of the other dead men showed signs that their flesh had been eaten. Now, fifteen years later, in total darkness, feeling his way along frozen edges of a shore line, Peary found the fort: *Biscuits were scattered in every direction, overturned cups etc., seemed to give indications of a hasty departure. To my surprise, the biscuits on the table, though somewhat tough, were not mouldy or spoiled. These things were meted out while a fire was being started in the range. Coffee in the bottom of one of the tins opened for sixteen years was found to have sufficient strength that by using a double amount drinkable coffee could be made.* But while sipping this coffee, Peary suddenly realized something had happened to his right leg. One of the Eskimos carefully removed his kamiks and Dr. Dedrick then removed the frost from his legs. Toes on both feet were badly frostbitten and had to be amputated. Parts of seven toes were removed by Dedrick in a primitive operation. Later, Peary put down his feelings: *Here I lay helpless on my back for six weeks . . . listening to the howling of the winter winds and the cries of my starving dogs, until in the latter part of February there was sufficient daylight to enable us to attempt to return to the ship. Throughout these interminable black days, though I could not at times repress a groan at the thought that my God-given frame was mutilated forever, still I never lost faith.* The two-hundred-and-fifty-mile journey back to the ship in temperatures that dropped to sixty-four below zero took eleven days.

The two Eskimos they left behind had returned to the ship, but they had been forced to eat some of the dogs.

Morris Jesup, backer of Anthony Comstock, had organized a group of wealthy businessmen to give financial support to Peary and his Arctic explorations. The group, the Peary Arctic Club, sent the ship *Diana* as its first contribution. When Peary arrived at home base, Herbert Bridgman, secretary of the club, welcomed him to the *Diana*, his new supply ship. Bridgman learned of Peary's hardships, his frostbite and resultant amputations of all but the little toe of each foot. After some walrus hunting, the *Diana* sailed home and Peary, Henson and Dedrick remained, using the Eskimo Village in Greenland as their home base and Fort Conger as their advance base.

It had been seventeen months since Dewey's victory in Manila when he started for home. He arrived in the latter part of September, 1899. Pulitzer, looking for a candidate other than William Jennings Bryan to run for President on the Democratic ticket, picked Dewey. He was so popular he could have the presidency for the asking. Pulitzer had sent an agent to the Orient to feel him out, without knowing whether the Admiral was a Democrat or a Republican. Dewey stated modestly: *I have no desire for any political office. I am unfitted for it, having neither the education nor the training. He added*

Governor Roosevelt welcomes Dewey back from Manila.

his health was so-so and that he was sixty-one, too old.

But the country was wild about Admiral Dewey. Gum was named "Dewey Chewies," girls wore Dewey hats, his likeness appeared on anything and everything, including a laxative called "The Salt of Salts."

At that time everyone kept a diary, including Dewey: *From all parts of the United States had come requests for a journey across the country by rail. Our inland cities seemed to be vying with one another in plans for magnificent receptions. Towns, children, and articles of commerce were named after me. I was assured that nothing like the enthusiasm*

Even the Brooklyn Bridge says "Welcome Dewey."

for a man and a deed had ever been known. I knew what to do in command of the Asiatic squadron, but being of flesh and blood and not a superman, it seemed impossible to live up to all that was expected of me as a returning hero . . . Dewey arches, Dewey flags, and **WELCOME DEWEY** *in electric lights on the span of the Brooklyn Bridge!*

From September 27 to September 30, New York was on a holiday. Army and Navy maneuvers were carried out on both rivers. The parade up Fifth Avenue for the Dewey reception was led by Governor Teddy Roosevelt, on horseback, in formal attire. The avenue leading up to the hundred-foot-high Dewey Triumphal Arch was lined with decorated double columns the same height as the arch. The *Cincinnati Enquirer*, owned by the man who had sold the *Journal* to Hearst, John McLean, proclaimed in headlines:

New York's Governor salutes as he passes Admiral Dewey and the Court of Honor.

The massive columns leading up Fifth Avenue to the Dewey Arch at Madison Square.

DEWEY'S WHITE TRIUMPHAL ARCH IS MODELLED AFTER THAT OF TITUS. WAS A LABOR OF LOVE FOR THE SCULPTORS. BEST TALENT OF AMERICA WORKED UPON IT. ALMOST READY FOR OUR HERO TO RIDE UNDER WHILE NEW YORK GOES INTO A FRENZY.

The arch was temporary, made of wood, plaster and lathe. A subscription was already under way to raise money by popular support for a permanent arch of granite and marble.

Another subscription was under way to raise money to purchase a house for the Admiral in Washington. Pulitzer personally gave a thousand dollars. A month after his grand reception, the newspapers quoted Dewey as saying he wanted *a simple house, dining room to seat but eighteen.*

Two months after his return the Admiral married publisher John McLean's sister, the widow of General Hazen. The ceremony was performed at St. Paul's Catholic Church in Washington. Although she had been born a Protestant, his bride had converted to the Catholic faith. She was the heir to millions but Dewey deeded over to her the fifty-thousand-dollar gift house from the public in Washington. Derisive voices protested that the mansion would become the seat of the papacy in Washington.

The last time Pulitzer had checked to see if Dewey would run, he had first sent someone to see his personal physician. There was no question but that the Admiral was in good health. But Dewey said he was now sixty-two, had enough honors and no political talent he knew of. He then told the reporter to tell Mr. Pulitzer to *drop it.*

However, there was still time and Pulitzer wired the Washington office to have another try at Dewey. Horace Mock took Pulitzer's teletype and dropped by Dewey's home and simply handed the message to him. Dewey put on his glasses and read it. *Yes,* he then said, *I have decided to become a candidate.* Dewey invited the reporter in and told him that if the American people wanted him to serve in this high office, he would. In his statement published the next day underneath his photograph he stated: *Since studying the subject I am convinced that the office of the President is not such a very difficult one to fill, his duties being mainly to execute the laws of Congress. Should I be chosen for this exalted position I would execute the laws of Congress as faithfully as I have always executed the orders of my superiors.* That was all he would say. He would not say what party he belonged to or on what platform he would stand. *The New York Times* claimed it sounded more like Mrs. Dewey's ambitions than the Admiral's. When cornered once again by a *New York World* man to find out his party affiliation, Dewey said: *Mrs. Dewey will speak to you.* Mrs. Dewey quickly interjected: *The Admiral has a mind*

Admiral Dewey with his sword, gift of a proud people in memory of his victory at Manila Bay.

of his own. He does his own thinking. In the press the comic Mr. Dooley said it all: *When a grateful republic . . . builds an arch to its conquering hero, it should be made of brick, so that we can have something convenient to hurl after him when he had passed by.* The money raised for the permanent Dewey Arch was returned to the donors and the plaster-and-wood model reduced to rubble and carted away in horse-drawn vans.

John Stark had been a farmer before going into the music business. An honest man with a lively Irish imagination, he was well liked in Sedalia, Missouri. He had sent his daughter to Europe to study with Moskowski and she showed great talent and the promise of becoming a concert pianist. At that period songs were bought outright for five or ten dollars. But when Stark heard the "Maple Leaf Rag" played by its composer in the Maple Leaf Club, he asked the man to come to his music store the next day. He then gave Scott Joplin fifty dollars and a contract for royalties on the song. The "Maple Leaf Rag" went on sale in September, promoted solely by Joplin playing it on the piano. Within six months it was a smash. Scott Joplin had been right when he had told a friend who admired the song that it would make him *king of the ragtime composers.* Stark moved his family and business to St. Louis and Joplin soon followed. Slowly America began to recognize she not only had a Navy, she had an original music. Within a year headlines would proclaim American music, ragtime, the rage of Europe. It would sweep Paris under the baton of John Philip Sousa as Parisians clamored for *le temps du chiffon.* But it would take time before music by black musicians would be accepted at Bar Harbor, Newport or Fifth Avenue. Americans were still too busy being English.

Three-hundred-pound William Howard Taft headed the weighty committee sent to the Philippines. Veblen referred to the "popular predilection for the dignified bearing and portly presence that are by vulgar tradition associated with opulence in mature men."

The Summer-Time Erect Forms

are now on sale by retailers the land over. All the popular Erect Form models have been duplicated in Bolinte of exquisite texture, combining the lightness of a feather and the sturdiness of leather. A wonderful weave this material—cool and woven so firmly that it will always hold shape.

Erect Form 918—Fan Front Summer Corset for $1.00
are now on sale by retailers the land over. All the popular Erect Form models have been...

Summer Erect Form 814 (Medium)
low bust—long in front—cut away....... $1.00
Slightly between hip and bust. Also
in Sterling Cloth and Black Sateen.
Sizes 18 to 30. Price.

Summer Erect Form 949 (Average)
Low bust—long hip and bust $1.00
Also in Sterling Cloth and Black Sateen...

Summer Erect Form 926 (Stout)
Low bust—long hip and bust closely $1.50
stitched fan-front. Sizes 19 to 36. Also...

The above models are all made in finer qualities at $1.50, $2.00 and $3.00 per pair

WEINGARTEN BROTHERS, DEPARTMENT A, 377-379 BROADWAY, NEW YORK

"The corset . . . is a mutilation undergone for the purpose of lowering the subject's vitality and rendering her permanently unfit for work."—Veblen.

The Perfect Poise

Of the woman who wears a FERRIS WAIST is easily distinguishable. She rides with easy grace because every motion, every muscle is absolutely free. She rides without fatigue because she enjoys perfect respiration. Ferris' Bicycle Corset Waist is constructed with elastic sides which yield to every motion of the wearer. The hips are short and pliable, the bust is made to give support without restriction. Every woman who rides a wheel or a horse, who plays tennis or golf, should wear the

FERRIS Bicycle Corset Waist

They are shown in all their beauty in the Ferris book of corset styles. Sent free. Ferris' Good Sense Corset Waists are sold by all leading retailers. Do not take substitutes. Ladies', $1.00 to $4.25; Misses', 50c. to $1.00; Children's, 25c. to 50c. Made only by

THE FERRIS BROTHERS COMPANY
341 Broadway, New York

For Smart Dressers

Who own a corset gains a perfection of line of fine slender figure-line grace of slim waist to be claimed by no other way. Many without a corset it is so difficult but equally can attain the perfect line which desire by the aid of the stylish model who adorns the ideal waists by means of the

Kabo Bust Perfector

distinctly moulds, adjusted and delightfully comfortable. Satisfactorily to ladies who lack perfect proportions, to maidens alike. Correctly every imperfection. It will be in every way a relief to the stout, smartly dressed...

Kabo Corsets Are Celebrated for Style, Fit and Comfort
NO BRASS EYELETS
$1.00 to $3.00. All Leading Dealers
CHICAGO CORSET CO.
205 Monroe Street, Chicago. 383 Broadway, New York

Photograph of Style No. 202.

Grace of Bearing

beauty of proportion, suppleness of figure and improved health follow constant exercise in a

Ferris Good Sense ATHLETIC WAIST

Stylish enough for dress.
Easy enough for exercise.

Observe its moulded bust and elastic sides, permitting full expansion of ribs and chest at every breath.

NOTE.—Ask for the genuine with "FERRIS GOOD SENSE" sewed in red on each Waist.

Illustrated Ferris Book mailed free

THE FERRIS BROS. COMPANY
341 Broadway, N.Y.

AMERICAN BEAUTY CORSETS

STYLE 93
New Fan Front Effect. Extra Quality Sterling Cloth.
Wide Lace Trimming with Silk Bow White, Drab and Black.
Style 495. Same Style as above. Extra Quality Batiste.
Sent by mail, charges paid, for $1.00 if not for sale by your local dealer. State which material desired.
Other Styles, $1 to $5

FIVE HUNDRED PRIZES

will be given away to still further popularize American Beauty Corsets, which are worn by more American women to-day than any other corset made.

The Grand Prize **Packard** PIANO Made by The Packard Co. Ft. Wayne, Ind.

and one of the most beautifully toned instruments in the world, will be given to the lady who sends the largest list of words in the English language, beginning with "A and B" made from the letters

"A M E R I C A N B E A U T Y"

In addition to the above prize, we will give 499 American Beauty Corsets in any style or color retailing at $1.00 to the 499 ladies (contestants tied for first prize will be required to submit article on these corsets to decide the winner) whose lists have the next largest number of words.

Each list of words must be accompanied by the two end labels from an American Beauty Corset box. These corsets are for sale by first-class dealers everywhere, and we prefer that you purchase from your dealer; if he cannot supply you we will forward any style, charges prepaid, upon receipt of retail price. Ask for our retail price list, showing fifty new and up-to-date styles and other information desired about this contest. Contest closes July 1, 1904.

KALAMAZOO CORSET CO.
EXCLUSIVE MAKERS
212 ELEANOR ST. KALAMAZOO MICH.

On a windy day in the beginning of February, President McKinley appointed a United States circuit judge, William Taft, to head a Philippine Commission. It would be the task of the five-man commission to establish civil government on those islands. The average weight of the commissioners was two hundred and twenty-seven pounds. Taft himself weighed three hundred. The Filipinos regarded these Americans as an imposing spectacle, while Taft called them *little brown brothers.* Thorstein Veblen had already diagnosed the fat man's pecuniary reputability, referring to the *popular predilection as there may be for the dignified (leisurely) bearing and portly presence that are by vulgar tradition associated with opulence in mature men.*

And the opposite had become true for women. A man could put his two hands around the twenty-inch waist of T.R.'s daughter Alice. Veblen refers to woman *as dictated to by the canons of conspicuous waste, useless and expensive, and she is consequently valuable as evidence of pecuniary strength. It results that at this cultural stage women take thought to alter their persons, so as to conform more nearly to the requirements of the instructed taste of the time; and under the guidance of the canon of pecuniary decency, the men find the resulting artificially induced pathological features attractive. So, for instance, the constricted waist . . .*

Sigmund Freud said: *I am of the opinion that the unquestionable fact of the intellectual inferiority of so many women is due to the inhibition of thought imposed upon them for the purpose of sexual repression.* Havelock Ellis, comparing prostitution with marriage, found that the difference between the

Mrs. George Gould exhibits her distinctive five-hundred-thousand-dollar pearls. "Great as is the sensuous beauty of gems, their rarity and price add an expression of distinction to them which they would never have if they were cheap."—Veblen.

"If in addition to showing that the wearer can afford to consume freely and uneconomically, it can also be shown in the same stroke that he is not under the necessity of earning a livelihood, the evidence of social worth is enhanced. . . ."—Veblen. In pristine white trousers, Harry Lehr.

woman who sells herself in prostitution and the woman who sells herself in marriage was only a difference in price and duration of contract. He considered the prostitute well paid for how little she gives in return, and the wife badly paid for how much she gives and necessarily gives up.

Early in 1900, while Pulitzer was at Lakewood, his home on Fifty-fifth Street was destroyed by fire. The housekeeper and a governess were trapped and lost their lives, while seventeen other servants, Mrs. Pulitzer and the children escaped without harm. On his return, Pulitzer stayed at the Netherland Hotel. William Waldorf had it built because there was not a proper place, including his Waldorf-Astoria, for a gentleman to stay. Later, Pulitzer would have Stanford White draw up plans for a two-hundred-and-fifty-thousand-dollar home on East Seventy-third Street. One of White's letters to him said: *I feel certain . . . the house will be as fine a one as we have ever built.* Sharp orders from Pulitzer proscribed fanciness and undue display: *no ballroom, music room, or picture gallery under any disguise . . . no French rooms—least of all old furniture. . . . I want an American home for comfort and use, not for show or entertainment.* When completed, the house had a ballroom, music room, pipe organ and swimming pool.

John Jacob Astor IV built the Knickerbocker Hotel after William Waldorf put up the Netherland. William then built the Astor Hotel and John Jacob allowed his son Vincent to apply his mechanical aptitude to his new St. Regis. It became the first hotel with individually controlled air conditioning and heating in every room.

Stanford White finished a residence for Stuyvesant Fish and his wife Mamie at Seventy-eighth Street and Madison Avenue. Mrs. Fish, with the aid of one Harry Lehr, was in competition with *the* Mrs. Astor as Society's leader. When Lehr became interested in Elizabeth Drexel Dahlgren, he asked her to lunch with his four best friends. They were: Mrs. Astor, Mrs. Oliver Belmont, Mrs. Hermann Oelrichs and Mrs. Fish.

Elizabeth Drexel's family were of Philadelphia and New York. Part of the family was in partnership with J. Pierpont Morgan, whose home was across the street from the Drexels' on Madison Avenue. When her father died during the Blizzard of '88, her mother, whose ideal was Queen Victoria, insisted the family go into a prolonged period of mourning. Four years in black, two years in crepe veils. However, when Elizabeth fell in love with John Dahlgren, son of the Admiral, her mother relented and the two were married in St. Patrick's Cathedral on Fifth Avenue. Within a year, just before a son was to be born, John Dahlgren took ill and died. A year later, Elizabeth met Harry Lehr when Mrs. George Gould coaxed her out of mourning to an opera party. Mrs. Gould had described Mr. Lehr as the most amusing man in New York.

Elizabeth fell in love with Harry Lehr, and as he traveled about, he would send letters, from the Goulds' home at Lakewood, from Wanamaker's house in Philadelphia. The afternoon after the luncheon with his four "friends," Harry asked Elizabeth if she would marry him. He told her he loved her and she needed him and would love him someday. Elizabeth told Harry she was going to visit her mother at Pen Rhyn and he should come out and she would then give her answer. At Pen Rhyn she prayed for guidance, and when Harry Lehr arrived and kissed her, she wrote in her diary: *I honour him and I love him. He told me many things, which all went to strengthen my admiration for his character and virtues. He said he was not 'animal' or 'emotional.'*

Later, when she noticed his concern about the fortune her father had left her, she assured him he did not have to worry about money. *I told him you know I will give you everything, as much as ever you want. I understand perfectly that you have to provide for your mother, and we will arrange all that. . . . I don't suppose you have any idea of the way I live,* he answered, and then enlightened her. *I live not on my wits, but on my wit. I make a career of being popular.* Kaskel and Kaskel supplied him with the latest in shirts and pajamas. Wetzel made his clothes free, thinking it worth the cost to outfit the man the newspapers said "set the fashion" for American manhood. Black Starr lent him jewels. His rooms over Sherry's cost him nothing. They were part of Tom Wanamaker's apartment, and Wanamaker thought him amusing. Meals at Delmonico's and the Waldorf were on the cuff; the proprietors knew his socially eminent guests would honor them. Postage stamps involved expense, so thanks to Mrs. Clarence Mackay, he sent cables. He traveled on trains belonging to the husbands of Mamie Fish, Mrs. Gould and Mrs. Vanderbilt, who got concessions from their various mates for the ebullient "funster" Harry Lehr. He explained that all that was possible only so long as he was a bachelor. It would stop the moment he married. Elizabeth understood and later, with Tom Wanamaker and Sam Newhouse as witnesses, signed an agreement providing Harry with twenty-five thousand dollars a year as pocket money plus all expenses of their life together. They celebrated with lunch at Sherry's.

All of fashionable New York turned out for the wedding, not to see the bride but rather to see Society's most popular bachel take the vow. That night, Elizabeth, now Mrs. Harry Lehr, ordered Harry's favorite dishes served in the adjoining dining room their honeymoon suite. His favorite champagne, his favorite after-dinner cigars, cav quails in aspic, everything he could desire. Suddenly a flustered maid came to announ *Mr. Lehr wishes his dinner sent to his own room. He said Mrs. Lehr will dine alone to night.* Making excuses, Mrs. Lehr explaine her husband wasn't feeling well. A few mi utes later, Harry came in, shut the door an stood facing his bride: *There are some thin I must say to you, and it is better that I shoul say them now at the very beginning so that there can be no misunderstandings between us. You have just heard my orders to the se ants, I presume?* Startled, eyes wide in disbelief, she listened as he explained: *Since y force me to do so, I must tell you the unflattering truth that your money is your on asset in my eyes. I married you because the only person on earth I love is my mother.* went on to tell her that he had taken her to lunch with his four "friends" for their approval. Had they rejected her, he would never have jeopardized his social position b marrying her. While he would never be he lover, at least she would have a wonderful position in Society. Their marriage lasted twenty-eight years.

Augusta Saint-Gaudens found out about her husband's relationship with his lithe mo Davida. She also found out about their littl boy Novy. The Saint-Gaudens had been ir Europe together, then Augusta had return home. Davida then showed up in Europe a Augusta wrote a scathing letter to her husband. He answered: *Dear Gussie, sweetnes and kindness in a woman is what appeals*

ABOVE LEFT: *"The only person I love on earth is my mother."—Harry Lehr to Elizabeth Drexel on their wedding night.*

RIGHT: *Davida, the peccadillo which caused Saint-Gaudens misery of mind.*

ABOVE RIGHT: *"... a blessed charity for human failings makes one beloved."—Saint-Gaudens to Mrs. Saint-Gaudens.*

mostly to men and a blessed charity for human failings makes one beloved. The quiet dignity of Mrs. MacMonnies and Mrs. White toward the gross actions of their husbands is far finer and commands a deeper respect than any other attitude they could possibly have taken and way down deep in their hearts their husbands respect them all the more. Although my action is a mere peccadillo in comparison to them, it had caused me a misery of mind you do not dream of.

When Jo Peary returned on the relief ship to Greenland to await her husband, she was greeted joyously by the pretty Allakasingwah. Boasting happily of her life with Pearyksuah, Ally showed Jo their baby.

The reform candidate for district attorney, William Travers Jerome, fell in love with Ethel Stewart Elliot. He was forty-four and married, she was twenty-two and recently widowed. Divorce or scandal would ruin his promising career. Their relationship remained concealed until his death.

Another misalliance, that of Boss Platt and Teddy Roosevelt, was difficult to dis-

85

solve. The first clash came when Governor Roosevelt listened to Platt's choice for public works commissioner, then appointed his own choice. The second came when T.R. championed a special tax on public service corporations, a bill already twice defeated. Roosevelt was threatened by Platt, then pleaded with, but he insisted on pushing the bill to the floor of the Assembly. When the speaker read a message from the governor, he tore it up. T.R. persisted, forcing the bill's passage. Big business was enraged. After all, they paid the party organization for protection against just this type of legislation. Boss Platt sent a nasty letter to T.R. The governor snapped back a reply that Republicans must oppose improper corporate influence.

When the former lobbyist for Jay Gould, Lou Payn, came up for reappointment as insurance commissioner, T.R. refused to reappoint him. To Platt, Payn was an essential link in the sale of securities of Republican corporations to the insurance companies. T.R. had to be pushed out of New York so the Republican machine could be saved. McKinley's Vice President had died in office and the bosses had the brilliant idea of "promoting" Roosevelt to the vice presidency. T.R., for one, objected. And Mark Hanna, wealthy party chief who had helped elect McKinley the first time, refused to consider the crazy cowboy for the nomination. William Jennings Bryan, after Dewey had been rejected, had already begun campaigning against the growing imperialism since the Spanish-American War. Cabot Lodge felt T.R. should accept the vice presidential nomination because it could lead him to the presidency. At the Philadelphia convention, New York Boss Platt fought for Roosevelt's nomination while others protested. Roosevelt had not wanted the job, but when he strode into the hall wearing his Rough Rider sombrero, the delegates recognized it as his acceptance hat. Twenty thousand persons cheered and started chanting: *We want Teddy! We want Teddy!* Up and down they paraded, shouting in unison for Teddy. Mark Hanna, frightened, asked his colleagues: *Don't any of you realize that there's only one life between this madman and the White House?* Later, Hanna told President McKinley: *Now it's up to you to live.* The ticket was: William McKinley, the Western man with Eastern ideas, and Theodore Roosevelt, the Eastern man with Western characteristics.

The choice for anti-imperialists was between McKinley the imperialist and Bryan the evil anti-imperialist. A meeting was held in the Plaza Hotel to form a third party to seek a third choice. Andrew Carnegie immediately subscribed twenty-five thousand dollars for that purpose. But at that time negotiations were under way for the sale of the Carnegie Steel Works and he was informed that if he persisted with his third party the sale was off. Carnegie then backed out of the third party movement and it fell apart. Anti-imperialists decided they would have to hold their noses and vote for Bryan.

Hearst, now seeking a political career for himself, took to wearing Eastern clothes and attacking imperialism and McKinley. T.R. did most of the campaigning for the Republicans accompanied by mounted Rough Riders. Hats waving in the air, they rode by his train across the plains and prairies of the country to the accompaniment of bugles.

Hearst's vitriolic attacks on President McKinley described him as "the most hated creature on the American continent." One unsigned indictment against McKinley read

If bad institutions and bad men can be got rid of only by killing, then the killing must be done. When Governor Goebel of Kentucky was shot, Ambrose Bierce, the California journalist, wrote for Hearst:

> The bullet that pierced Goebel's breast
> Can not be found in all the West;
> Good reason, it is speeding here
> To stretch McKinley in his bier.

Sometime before the campaign began, Pulitzer had ended his war with Hearst and returned his *World* to accuracy and the public good.

In 1900 Hanna, running McKinley's campaign again under the slogans "Republican Prosperity" and "the full dinner pail," found it easy to raise two and a half million dollars from a few corporations and wealthy men. Although Hawaii and Puerto Rico wished to be made states, they became territories instead and America had dominion over ten million non-English-speaking people.

At the Casino Theatre in New York *Florodora* opened, and although *Cosmopolitan* raved about the "sestet," the rest of the press called it a "sextette."

King Humbert of Italy was assassinated by an anarchist from Paterson, New Jersey. Workmen on the Croton Dam struck for an advance from one dollar and twenty-five cents to one dollar fifty a day. The average wage in America in 1900 was four hundred and ninety dollars a year. Over a million and a half children still labored for as little as twenty-five cents a day. The complaint of the average man was answered with arrogance: *We own America, we got it, God knows how, but we intend to keep it.* One

Hearst writer Ambrose Bierce who predicted a bullet speeding toward President McKinley.

of the super-rich, George Baer, president of the Philadelphia Reading Railway, said: *The rights and interests of the laboring man will be protected and cared for—not by labor agitators, but by the Christian men to whom God in his infinite wisdom has given the control of the property interests of the country.* The senator from Indiana, Albert Beveridge, stated: *God has marked the American people as His chosen nation to finally lead in the regeneration of the world. This is the divine mission of America and it holds for us all the profit, all the glory, all the happiness possible to man.* John D. Rockefeller announced piously: *God gave me my money.*

Religion had become the opiate of the rich.

Mrs. Nesbit had moved to Philadelphia in 1899, when her daughter Evelyn was fourteen. There they existed on the child's meager earnings as an artist's model. In 1900

"We didn't have anything to eat sometimes for days but bread—sometimes coffee."—Evelyn Nesbit at seventeen.

they decided to try New York. Her mother still could not find a position. Evelyn said: *She kept failing all the time, and we lived in a little back room on the second floor, and things got very bad. We didn't have anything to eat, sometimes for days, but bread— sometimes coffee. And then mother took this Phillips photograph of me to Mr. Carroll Beckwith. I think it was in December of 1900. Mr. Beckwith told her that if she would bring me up there to his studio he would surely give me some work to do. Beckwith taught life classes at the Art Students' League and his studio was on Fifty-seventh Street at Sixth Avenue.* James Montgomery Flagg and Charles Dana Gibson used her, too, but photographers paid more and Evelyn soon became a photographer's model. Her weekly earnings reached eighteen dollars. She was the sole support of her mother and younger brother.

On March 3, 1901, the financial pages carried an announcement headlined: **OFFICE OF J. P. MORGAN & CO.** In smaller type: *To the stockholders of Federal Steel Company, National Steel Company, National Tube Company, American Steel and Wire Company of New Jersey, American Tin Plate Company, American Steel Hoop Company, American Sheet Steel Company. I* stated that the *syndicate* had arranged for the acquisition of substantially all the bonds and stock of the Carnegie Steel Company, including Mr. Carnegie's holdings. The signature at the close of the announcement said simply: *J. P. Morgan & Co. Syndicate Managers* Under the liberal laws of the state of New Jersey, the United States Steel Company had been formed. Carnegie had dropped out of the third party movement he believed in because of these negotiations with J. P. Morgan Less than a year before, Andrew Carnegie had formed his colossus, the Carnegie Steel Company, with the huge capitalization of one hundred and sixty million dollars. Now United States Steel was taking over Carnegie's holdings. Two years before, Carnegie had set his price for selling out at just under one hundred and fifty eight million. The deal collapsed. Rockefeller then asked Carnegie the price for Carnegie Brothers Steel and Frick Coke. *Two hundred and fifty million,* Carnegie replied, *half in cash.* The deal was turned down and the Scottish Steel King, like the tribal warlord of an ancient clan, declared war on Rockefeller, the Pennsylvania Railroad, the National Tube Company and the American Steel and Wire Company. He set a corps of engineers and surveyors to mapping a railway from Pittsburg to the ocean, announced a new twelve-million-dollar tube works on five thousand acres and proclaimed loudly that ten million dollars would be spent on plant improvement. He also had a defensive motive, for the Morgan and Rockefeller steel interests were encroaching on his territory. The other financiers of steel and rail empires panicked. They sent for Morgan. Carnegie himself sent for Charles M. Schwab and worked out the figure of just under a half-billion dollars. The price was quoted to Morgan, and within three hours the deal was agreed upon. *Hurrah! I am out of business,* cried Carnegie, retiring on a pension of over thirteen million a year, or forty-four thousand dollars a day. He added: *I never found my business anything more than mere play, golf is the only serious business of life. Landing a huge pickerel is better than making a hundred thousand dollars.* Wistfully, he said: *I would give all the millions I own if I could only be a boy again.* Years later, on an ocean liner of the White Star Line with Morgan, Carnegie suggested that he had made a mistake in the price: *I should have asked you for another hundred million.* Morgan, without a moment's hesitation, replied: *If you had, I should have paid it.*

It was said that it was fortunate for Carnegie that he was dealing with a: *careless and poor bargainer.* People were referring to J. P. Morgan, and they were wrong. All Morgan would get was a banker's commission on the reorganization, banker's interest on money lent, banker's profit on the floating and underwriting of the bonds and stocks—plus control. The United States Steel Company was floated at one billion four hundred million dollars. Less than seven hundred million represented cash investment in property and plants. Over seven hundred million, more than half, represented promoters' profits, speculation and fees. This was called "water." Morgan and his underwriting syndicate received sixty-two million dollars' worth of stock. This huge illegal merger was announced on March 3. The following day the syndicate's friend, President William McKin-

ABOVE: *"Hurrah! I'm out of business."—Carnegie.*

BELOW: *"I would give all the millions I own if I could only be a boy again."*

89

President McKinley and Vice President Theodore Roosevelt. "If I get through the Vice Presidency, I should like to get a position in a college."—T.R. looking for future work.

ley, was inaugurated for his second term. Mark Hanna was the only one with trepidations, for McKinley's Vice President was Theodore Roosevelt. But New York's Tom Platt was smiling as he watched Roosevelt take the veil. There was already a joke about the U.S. Steel combine: *God made the world in four thousand and one* B.C. *but it was reorganized in nineteen-o-one by James Hill, J. Pierpont Morgan and John D. Rockefeller.* When J. P. Morgan remarked: *I like this country,* William Jennings Bryan retorted: *When he finishes with it the American people would be pleased to have it back.* Morgan roared: *I owe the public nothing.*

The only unhappy man of the period was Theodore Roosevelt. After two months in the vice presidency, he wrote to Governor Thompson: *If I get through the Vice Presidency, I should like to get a position in a college where I could give lectures on United States history to graduates, and at the same time start to write a history of the United States.* Roosevelt wrote to another fellow

New Yorker, Supreme Court Justice John Clarke: *Just a line in reference to my studying law. I have been one year in the law school, and at that time was also in my cousin John's office. Now, could I go into an office in New York—say Evarts & Choate —or study in New York or here in Oyster Bay, so as to get admitted to the bar before the end of my term as Vice-President?*

At this time Saint-Gaudens began to receive almost daily missives from the director of the Fine Arts Division of the coming Pan-American Exposition to be held in Buffalo. William Coffin, the director, wanted the equestrian Sherman for the exposition. He had already made plans for a cast of the Shaw memorial and other works of Saint-Gaudens, but most of all he wanted the Sherman. He was also insisting that Saint-Gaudens accompany the Sherman to Buffalo. But the sculptor had recently had an operation for the removal of an intestinal tumor. The surgeon was not optimistic and Saint-Gaudens was to be kept from worry. His son Homer was forbidden to mention his disastrous grades at Harvard. A year before, Homer had forgot-

Beneath the General Sherman plaster, Saint-Gaudens, third from left.

President McKinley stayed home to take care of his ailing wife while Alice helped her father open the Buffalo Exposition.

ten to register at Harvard on time, then flunked French and math.

Another father who would be disappointed in his son was Joseph Pulitzer. Young Joseph would barely slide through one year, then cut classes, do poorly, be warned and finally get the ax from Harvard. Pittsburger Harry Thaw had an even briefer stay at Harvard, where he seemed to have majored in poker. But a forty-two-year-old Harvard graduate was called upon to officiate at the opening of the Buffalo Exposition. It was Vice President Theodore Roosevelt, accompanied by his pert daughter Alice. President McKinley could not officiate because his wife was ill and he had to stay with her in Washington. He would come to Buffalo later, on September 6, for President's Day.

Emma Goldman had visited friends in Chicago after staying four months with her patient, Mrs. Spenser. While there, a young man named Nieman told her he was from Cleveland. He found the socialist organization there dull. What could she recommend

he read? He had heard her speak in Cleveland in May of that year on anarchism. But Emma was catching a train to Rochester and had no time, so she passed him along to her friends to help. Later, while in Rochester, she received a socialist paper, *Free Society*, with a warning against Nieman written by the editor. Emma wrote demanding proof against the handsome youth. The editor wrote back that he had aroused suspicions by trying to get into anarchist circles and talking about acts of violence. They therefore concluded he must be a spy. But Emma wanted to visit Niagara Falls, and the Pan-American Exposition at **Buffalo** interested her; she had no time to do **anything** about young Nieman.

Saint-Gaudens felt well enough to go to see his sculptures at the Buffalo Exposition. He had sent a talented young sculptor, Henry Hering, to set up his exhibit, which also entailed bronzing-with-paint plaster casts of some of the work, including the Shaw memorial. The Sherman itself was either to be indoors or outside in front of the Fine Arts Building. Saint-Gaudens insisted it be outside because it was designed for such a location and needed the space and light and shadows. In making the new cast of the Sherman, he had used another model rather than Davida, and the figure of Victory walking in front of the mounted Sherman had the strong face of Alice Butler. On his short visit to Buffalo, Saint-Gaudens was pleased with the placement of the Sherman but had the feeling the horse was trotting toward the stables rather than charging out of them.

Emma Goldman left Rochester with her sister's children. *In merry anticipation of the adventure, I took the older children to Buffalo. We were treated to a round of festivities, "did" the Falls, saw the Exposition, and enjoyed music and parties, as well as gatherings with comrades, at which the younger generation participated in the discussions on a footing of equality.* She then returned with the children to the house of her sister Helena in Rochester.

T.R. did not attend President's Day at the Buffalo Exposition, preferring the outdoor life advocated in his newly published book, *The Strenuous Life.* His family waited for him in the Adirondack Mountains, where he intended to get in some climbing. But first he went to Lake Champlain for an outing of the Vermont Fish and Game League.

President McKinley did go to the Buffalo Exposition, and on the afternoon of September 6 shook hands with well-wishers at the reception in his honor. It was a sunny afternoon, and lines of men and women waited patiently under parasols to gain entry to Buffalo's Temple of Music to shake the Pres-

ident's hand. Nieman, the man who had asked Emma Goldman for advice on socialist literature, stood in line, his right hand covered by what appeared to be a bandage. It was a handkerchief. Behind him was a Negro man, also waiting to shake hands with the President. The concept of a stateless society, without ownership of property or restrictive laws protecting owners, had caused the assassination of President Carnot of France, Premier Canovas of Spain, the Empress Elizabeth of Austria and King Humbert of Italy, all within the last seven years. It was their vision of justice and equality for all that caused anarchists to murder and destroy, justifying their acts (as did the barons of business) with the slogan "the end justifies the means." Nieman's turn came to shake the hand of President McKinley. He raised the covered hand and two explosive shots were heard. The Secret Service man was too shocked to move but the Negro behind Nieman struck him on the back of the neck and wrestled him to

THE
STRENUOUS LIFE

ESSAYS AND
ADDRESSES

BY

THEODORE ROOSEVELT

NEW YORK
THE CENTURY CO.
1902

the ground before he could discharge another bullet into the President, still standing six inches away from the raised revolver. The first bullet struck a button of the President's coat and was harmlessly deflected. The second entered the fleshy part of his stomach. McKinley, still conscious, was helped to a chair. His first concern was that they not tell his wife for fear of worrying her.

Nieman's real name was Leon Czolgosz. Born in America, he had been raised on a small farm in Ohio. His family considered him an intellectual because of his fondness for reading. He had broken with the Catholic Church and read pamphlets on political radicalism. He felt McKinley responsible for the suppression of the Filipinos after liberating the Philippines from Spain, although this conflict had ended almost a year before. In his statement before his execution he blamed McKinley for shouting prosperity in his campaign when there was none for the poor man. He continued: *I know other men who believed what I do, that it would be a good thing to kill the President and have no rulers . . . I am an anarchist. I don't believe in marriage. I believe in free love.* Roosevelt was notified the night of September 6 of the shooting and hurried from Lake Champlain to Buffalo.

Emma Goldman had received a letter from Sasha telling her his privileges had been restored because there was a new inspector and the old warden, seriously ill, had been replaced. Perhaps Emma could visit as his "sister." After nine years Emma stood waiting in the Western Penitentiary for this meeting with her beloved Sasha. At last she heard his footsteps echoing in beat with the clanging of iron gates. *Sasha! I rushed forward with outstretched arms. I saw the guard, be-*

side him, a man in a grey suit, the same greyness in his face. Could it really be Sasha, so changed, so thin and wan? He sat mute at my side . . . I waited tensely, listening for a word. Sasha made no sound. Only his eyes stared at me, sinking into my very soul. Sasha had just been released from a year in solitary confinement with never a chance to exchange a word with another human being, or to hear a kindly voice. You grow numb and incapable of giving expression to your longing for human contact. In tears, Emma left Allegheny City and went to St. Louis.

The next day she heard the newsboys crying *Extra! Extra! President McKinley shot!* The following day the headlines read: **ASSASSIN OF PRESIDENT McKINLEY AN ANARCHIST. CONFESSES TO HAVING BEEN INCITED BY EMMA GOLDMAN. WOMAN ANARCHIST WANTED!** Inside the paper there was a picture of the assassin, Leon Czolgosz. Emma Goldman studied the picture, then gasped: *Why, that's Nieman!*

In trouble along with Emma Goldman was William Randolph Hearst. On their front pages Republican newspapers were connecting the vitriolic attacks on the President by Hearst with Czolgosz' deed. Hearst was burned in effigy in small towns and cities across the nation. When Emma Goldman was finally caught in Chicago and imprisoned for questioning, she received an offer of twenty thousand dollars for an exclusive with Hearst in New York. Her friends warned against it, Hearst's was already the loudest voice demanding the extermination of the anarchist; Emma would be an out for him.

As for Emma Goldman's life in the Chicago prison, at first it was hell. She was questioned hours on end, water was placed just out of her reach and fifty detectives constantly shook their fists in her face, declaring they had seen her with Czolgosz in Buffalo. Suddenly Chief of Police O'Neill appeared, sat down and listened to her account of her whereabouts leading up to the assassination. She convinced him, and the attitude of her jailors changed drastically. Her cell door was left open; she now received gifts, food and visitors, including the press. But she refused to attack Czolgosz and wondered what the forces were that had driven him to this doom. In an interview with the press Goldman refused to condemn Czolgosz but admitted that she would nurse President McKinley if asked. She tried to explain to a puzzled reporter: *The boy in Buffalo is a creature at bay. Millions of people are ready to spring on him and tear him limb from limb. He committed the act for no personal reasons or gain. He did it for what is his ideal: the good of the people. That is why my sympathies are with him. On the other hand, William McKinley, suffering and probably near death, is merely a human being to me now. That is why I would nurse him.* The next day, the headline read: **EMMA GOLDMAN WANTS TO NURSE PRESIDENT; SYMPATHIES ARE WITH SLAYER.**

Perhaps they should have let her nurse the President. The bullet lodged within the President was not fatal, and Roosevelt had left McKinley recuperating in a friend's home in Buffalo and returned to his own family in the Adirondacks. After McKinley was shot, he was rushed by auto-ambulance to the little hospital on the Exposition grounds. As he watched doctors arriving from all over town, the President whispered to his secretary, G. B. Cortelyou, *Be careful of the doctors, I leave all that to you.*

It was the president of the Exposition who picked the doctor to operate on McKinley. The man selected was the distinguished gynecologist Matthew Mann. They could have waited till seven o'clock when Dr. Park, the Exposition's medical director and also the president of the American Society of Surgeons, would arrive, but decided speed was more important. The gynecologist was therefore given the go-ahead. The doctors did not bother to put on caps or gauze masks. They probed for the bullet, decided it was lodged in a back muscle and might be left alone. They closed up the incision without leaving a clean excision of the bullet's track. When Dr. Park arrived, the operation was almost completed and he refused to take over the case. He left draining of the wound up to Dr. Mann. The wound was then sewed up without benefit of drainage.

The gun Czolgosz had used was a 32-caliber nickel-plated Iver Johnson. The Sears Roebuck catalogue advertised this item for three dollars and ten cents plus postage of seventeen cents.

Materia medica and Christian Science do not mix. Although Emma Goldman would have nursed President McKinley, Mrs. Mary Baker Eddy could not. She had started her new religion for healing purposes, and opened her Massachusetts Metaphysical College for medical purposes in 1881. At the time of the shooting, she was eighty years old. Had she been on the case, the President might have survived, for he died not from the bullet, but from the operation. For a week he had seemed to improve, then ate a piece of toast and began to fail. He muttered bravely: *Good-bye, God's Will be done, not ours.* An autopsy showed he had died of gangrene.

Leading the strenuous life he advocated,

T.R. was busy scaling one of the Adirondacks' most challenging peaks, Mount Marcy, when word reached him of the President's condition. Roosevelt began his race against time to reach the President before his death. But by the time he came down from the mountain, a telegram informed him that McKinley had died. He was now President of the United States.

Mark Hanna, the industrialist who had been McKinley's campaign manager for so many years, was at his side when he died. Roosevelt was rushed to the Ansley Wilcox home in Buffalo to be sworn in. He stated prior to the brief ceremony: *I will show the people at once that the administration of the government will not falter in spite of the terrible blow . . . I wish to say that it shall be my aim to continue absolutely unbroken the policy of President McKinley for the peace, the prosperity, and the honor of our beloved country.* Judge Hazel then administered the oath of office. Senator Mark Hanna's comment is famous: *Now look, that damned cowboy is President of the United States!*

Back in Washington, Secretary of the Navy Long pulled out his diary and made a note on the page dated April 25th, 1898, where he had criticized T.R. for resigning from the Navy to fight in the Spanish-American War. He wrote: *P.S. Roosevelt was right and we his friends were all wrong.*

1900 Ladies' Home Journal *advertisement.*

"*Now look, that damned cowboy is President of the United States.*"—Senator Mark Hanna.

Archie and little Quentie at the changing of the White House guard.

His going into the army led straight to the Presidency.

The *New York Tribune* and other journalistic enemies of Hearst were pillorying the *Journal* by reprinting the Ambrose Bierce quatrain and the inflammatory Hearst articles that had appeared before the assassination. They even reported, falsely, that a copy of the *Journal* was found in Leon Czolgosz' pocket at the time of the shooting. But Pulitzer sent word that the *World* should report accurately, refusing to kick Hearst while he was down.

After reassurances from the new President that he would "go slow" and after receiving his pledge to continue McKinley's policies, Republican newspapers lauded the cowboy: *Theodore Roosevelt is a man on whom the American people can rely as a safe and sagacious successor to William McKinley.* And Hanna stated: *Mr. Roosevelt is an entirely different man today from what he was a few weeks since.*

The changes started as soon as T.R. moved into the White House. He ordered his architects, McKim, Mead and White, to get rid of the "dreadful" screen made by Louis Comfort Tiffany. He welcomed reporters in for informal, outspoken visits. He announced that if he couldn't find qualified Republicans, he would appoint Democrats to office, and did so two weeks later. The writing was on the wall years before when Roosevelt, the loyal Republican, wrote Lodge: *The ugly feature in the Republican canvass is that it does represent exactly what the Populists say, that is corrupt wealth. The Pierpont Morgan type of men forced Fitch on the ticket; and both Platt and Tracy represented the powerful, unscrupulous politicians who charge heavily for doing the work, sometime good, sometimes bad, of the bankers, railroad men, insurance men, and the like.*

Edward Harriman, a mousy, scraggly moustachioed little man who had once been a stockbroker, was now a Napoleon of railroads. He had taken the defunct Union Pacific Railroad and rebuilt it into an empire. James Hill had reorganized the Northern Pacific with the aid of J. P. Morgan. Both Hill and Harriman now sought control of a serious link, the Burlington. When Hill denied he was trying for control and then proceeded to take over the Burlington, Harriman said: *Very well, this is a hostile act and you must take the consequences.*

Hill and Morgan had used the Northern Pacific to carry out the purchase. Although they had control of the Northern Pacific, they did not have the majority of the stock. Harriman saw this Achilles' heel and decided to gain control of the Burlington by grabbing the huge Northern Pacific, which controlled it. Morgan and Hill relaxed, figuring it would take seventy-eight million dollars to take over the Northern Pacific. They couldn't guess that Harriman would hock everything he owned in the pursuit of more.

Slowly he began acquiring stock and slowly the stock began to climb. One-hundred-one, one-hundred-nine a few days later. The Hill-Morgan group had expected the Northern Pacific stock to rise after the acquisition of the Burlington, and a Morgan associate dumped thirty-five thousand shares; the Northern Pacific sold thirteen thousand, the Morgan group another ten thousand. Hill, a railroad man, was puzzled by the trading in three days of half a million shares of Northern Pacific, and raced from Seattle to New York, straight to the offices of Jacob Schiff of Kuhn, Loeb, the buyers of the stock. Schiff assured him that it was true Mr. Harriman was purchasing stock in the Northern Pacific, but only to safeguard himself as to the Burlington and that he would want Hill to stay on and run the Northern Pacific. The war was on. When the Morgan

men leaped into the buying fracas, Northern Pacific stock began to soar—one-fourteen, one-twenty-two, one-twenty-seven.

The speculators moved in. The stock was already too high and sure to drop. They would sell shares they didn't own, then borrow them. Later, when the price dropped, they would buy the shares and return them to their lenders. This was called going "short." But the stock continued to skyrocket, past one-thirty, one-forty. As it kept soaring, other stocks began to plummet because the "shorts" were unable to borrow the stocks they had sold and were scrambling to buy at any price. Three hundred, four hundred, six hundred dollars a share. Standard Oil dropped one hundred and fifty points. What the shorts couldn't see was that there were only one hundred and seventy thousand shares outstanding, and that they had sold over five hundred thousand shares, an impossibility. Harriman and Morgan finally declared a truce and allowed the shorts to settle at one hundred and fifty dollars a share. The market began to settle back, but many had already been ruined. Hill and Harriman, and Morgan and Schiff formed a holding company in New Jersey called the Northern Securities Company, with Morgan in control but with Harriman protected and on the board. It was capitalized at four hundred million dollars, one hundred and twenty-two million of which was "water."

In his first address to the Congress, Roosevelt warned that he was against "bad" trusts. He would draw the line *on conduct, not on size.* He believed financial manipulators' wealth "tainted," "wrong." Secretly he asked Attorney General Knox if the new rail merger was illegal. Not only did Knox believe it illegal, he felt he could prove it in court. T.R. told him to go ahead, quietly.

Saint-Gaudens bas-relief of Jacob Schiff's children. Mortimer, the little boy, named his daughter Dorothy.

But now T.R. himself came under vicious attack. He had asked Booker T. Washington to the White House to give him suggestions on Negro appointments. This was fine. But then he had lunch with him. One Southern paper declared: **THE MOST DAMNABLE OUTRAGE EVER COMMITTED.** Another: **A STUDIED INSULT.** The clearest comment on the sordid affair was Pulitzer's editorial: *An American named Washington, one of the most learned, eloquent, most brilliant men of the day—the President of a college—is asked to dinner by President Roosevelt and because the pigment of his skin is some shades darker than that of others a large part of the United States is convulsed with shame and rage. The man is a negro.*

T.R. with Booker T. Washington at Tuskegee Institute. "The most damnable outrage ever committed."

Therefore in eating with him the President is charged with having insulted the South. This man may cast a ballot but he may not break bread. He may represent us in the Senate Chamber, but he may not "join us at the breakfast table." He may educate us; but not eat with us; preach our Gospel, but not be our guest . . . die for us but not dine with us.

Roosevelt knew all this; his mother had been a Southern belle from Savannah. Her brothers, T. R.'s uncles, had all fought for the Confederacy. Pulitzer also knew all this too; he had been friendly with Jefferson Davis after the Civil War (his wife, Kate Davis, was a distant cousin of Jefferson Davis). What neither Roosevelt nor Pulitzer knew was that they would soon be locked in battle against one another with William Travers Jerome in the middle.

Scott Joplin read about the Roosevelt-Washington lunch, and named his new rag . . . "A Strenuous Life."

Emma Goldman continued to defend Leon Czolgosz and men like him in an article entitled "The Tragedy of Buffalo": *Far from being depraved creatures of low instincts they are in reality supersensitive being unable to bear up under too great social stress. They are driven to some violent expression, even at the sacrifice of their own lives, because they cannot supinely witness the misery and suffering of their fellows.* Of course, she was referring to Sasha. At the same time, the police were searching out all anarchists. Her sisters in Rochester were questioned and harassed by the police and Emma's niece Stella was held at the police station all day. In school it was worse for the children; they were taunted with: *Your Aunt Emma Goldman is a murderess.* And everywhere Emma went she was called a murderess. Friends were afraid to be seen with her. She was forced to change her name to E. G. Smith to find work. Antianarchist bills began to flow from congressional sponsors after President Roosevelt's message to that body to strike a blow at anarchism. Senator Hawley declared he would *give a thousand dollars to get a shot at an anarchist.*

Then, a letter from Sasha was smuggled

from prison to Emma: *I pressed my lips to the precious envelope, opening it with trembling fingers. It was a long sub rosa letter . . . written on several slips of paper in the very small script Sasha had acquired, each word standing out clear and distinct.* The letter began: *I know how your visit and my strange behaviour must have affected you. The sight of your face after all these years completely unnerved me. I could not think, I could not speak.* Further in the letter he referred to recent events in Buffalo: *If the press mirrored the sentiments of the people the nation must have suddenly relapsed into cannibalism. There were moments when I was in mortal dread for your very life, and for the safety of the other arrested comrades. . . . I was especially moved by your remark that you would faithfully nurse the wounded man, if he required your services, but that the poor boy, condemned and deserted by all, needed and deserved your sympathy and aid more than the President.* Sasha then went on to say how they had both changed, grown: *We should have considered it treason to the spirit of revolution; it would have outraged all our traditions even to admit the humanity of an official representative of capitalism.* He marveled that they should have reached the same evolutionary point after ten years along divergent paths. But as Emma read on, suddenly she was being told that Leon Czolgosz' "deed" should have been resorted to only as a last extremity . . . and only against an immediate enemy of the people. Then she read: *I do not believe that Leon's deed was terroristic, and I doubt whether it was educational, because the social necessity for its performance was not manifest.* Sasha continued: *. . . as an expression of personal revolt it was inevitable, and in itself an indictment of existing conditions. But the background of social necessity was lacking, and therefore, the value of the act was to a great extent nullified.* The letter dropped from her hand. She realized Sasha was using the same argument against Leon that Johann Most had used against Sasha. She broke down in tears.

The background of the musical that opened in 1900 was a mythical Philippine island. It became a huge success and after more than three hundred performances moved to a larger theater. The musical, *Florodora*, featured a sextette of Gibson girls and a show-stopping number sung by six Gibson men: *Tell me, pretty maiden, are there any more at home like you?* Stanford White saw this number forty times. It was his favorite. At the same time, a former Art Students League youth, now a reporter and sketch man, fell in love with seventeen-year-old Evelyn Nesbit, two years his junior, one of the members of the sextette. The reporter, John Barrymore, got his job because the *Journal*'s editor admired his sister Ethel when she appeared in *Captain Jinks of the Horse Marines.* When White met

A mythical Philippine Island called Florodora.

young Evelyn, she was about to marry Barry-more against her mother's wishes. The *New York Herald* wrote about Evelyn's love affair: *Gay and joyous with the freshness of youth, Evelyn Nesbit danced and sang her way into the hearts of all, but she showed preference to none until Jack Barrymore paid sudden and tempestuous court. . . . Nightly he waited for her at the stage door, whence she would emerge with a huge bouquet of violets as her corsage, the tribute of* *her admirer. In the afternoons they would drive or walk through the Park. They foun each other congenial and all else dross. . . .*

But Barrymore, who came from a strang theatrical family, drank his suppers and survived on free lunches. He was fired shortly after starting with the *Journal*. Evelyn told of the time she, White and Barrymore were together in Stanford White's tower in Mad son Square Garden. Barrymore proposed ar

John and Ethel Barrymore in 1912.

Copyright 1912
Charles Frohman

White asked what they would live on. Barrymore laughed and said love. Mrs. Nesbit was worried about her daughter running off with Jack Barrymore and asked White to do something. White then suggested sending Evelyn off to Mrs. De Mille's school in New Jersey.

At this time, Ethel Thomas was going out with Harry Thaw: *At first he lavished much affection on me. He took me on automobile rides, to theatres and other places of amusement, and bought flowers and jewelry for me. . . . One day, however, I met him by appointment, and while we were walking towards his apartment he stopped at a store and bought a dog whip. I asked him what that was for, and he replied laughingly, That's for you, dear. I thought he was joking but no sooner were we in his apartment and the door was locked than his entire demeanor changed. A wild expression came into his eyes, and he seized me and with his whip beat me until my clothes hung in tatters.* Harry Thaw began to send flowers and money backstage at *Florodora* to Evelyn Nesbit.

In February of 1902 J. Pierpont Morgan, while at dinner in his brownstone mansion on Madison Avenue, was summoned away from his guests to an urgent telephone call. He learned to his great dismay that the President had ordered Attorney General Knox to take legal action against the Northern Securities Company for violation of the Sherman Antitrust Act, which forbade combinations in restraint of trade. America had been the land of opportunity, the best man, men or combinations winning out with no restraint to interfere with this "natural order." John D. Rockefeller's trust in the oil industry was justified by "God" and his beneficence. The wire nail trust had been organized in 1895 with a keg of nails priced at a dollar twenty. A year later the price was up to two twenty-five. Morgan's U.S. Steel had so much "water" in the financing that steel rails were priced at twenty-eight dollars a ton, twice their real cost. Boss Platt defended the game, demanding *the right of a man to run his own business in his own way, with due respect of course to the Ten Commandments and the Penal Code.* Andrew Carnegie, by threatening to compete

Ford and his first.

Thorstein Veblen.

with the rail, coke and steel magnates, had panicked them into buying him out. Before that, Consolidated Steel and Wire had combined with several other companies to form American Steel and Wire, with every hundred-dollar share being exchanged for a three-hundred-fifty-dollar share in the new conglomerate. When Morgan's U.S. Steel absorbed that organization, the stock was again exchanged, this time for four hundred and ninety dollars a share.

At the same time in Detroit a mechanic quit and left the car he had made with the financiers who had backed him. They had insisted that he put the car he had designed and built on the market, ready or not. He was interested in making a good car; they were interested in making good money. He took his name with him—the Ford Motor Company—and left the car with them. They called it the Cadillac.

Thorstein Veblen, still at John D. Rockefeller's University in Chicago, began his second book, *The Theory of Business Enterprise*. Veblen saw a distinct difference between industrial and business functions. The former he saw as productive and contributing to the well-being of the community. The latter he saw as "pecuniary" and enriching one segment of the community. In the new machine age, industry and its engineers were interested in the production of goods. Industry was tied to industry and the machines' aim in life was the creation and continued production of goods of the same dimensions in feet, inches and millimeters, and the identical weight in tons, pounds, ounces and grams. But the businessman or financier was a saboteur. He could benefit from disruption, and often caused it. His motive was pecuniary gain and the usual desired outcome was the accumulation of wealth for himself. Veblen saw that the businessman's viewpoint had shifted from surveillance and regulation of an industrial process to an alert redistribution of investments from less to more gainful ventures and to a strategic control through shrewd investments and coalitions with other businessmen. And so the business community was tied together almost as a single, comprehensive balanced mechanical process. A disturbance of the balance at any point meant an advantage or disadvantage to one or more of the owners of the subprocesses between which the disturbance fell. Veblen saw that industry depended on the businessmen for its smooth operation. But men like John "Bet-a-Million" Gates, Frick, Carnegie and Morgan were interested only in pecuniary gain, whether it could be gotten by a smooth-running industry or by its exact opposite. The pecuniary operations of these captains of industry were of gigantic scope and their fortunes commonly were not bound up with the smooth working of a given subsystem of the industrial process. Their endeavors were mainly directed to the temporary control of properties in order to close out at an advance, or to gain some indirect advantage for strategic purposes. The control of rail lines, coke mines, iron mills, was the basis for further transactions out of which gain was expected. The businessman's interest in the industrial equipment and worker was altogether transient and of a factitious character. Although the community at large would gain from the smooth and uninterrupted interplay of the various processes that made up the industrial system, this was not necessarily true for the captains of industry. Their gains and losses were related to the magnitude of the disturbances that took place.

The creation of U.S. Steel was caused by two factors: one, the disruptions threatened by Carnegie; two, the pecuniary rewards of such a conglomeration. Carnegie, Henry Clay Frick and Morgan took away in bonds, preferred stock and common stock more than the whole of U.S. Steel was worth. Frick knew this and began immediately to unload his twenty-one million dollars' worth of common stock, then priced at fifty dollars a share. By selling in small lots and on rebounds, he managed to get clear before the stock plummeted to nine dollars two years later.

Although Morgan would have pulled through, the company itself was saved by a mechanic in Detroit who was honestly trying to mass-produce exactly alike automobiles at the lowest possible price. He also had the startling concept of paying workers enough that they could afford to buy the product they were producing—Ford cars. When he worked out the assembly line, he was able to lower the price of the car, change the lives of millions of Americans and boom the U.S. Steel Company with orders for sheet steel. He hated financiers and Wall Street and had little interest in accumulating wealth. His dream was to produce an inexpensive car for the masses so that they would demand better roads and the need for his cars would grow. There were to be no accessories, and you could have your choice of any color provided it was black.

Henry Ford was Thorstein Veblen's vision of the future, the pure mechanic or engineer. Ford was not expelled from Harvard, he never finished grammar school.

The *New York World* published a cartoon of President Roosevelt wearing a gun belt,

J. Pierpont Morgan. "The
walking-stick . . . comforting to
anyone who is gifted with even
a moderate share of ferocity."—
Veblen.

holding a globe of the world in one hand, a club or "big stick" in the other. T.R. had confided in a friend: *I am trying to make tropical American peoples understand that on the one hand they must behave themselves reasonably well, and on the other I have not the slightest intention of doing anything that is not for their own good.*

A revolution in Venezuela had delivered that country into the hands of Cipriano Castro, whom Roosevelt thought *an unspeakably villainous little monkey*. Because of Castro's cavalier actions regarding his nation's debts, both Germany and England sent warships to bombard that country. Finally, at T.R.'s urging, arbitration was agreed upon. Roosevelt had written to a friend two years before: *I have always been fond of the West African proverb: Speak softly and carry a big stick.* Another man never seen to walk without his stick or walking cane was J. Pierpont Morgan. His favorite walking stick had a gold head.

A walking stick may be a cane, but to Thorstein Veblen: *The walking-stick serves the purpose of an advertisement that the bearer's hands are employed otherwise than in useful effort, and it therefore has utility as an evidence of leisure. But it is also a weapon, and it meets a felt need of barbarian man on that ground. The handling of so tangible and primitive a means of offense is very comforting to anyone who is gifted with even a moderate share of ferocity.*

J. P. Morgan went to Washington a few days after learning of the suit against the Northern Securities holding company. He was a man of action and direct, and so was the man he was calling on. He complained immediately of the failure of the administration to give him advance notice of the suit. *Just what we did not want to do*, chirped Roosevelt. Morgan then made his famous response: *If we have done anything wrong, send your man to my man and they can fix it up. It can't be done*, snapped the Rough Rider. Anxiously, Morgan retreated to other grounds: *Are you going to attack my other interests? . . . Certainly not, unless we find out that in any case they have done something that we regard as wrong*, came the response. The suit began in March and ended two years later with a complete victory for President Roosevelt.

But before the suit had hardly begun, there was further strife between the two factions. The anthracite coal strike began in May of 1902 and now it was October. The politicians were in a panic over the coming elections. T.R. decided he would send in troops as Cleveland had done in the disastrous Pullman strike, but with a difference. The troops would take over the mines. Roosevelt sent his Secretary of War, Elihu

Root, to see Morgan aboard his yacht, the *Corsair*. When he heard Roosevelt's plan to take over the mines, Morgan feared it was the advent of socialism. He got the mine owners to agree to arbitration, but only provided the board of arbitrators did not include a union man. A sociologist, however, was deemed acceptable. Roosevelt learned something: *It gave me an illuminating glimpse into one corner of the mighty brains of these "captains of industry . . ." All that was necessary for me to do was to commit a technical and nominal absurdity with a solemn face.*

William Randolph Hearst changed to dark frock coats, became a family man. His aim, the Presidency.

Impressionistic photograph of the Flatiron Building by Edward Steichen in 1905.

This I gladly did. I appointed the labor man I had all along had in view, Mr. E. E. Clark, the head of the Brotherhood of Railway Conductors, calling him an "eminent sociologist."

With the invention in the 1850s of the elevator by Elisha Otis, the face and value of New York changed. Family upon family and business upon business could be stacked one atop the other. John Jacob Astor's original land holdings in the city doubled, tripled, quadrupled in value. This was instantly recognized with the completion of the twenty-two-story Flatiron Building at the south end of Madison Square. D. H. Burnham, who had been in charge of the Chicago Exposition in 1893, was the architect who designed New York's first skyscraper.

When William Randolph Hearst decided to make his overt political move, he sent Arthur Brisbane to Boss Croker of Tammany

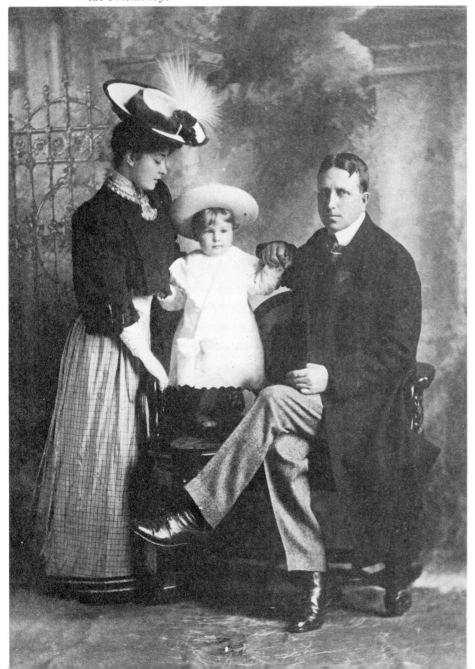

Houdini used the Kaiser.

Hall, and after agreeing on a sizable donation to the campaign managers, was given the nomination of congressman for the Tenth New York Assembly District. On his election on November 4, 1902, to celebrate and get full publicity for his victory, he tried to make arrangements with the Flatiron Building for a fireworks display from its roof. The building's managers would not allow this from New York's finest edifice. The display was set up instead on Madison Avenue between the park and Madison Square Garden. There was a gigantic election celebration taking place and the area was packed with celebrants when the fireworks accidentally exploded. Seventeen persons were killed, an equal number maimed. District Attorney William Travers Jerome lamented to the press the huge waste of life from such a large amount of explosives: *in this case, the collecting together of such a quantity was only for celebration purposes and for the amusement of the people.* Hearst never forgave Jerome for the remark. The lawsuits that piled in would be fought by Hearst for nearly twenty years.

Hearst's father had attempted to do what Harry Thaw's father failed to do—limit the money available to a wastrel son. In each case the mother ignored the express wishes in her late husband's will and gave generously to her offspring. Whereas William Randolph Hearst, as the male offspring, should have received millions from his father the will left him nothing. But his mother supplied Hearst with the money he required to buy and run his papers. Both Thaw and Hearst had been expelled from Harvard, and Hearst now chased a chorus girl appearing in *The Girl from Paris* at the Herald Square Theatre, while Thaw pursued a *Florodora* girl. In April forty-year-old Congressman William Randolph Hearst married show girl

Millicent Willson and she dropped out of the chorus for a European honeymoon on the *Kaiser Wilhelm II*, a superliner of the North German Lloyd line. For the sake of his ambition for the presidency, Hearst had married and changed his wardrobe. He now appeared in long black frock coats and black slouch hats. He wanted the public to forget the image of a man in a checkered suit with a pretty girl on each arm, and visualize instead a statesman, serious and married, worthy of the Executive Mansion.

At the same time that T.R. had started the federal suit against Morgan, Harriman and the Northern Securities Holding Company, and the suits began against Hearst for the fireworks deaths in Madison Square, Houdini became embroiled in a lawsuit against a German official. Werner Graff had written an article accusing the American escape artist of being a fraud. Graff, a powerful police official in the Kaiser's Reich, found that Houdini had claimed in his ads that he could escape from anything and everything. Since no one could do that, Graff claimed misrepresentation and fraud. When Houdini finally came up with a German lawyer willing to fight a German official in a German court, he brought suit. They then maneuvered the official, Graff, into challenging Houdini. Graff had claimed that Houdini was an illusionist who could escape from his own trick cuffs, leg irons or chains. In court Houdini's lawyer had an officer put on Houdini the regulation wrist chains and padlock with which he was already familiar, and from which he immediately freed himself, winning the case. Officer Graff took the case to a higher court with similar results, and Houdini became famous and a hit in Germany.

In November of 1902 Peary returned to the States after another defeat in his attempt to reach the Pole. He received a letter from his nine-year-old daughter Marie regarding a report in the *New York Herald* that the Peary Arctic Club wanted him to make another exploration of the north. Marie had been born in Greenland on one of the two trips on which Peary had taken his wife. When Marie was born, natives had come from miles around to see the "snow baby," and only on touch were they convinced she was flesh and blood. The name stuck, and Snow Baby, at nine, wrote an impassioned plea to her father: *My dear, dear Father— Of course, I know the papers are not always right, but I read that the Peary Arctic Club is trying to get your consent to go north again. I think it's a dog's shame . . . I know you will do what pleases mother and me, and that is to stay with us at home. I have been looking at your pictures, it seems ten years, and I am sick of looking at them. I want to see my Father. I don't want people to think of me as an orphan. Please think this over. Your loving, Marie.*

But the papers were right, and the new President sympathized with Peary's cause, approved of it and wanted it for the national pride. Peary was at work on a new ship that could take him further into the frozen north. He named it the *Roosevelt*.

When Katherine Duer married Clarence Mackay, she asked her father-in-law to build them the finest estate on Long Island. The old man granted this wish by calling in Stanford White. The result, completed in 1902, was the finest French Renaissance mansion in America, Harbor Hill. Although the old man was one of the rough and tumble Irishmen who mined the Comstock lode and was snubbed by New York society for so many years in spite of his wealth, this house would make the family acceptable even to royalty.

Mrs. Nesbit appealed to Stanford White to get Evelyn away from ne'er-do-well John Barrymore. Hearst had fired Barrymore.

In Newport White designed and was building a forty-room château inspired by Marie Antoinette's Court of Love at Grand Trianon for Mrs. Hermann Oelrichs, whose father had been one of the Comstock partners with Mackay. Although the mansion overlooked the sea, you could not view the harbor. When Mrs. Oelrichs gave her famous White Ball, she commanded all the guests to wear white and had a small navy of full-scale, white-hulled, white-sailed boats anchored in view of her white ballroom.

While those two mansions were being built, White was also building a residence for the James Pyle family in Morristown,

New Jersey, and finalizing the plans for the Charles Dana Gibson home as well as the new residence of Joseph Pulitzer. The latter was to be his most difficult client; he could not see the sketches so he demanded a model of the house so that he could "see" with his fingertips whether the exterior was too ornate.

White was also designing a porch with three graceful arched doorways for St. Bartholomew's Church, a gift of the Vanderbilts. But White also found time that same year to come to the aid of Mrs. Nesbit and her seventeen-year-old daughter. He had been giving the family financial help for over a year and had put them up in an apartment in the Hotel Audubon. Now, Mrs. Nesbit wanted him to get her daughter away from the ne'er-do-well Jack Barrymore, who had lost his job at the *Journal* and showed too much talent for alcohol. So White paid to have Evelyn enter Mrs. De Mille's School in Pompton, New Jersey. In her diary, Evelyn describes the school and Cecil B.: *When we drove up, Mrs. De Mille's son came out to meet us smoking a pipe. He was certainly a pie-faced mutt, as Stanford White would say. . . . I was taken in and shown my room. It was neither large nor small, had a Japanese paper on the wall and contained a "virtuous" white bed.* She went on to describe the other girls: *These girls have been kept from the world and they know little or nothing of the mean side of it, but there is not one of them who will ever be anything. . . . They may be good wives and mothers, but I'm going to be what's better.* A few months later she had to leave the school for unidentified medical treatment and an operation. (Years later, District Attorney Jerome would ask Evelyn Nesbit if she had had a criminal operation caused by Mr. Barrymore and if Stanford

White hadn't wanted Mr. Barrymore arrested for seduction.)

After she recuperated, Evelyn and her mother sailed for Europe—and so did Harry Thaw, who bought their tickets. On her return from the "trip," Evelyn filed an affidavit with Stanford White's lawyer to bring suit against Harry Thaw. While her mother remained in London, Evelyn had gone on an odyssey: *Mr. Thaw and I then traveled throughout Holland, stopping at various places to catch connecting trains, and then we went to Munich, Germany. We then traveled through the Bavarian Highlands, finally going to the Austrian Tyrol. During all this time the said Thaw and I were known as husband and wife, and we were represented by the said Thaw and known under the name of Mr. and Mrs. Dellis.* She then described tripping together for five or six weeks, finally renting the castle in Tyrol known as the Schloss Katzenstein. It was situated halfway up an isolated mountain and they had rented one end of the castle consisting of two bedrooms, parlor and drawing room. The servants were in another wing. Her document goes on: *The first night we reached the "schloss," I was very tired and went to bed right after dinner. In the morning I was awakened by Mr. Thaw pounding on the door and asking me to come to breakfast, saying the coffee was getting cold. After the breakfast the said Thaw said he wished to tell me something, and asked me to step into my bedroom. I entered the room, when the said Thaw, without provocation, grasped me by the throat and tore the bathrobe from my body, leaving me entirely nude except for my slippers. I saw by his face that the said Thaw was in a terrific, excited condition and I was terrorized. His eyes were glaring, and he had in his right hand a cowhide whip. He seized hold of me and threw me on the* bed. *I was powerless and attempted to scream, but the said Thaw placed his fingers in my mouth and tried to choke me. He then, without any provocation and without the slightest reason, began to inflict on me several severe and violent blows with the cowhide whip. So brutally did he assault me that my skin was cut and bruised. I besought him to desist, but he refused. I was so exhausted that I shouted and cried. He stopped every minute or so to rest, and then renewed his attack upon me, which he continued for about seven minutes.*

Evelyn goes on in the sworn affidavit to tell of her inability to leave her bed for three weeks. She then discovered *a little silver box, oblong in shape, and about two and a half inches long, containing a hypodermic syringe and some other small utensils. I went to the said Thaw and asked him what it was and what it meant, and he then stated to me that he had been ill, and tried to make some excuse, saying he had been compelled to use cocaine. I realized then, for the first time, that the said Thaw was addicted to the cocaine habit. I also frequently saw the said Thaw administer cocaine to himself internally by means of small pills. On one occasion he attempted to force me to take one of these pills, but I refused to do so. . . . During this*

"*His eyes were glaring and he had in his right hand a cowhide whip.*"—*Evelyn Nesbit.*

entire period, while I was in this condition of non resistance, Thaw entered my bed and without my consent repeatedly wronged me. I reproved the said Thaw for his conduct, but he compelled me to submit thereto, threatening to beat and kill me if I did not do so. . . . I have been repeatedly told by the said Thaw that he is very inimical to a married man, whom he said he wanted me to injure, and that he, Thaw, would get him into the penitentiary; and the said Thaw has begged me time and again to swear to written documents which he had prepared, involving this married man and charging him with drugging me and having betrayed me when I was fifteen years of age. This was not so, and so I told him, but because I refused to sign these papers, the said Thaw not alone threatened me with bodily injury but inflicted on me the great bodily injury I have herein described.

The Republic of Panama was founded in Room 1162.

But while Evelyn Nesbit was dictating the above document to Stanford White's lawyer, Harry Thaw was writing to his lawyer, Frederick Longfellow: *The daughter cannot be with her mother because of superhuman neglect. A blackguard was allowed to drug the girl and ruin her.* Two years later, Evelyn would become Mrs. Harry Thaw. Her mother's financial worries would then be ended.

The Republic of Panama was founded in Room 1162 of the Waldorf-Astoria. In 1888, after ten years of work, the Ferdinand de Lesseps group that was building a canal through the Colombian province of Panama failed. The company declared bankruptcy and turned to the United States to see if it would be interested in buying concession rights the company had purchased from Colombia. It was now 1903. The rights would expire in 1904, the year of the next presi-

dential election. Roosevelt knew of no Vice President who had succeeded to the presidency and then been elected President. He believed his popularity as he traveled about the country was due to his office, not himself. Therefore his dream of a canal to tie in with his concept of naval power was urgent in his priorities for action.

The bankrupt canal company was reorganized as the New Panama Canal Company for the sole purpose of selling its rights in Colombia to the United States. The company hired a lobbyist-lawyer, William Cromwell, to see that Nicaragua, then favored, was not selected as the canal site.

In the 1880s there had been two exploratory expeditions to Nicaragua to assess the feasibility of the proposed canal. On both expeditions the engineer selected to survey the canal area was Robert Peary. Peary had met Matthew Henson in Washington, D.C., and Henson went with him to Nicaragua as his manservant. Although Peary favored Nicaragua, after Cromwell gave a sixty-thousand-dollar donation to the Republican campaign and a timely volcano erupted in Nicaragua, Panama was settled on. The New Panama Canal Company asked for over one hundred million dollars for rights, which would expire the following year. The committee contended forty million was all the rights were worth. The New Canal Company jumped at the offer. A treaty was drawn up in which Colombia would grant the United States a hundred-year lease on a six-mile-wide strip of land through Colombia's province of Panama. Colombia, in turn, would receive ten million dollars, and after nine years, two hundred and fifty thousand dollars in annual rent. The treaty also stated that the United States would pay the New Panama Canal Company forty million dollars for its rights

French engineer Philippe Bunau-Varilla, first Panamanian Minister to Washington.

set the date for the revolution—November 3. General Huertas, who was in charge of the detachment of Colombian troops stationed in Panama City, was to be commander-in-chief and the men who joined him were to receive a fifty-dollar bonus. The day following the revolution, the troops received their payment in gold. Dr. Amador, their new President, told them: *The world is astonished by your heroism. Long live the Republic of Panama! Long live President Roosevelt!* Thirteen days later, the Frenchman Bunau-Varilla, as Panamanian Minister to Washington, concluded a treaty conferring the ten-million-dollar down payment on the Republic of Panama, the same payment Colombia had previously rejected. The stockholders of the New Panama Canal Company, whoever they might be, were to receive forty million for their almost expired Colombian rights. (Eight years later T.R. bragged to University of California students that: *I took the canal zone and let Congress debate, and while the debate goes on the canal does also.* Colombia now demanded indemnity and Roosevelt's friends blocked any apology until after his death. The Harding administration then gave, in conscience money, twenty-five million dollars to Colombia.)

and that Colombia was not entitled to any part of that money. Colombia rejected the terms of the treaty. Furious, T.R. grumbled: *those contemptible little creatures in Bogota ought to understand how much they are jeopardizing things and imperiling their own future.* To his Secretary of State he said: *we may have to give a lesson to those jack rabbits.*

He had already decided the canal would be built and would not tolerate interference or delay. Philippe Bunau-Varilla, the French engineer working with lobbyist Cromwell, set up headquarters in the Waldorf-Astoria, and while his wife stitched a flag for the new Republic of Panama, he drew up a declaration of independence. He then met with Dr. Manuel Amador, company physician for the Panama Rail and Steamship lines, who was to be the first selected President. When Bunau-Varilla was informed ships of the U.S. Pacific fleet were being sent to Colombian waters, he

When President Roosevelt decided to take on the trusts and began with the captain of the captains, Morgan, and the Northern Security Holding Company, Pulitzer editorialized: *People will love him for the enemies he has made. Mr. Cleveland lost popularity among the Democratic masses by not enforcing this [antitrust] law. Mr. Roosevelt will gain by enforcing it. It cannot now be said that the Republican party is owned by the trusts. It cannot now be said that Mr. Roosevelt is owned by them.*

Ralph Pulitzer contacted his father to tell

Pulitzer declared the house that White built a "wretched failure."

him the President was very pleased and would like him to come around for lunch or dinner at his convenience. But now election time was drawing near and aggressiveness against the trusts diminished rapidly. Roosevelt began to panic and sent Cortelyou, the Republican National chairman, to raise more money for his campaign. The money came in, one hundred thousand from George Gould, fifty thousand from Harriman, one hundred thousand from Standard Oil, fifty thousand from Frick and one hundred and fifty thousand from J. Pierpont Morgan. Seventy-two percent of the two million raised had come from the big corporation men. Pulitzer fumed and his *World* asked how much the sugar, beef, coal and other trusts had given.

But Pulitzer had other worries. Hearst, now owner of eight papers, was using them for his own political ambitions; his goal was the White House. Hearst had turned the National Association of Democratic Clubs, which he headed, into his own powerful organization, with his own men in charge. Pulitzer threw his weight behind Judge Alton B. Parker, but worried that if Bryan suddenly

backed Hearst, Hearst would get the presidential nomination. However, Parker was selected and Pulitzer instructed his editor to treat Roosevelt with absolute fairness, crediting him with the Northern Securities decision and positive achievements, but: *then, having done him full justice, unroll the indictment. . . . My idea is that his real weakness and vulnerability lie in his jingoism, blatant militarism, unconstitutionalism, in the personal Government he has substituted for that of law.* The *World* began to question in its editorials the corporate contributions as well as the appointment of Cortelyou as Secretary Commerce and Labor. That meant Cortelyou the campaign manager who raised money from the corporations was now in charge of the bureau of corporations. In a later edition the *World* published a list of contributions and the names Morgan, Gould, Harriman beside the amounts given.

But Parker was buried in a Roosevelt landslide. Even T.R. was taken aback and wrote to his son Kermit: *I am stunned by the overwhelming victory we have won.* To his wife he said with new confidence: *I am no longer a political accident.*

Joseph Pulitzer declared the house that White built a *wretched failure*. Although he had approved the exterior design by running his fingers over a model of the house and found it not overly ornate, the interior was a failure; he heard a sound in his bedroom. His family had moved in before him and all had found the bedroom tomb silent. His secretaries, whom he trusted and spent more time with than his own family, also checked out the room. While some locked themselves in the room, the others jumped up and down screaming in the hall. Dead silence. But after all this testing, and just before Pulitzer moved in, a sump pump had been installed in the cellar to divert spring water. The heating system carried the heartbeat of the pump to Pulitzer's room. He then had a soundproof tower added to the house. It was known as the vault.

At twenty-six, Ralph Pulitzer worked for a salary and also received an allowance from his father. Pulitzer, in turn, received daily reports from his son's diary and sent back praise or blame, depending on the situation. When Ralph had paid attention to Mary Harriman, the *World*'s attacks on her railroad-baron father had broken up their friendship. Now he wished to marry the granddaughter of William Henry Vanderbilt. Frederica Vanderbilt Webb was the daughter of Eliza Vanderbilt and Dr. William Webb. The Webbs had inherited ten million dollars as their share of the Vanderbilt fortune. At the time of the marriage, Ralph's salary, in keeping with the rest of the staff's, was five hundred dollars a month. He was made a vice president and given an increased allowance. When the couple returned from their European honeymoon, another gift awaited them, a townhouse at Seventy-third Street, right next door to his father's house.

The same year that Ralph Pulitzer honeymooned in Europe, Nancy Langhorne met young Waldorf Astor, the heir to the British house of Astor. His father, William Waldorf Astor, had built the Waldorf and many other hotels before going into the political arena. When he was knocked out, he remarked *this was no place for a gentleman* and left the country. He settled in England and bought one of the great mansions of the world, Cliveden on the Thames. Both Nancy Langhorne and Waldorf Astor were twenty-six, having been born on the same day, May 19, 1879. William Waldorf Astor was unhappy with his son's choice of an American divorcee instead of a titled Englishwoman or at least the daughter of an aristocratic family. And again, no clergyman could be found who would perform the ceremony for a divorced woman. Finally, in secrecy, they were wed in London, at All Souls Church. William Waldorf then bestowed his blessings, which included as a wedding gift Cliveden.

In the fall of that year Stanford White wrote excitedly to Saint-Gaudens: *When I was in Syracuse years ago, I was perfectly ravished by a Greek Venus which they have there. I made a lot of drawings of her myself . . . but I never could find a photograph of her, and I have always regretted that I did not have one made. Lo and behold, in the Sunday* Herald *of October 8th they have a photograph of her, and I send it up to you and want to know if you do not think that she is the 'most beautifullest' thing that ever was in this world.*

Since Stanford White was a married man and Jack Barrymore a ne'er-do-well, Mrs. Nesbit allowed her daughter Evelyn to travel once again to Europe with the eligible bachelor Harry K. Thaw. In their suite in a Paris hotel Harry announced: *It's all over, everything is all over. I have taken laudanum.* Evelyn found an empty bottle that had contained the opium preparation and hastily summoned a doctor. In the meantime, Thaw became sick and wretched. By the time the doctor arrived, Harry had passed most of the poison from his system. The reason for his attempted suicide: depression over *that blackguard who ruined my life and yours,* meaning Stanford White.

On their return to America, Thaw called

Morgan's Corsair.

J. Pierpont Morgan at home on his Corsair.

on the Society for the Suppression of Vice. Anthony Comstock thought Thaw had come to him out of the purest of motives: *He seemed to think White was a monster who ought to be put out of the community.... On the strength of his information and from that received in anonymous letters which corroborated Thaw's statements, I endeavored to get at the truth about White.... I made application for a room in the tower next to the rooms occupied by Stanford White ... the result was that, although I was morally convinced of White's guilt, I had no substantial evidence to offer in a legal action.... I was therefore compelled to drop the idea of having White indicted. My ill success in not bringing White to trial seemed to depress Thaw ... and everything I heard about Mr. Thaw himself was highly commendable to him.*

One of the major financial backers of Anthony Comstock and his Society for the Suppression of Vice was J. Pierpont Morgan.

Maxine Elliott.

114

first actress to have her own theatre named after her. Although Morgan was accompanied by glamorous women on many of his voyages, his insistence on secrecy and complete privacy had kept most of their names among the unknown. But Maxine was proud of her accomplishments, and Morgan had to share her after her seduction of King Edward at Marienbad. Maxine then purchased a manor house in Hertfordshire and built a discreet stairwell to the King's suite on the second floor.

James Hazen Hyde had taken Alice Roosevelt to the horse show in 1904, and in 1905 invited her to his ball at Sherry's. Although she at first accepted, she was out of town the night of the ball and failed to participate. For Teddy Roosevelt, this was a stroke of luck. Sherry's seven-story building (designed by Stanford White) contained apartments for bachelors on its upper floors. Tom Wanamaker had rooms there and Harry Lehr had used Wanamaker's flat as his own before his marriage to Elizabeth Drexel Dahlgren. Sherry's itself contained

Morgan was never trailed, of course, but if he had been, Comstock would have found the married financier was also backing one of the prettiest actress-courtesans in the business. Maxine Elliott was often seen aboard Morgan's aptly named yacht *The Corsair*, both in this country and abroad. She was the

"On fine days, as often as he can get away, luncheon is packed in the row-boat and he takes the whole family rowing to some distant point on the shore, which even the Secret Service men have not discovered, and there they spend the day, the President pulling the oars going and coming."— Jacob Riis in Ladies' Home Journal, *1904.*

Madame Réjane with her host, James Hazen Hyde. In one year he would be thirty and the Equitable would be his.

the most magnificent ballroom in the country, with an extensive palm garden in the rear. (Years later, the Sherry-Netherland Hotel would be built by Sherry where William Waldorf Astor now had his Netherland Hotel.) Mrs. Harry Lehr described the hard work Stanford White had gone to in transforming Sherry's into the Court of Louis XVI, and the expense of dressing the musicians and staff in liveries of that period. Young Hyde had also engaged the famous actress Gabrielle Réjane to come over from France to perform for his guests. Hyde was so concerned with authenticity that he imported French statuary from the mother country. James Hazen Hyde had graduated from Harvard, but had also been educated in France and was at heart a Francophile. His father, in his will, made provisions for him to take over his precious Equitable Life Company, but not until his thirtieth birthday. At the time of the ball, he was twenty-nine. For the past seven years he had been executive vice president under the regency of his father's trusted friend, James Alexander, president of Equitable.

In the past guests had to travel to a studio to have their portraits taken. Now, for the first time photographers were on the scene, posing the guests in groups. The following day the press would have the portraits showing the guests in their exquisite French costumes. Although Alice was out of town, her cousin Franklin, recently graduated from Harvard, was an extra man on the stag line. The *New York World* applauded the event, recording the guest list and noting it wasn't the same old Four Hundred again but included names from the world of stage and opera. But concealed beneath the gayety lay an unseen plot. Alexander and his followers feared loss of control of Equitable the following year, when James Hyde turned thirty and could exercise his fifty-one percent inherited ownership in the company. So they plotted his ouster. Pulitzer's *World* got wind of the fallout, as did the other papers, and the ball turned sour. The press reported it as a scandal, printing rumors that the great French actress Mme. Réjane had recited indecencies and that she had performed the high-kicking can-can atop a table. (Evelyn Nesbit was accused of witnessing a cakewalk in the Dead Rat café in Paris with Harry Thaw.) Less than two weeks later, the *World* scored a scoop, revealing the ultimatum Alexander and twenty of the Equitable officials had issued to Hyde: either he would resign

E. H. Harriman and daughters at Hyde Ball.

or they would quit en masse. To avoid harsh publicity unfavorable to the company, the hierarchy tried to hush up their family troubles by denying all.

The *World* attacked in fury, exposing the waste and corruption with resultant mismanagement of policyholders' money, money supposedly held in trust for widows and orphans. The *World* then went after New York Life and Mutual Life, implying things were no better in these two giants than they were at Equitable. Pulitzer editorials demanded an insurance investigation. Finally Governor Frank Higgins, instead of instigating an investigation of the charges, requested his insurance superintendent, Francis Hendricks, make his own study. The results of the inquiry were denied to the press and public. Meanwhile, Pulitzer, deep at sea, cabled his editor to drop the Equitable thing because *it must be boring the public by now*. The governor, pressed for the contents of

the Hendricks report, said he had not seen it. District Attorney Jerome could not get a copy, the original being locked in Hendricks' safe in Albany. Pulitzer's *World* suddenly, in the middle of July, published the contents of the secret document. Reporter Louis Seibold had a friend on the inside in Albany who let him copy the entire report, which exposed the corruption only suggested in previous reports. It detailed how simple it was for an official to make twenty-five thousand dollars in three days. He simply had a friendly corporation that was trying to sell its stock to the insurance company pass its ownership to him, and then he sold the stock for a point more to his own company. James Hazen Hyde had done it, as had many other officials of the big three insurance companies. When Pulitzer returned to shore and learned what his editor Cobb and reporter Seibold had done, he suspended Cobb for three weeks and fired Seibold. The suspension was ignored (after all, Pulitzer hadn't

Seated, Mrs. Stuyvesant Fish. Tallest man, Stanford White. Photographed at the Hyde Ball.

been in the *World* building more than once since it was erected), and Seibold was forgiven by Pulitzer once he recognized the importance of his revelations. Don Seitz of the *World* began a series demanding that the recent investigator of the gas probe, Charles Evans Hughes, who was vacationing in Switzerland, be appointed chief investigator of the insurance field.

Hughes returned swiftly and began the investigation that led him from oblivion to the Supreme Court Bench. Hughes' technique was polite and steady as a steamroller. When a president of a company told him something was confidential, he would reply quietly: *There is nothing confidential about the insurance business now.* Richard McCurdy, the opulently corpulent president of Mutual, said his company was *a great beneficent missionary institution.* Hughes answered: *The question comes back to the salaries of the missionaries.* One of McCurdy's sons received almost two million dollars over a period of seventeen years. His son-in-law in one year pocketed one hundred and fifty thousand dollars, this in the days when there was no income tax. All in all, McCurdy's family had taken fifteen million from the company in "missionary" fees.

The New York Times, on April 5, 1905, carried on its front page the battle being waged to oust Hyde by Alexander, and Hyde's attempt to dislodge his opposition in return. Adjoining that column was a four-paragraph report of a wedding at the Third Presbyterian Church of Pittsburg. The headline said simply: **THAW WEDS MISS NESBIT.** The last paragraph noted: *It is conceded that Harry Thaw, whose allowance had been cut to twenty-five hundred dollars a year, will now enjoy his full allowance of eighty thousand dollars annually.*

Hughes' investigations carried the public's interest and suddenly he found himself boomed for the mayoralty nomination by William Randolph Hearst. By October Hearst, who had already been nominated b the Municipal Ownership League, was look ing toward the following year's gubernator elections and was afraid that if Hughes was still eligible he would get the public's nod. This would prevent Hearst from reaching this important rung in his grasp for the pres idency. Hughes, whom the Republicans no wanted out as his investigation neared their leaders, declined the nomination, fearing th investigation would be discredited if he accepted. Just as Hearst had feared, the following year he was defeated by Hughes, w became governor of New York State.

The Hughes investigation revealed that t big three insurance companies had divided the country into territories in which each company would fight, through lobbyists, u favorable legislation. Favorable reporting b papers was to be rewarded at the rate of a dollar a line of puffery.

Hughes also discovered the benefit of interlocking directorates. Morgan's partner, George Perkins, disposed of Morgan Company International Mercantile Marine bond at eight million dollars to George Perkins, the vice president and director of New Yor Life. When Hughes requested that Hanove Bank turn over its books so that he could determine the whereabouts of a forty-eight thousand-dollar payment, he was cautioned by Perkins: *Mr. Hughes, you're handling dynamite. That forty-eight thousand dollar was a contribution to President Roosevelt's campaign fund. You want to think very car fully before you put that in evidence.* But Hughes gave it little thought if any. He put the answer in evidence. Testimony continu

The Roosevelt, *built by Robert Peary with J. Pierpont Morgan's backing.*

and proved the *World* had been right in charging Roosevelt's campaign fund was all big-business contributions. Mutual and Equitable had each given forty thousand to the fund. Also benefiting from the generosity of the insurance moguls were New York's two senators, Tom Platt and Chauncey Depew. Depew received twenty thousand a year as a retainer from Equitable, and Platt ten thousand from Mutual now and then. Although no one was sent to jail, retribution was heavy. President Alexander was removed from his post at Equitable and died soon after in a sanatorium. McCall of New York Life resigned, started repayment of over two hundred thousand dollars to Mutual. McCurdy left the country for the Continent, where he died. Perkins resigned from the board of New York Life and repaid the forty-eight thousand dollars he had given the Roosevelt campaign fund with accrued interest. Young James Hazen Hyde, whose French ball had started it all, left on a short trip to France

after disposing of his stock in Equitable. He stayed there thirty-five years.

Early in March, 1905, Robert Peary's new hundred-eighty-four-foot ship, the *Roosevelt,* was completed. Stubby and powerful, it could twist through the icy seas and, if necessary, withstand the crush of ice cakes against its egg-shaped hull. Although the Navy, at T.R.'s prodding, offered to sponsor the expedition, it would not participate in the ensuing financial burdens. Morris Jesup, J. Pierpont Morgan and their Peary Arctic Club had then agreed to guarantee construction and raise half the fifty-thousand-dollar cost if Peary could raise the other half. Jo Peary launched the new vessel by smashing an ice-encased bottle of champagne against its prow. This time Peary was sure he would make it. He had had further surgery on his toes and skin from the bottom of his feet had been brought up to cover the stubs. He shuffled a bit, but he did not limp. Jo, pointing out his terribly unsettled mental and physical condition, urged him to forget about reaching the Pole. But his mind was made up, and in lectures to raise the necessary financing, he often declared he would sell his soul to the devil to have still another go at the Pole. In the blistering heat of mid-July the fledgling *Roosevelt* left its safe harbor for the Arctic. Captain Bartlett admired the steady way the ship handled, but a defective boiler forced them to cut their speed in half. In August they rendezvoused with the supply ship *Eric* in Greenland before setting off for the desolate far reaches of the north. When the *Roosevelt* sailed into Smith Sound, she encountered her first test with pack ice and Peary insisted Bartlett slam into the ice at full speed. With two hundred dogs and fifty Eskimo men, women and children atop deck, the *Roosevelt* plowed into the ice, shoving it aside or slicing through heavy packs like coconut pie. Later, in steep floes of pack ice she would squeeze under the pressure until her rounded wood hull vibrated her loose.

The assault on the Pole would not begin until February, but preparations had to be made and the ship's crew, expedition men and Eskimos cared for. Peary had excellent food, though they ate only two meals a day. Typical breakfast was cereal, sausage and eggs or beans with brown bread. Suppers included musk ox steak, trout, corned beef and vegetables, bread with butter, tea and a dessert. Peary also entertained his crew with snowshoe and sledge races for prizes he supplied, and there was a dinner for the Eskimos served by the *Roosevelt*'s officers. Peary also kept track of birthdays in his diary. On Christmas morning there were gifts from Jo. But for all the planning, the trip was doomed once again to failure.

Peary's plan was to divide his men into groups or divisions. The divisions would go off, one a day, for six days, each returning after going fifty miles past the last group. This way each would make a trail the next group could follow, and go another fifty miles and deposit its supplies, to in turn await the following division. The unforeseen was the drift eastward of the sea ice. Leads (open water) suddenly appeared as ice split and the division had to wait three or four days for the lead to freeze over to permit sledges, men and dogs to pass. And the ice they traversed shifted so that the trail was never straight between the first fifty-mile party and the next. Twenty days after Peary shoved off, he came upon three divisions waiting before open water. They had to wait six days before the ice was firm enough to move across. A blinding blizzard held them in its

grip for another six days, and Peary abandoned his plan. Instead, he decided to make a dash for it with Matthew Henson's group. Late in April they were trapped with moving ice, snow and uncertain murky water at eighty-seven degrees six minutes north longitude. No man had ever been this far north. But they had to give up. And the return trip proved more perilous than the getting there. At one point they were cut off by surrounding water and Peary recorded: *Each day the number of dogs dwindled and sledges were broken up to cook those of the animals that we ate ourselves. One day leads formed entirely around the ice on which we were, making it an island of two or three miles' diameter.* Peary then sent scouts out to study the predicament, and when they returned they reported a film of new ice extending from their floating island for two miles over the open lead. For Peary and his men it was now or perish. *I gave the word to put on snowshoes and make the attempt. I tied mine on more carefully than I had ever done before. I think every other man did the same, for we felt that a slip or stumble would be fatal. . . . We crossed in silence, each man busy with his thoughts and intent upon his snowshoes. . . . Once started, we could not stop; we could not lift our snowshoes. It was a matter of constantly and smoothly gliding one past the other with utmost care and evenness of pressure and from every man as he slid a snowshoe forward, undulations went out in every direction through the thin film encrusting the black water. The sledge was preceded and followed by a broad swell . . . near the middle of the lead, the toe of my rear kamik, as I slid forward, broke through twice in succession. I thought to myself, "This is the finish," and when a little later there was a cry from someone in the line, the words sprang from me of themselves: "God help him; which one is it?" But I dared not take my eyes from the steady, even gliding of my snowshoes, and the fascination of the glassy swell at the toes of them. . . . When we stood up from unfastening our snowshoes and looked back for a moment before turning our faces southward, a narrow black ribbon cut the frail bridge on which we had crossed. The lead was widening again and we had just made it.*

Further on he came upon another group led by Charles Clark, a fireman from their ship. Clark and his three Eskimos were near starvation, having subsisted the past few days on spare boots.

It is the alleged custom of the Japanese to declare war by attacking their adversary. They did this on the night of February 9, 1904, inflicting heavy losses on the Russian fleet at Port Arthur. President Roosevelt was well pleased with the Japanese victory, believing Russia was *behaving very badly in the Far East, her attitude toward all nations including us, but especially toward Japan, being grossly overbearing.* But as the Japanese victories continued, T.R. worried about the Philippines and proffered his personal services to the Russians to bring about peace. He wrote to his Secretary of War William Howard Taft: *My own view is that the Russians would do well to close with them even now; but the Czar knows neither how to make war nor to make peace.* Teddy then went off to hunt bears in Colorado, leaving Taft, as he put it, sitting on the lid. That summer the Secretary of War, with a party of congressmen including Nicholas Longworth as well as Alice Roosevelt, stopped off in Japan where he urged the Japanese Prime Minister to make peace with Russia. Taft then asked about the Japanese

Alice went to Japan, the President went hunting.

Kaiser Wilhelm turned to T.R.

chored at Oyster Bay. The President offered a toast to lasting peace and the delegates then departed for their peace conference in Portsmouth, New Hampshire. But while T.R. was still shooting bear in Colorado, another crisis had arisen. France and England had decided to squeeze Germany out of commercial interests in Morocco. England would have rights in Egypt, France in Morocco. When the Kaiser demanded a conference, France turned him down flat. The Kaiser then turned to T.R. to intervene in his behalf. (After all, Alice had dedicated his new American-made yacht only a few years before.) By the time T.R. returned from Colorado, a German warship was steaming toward Morocco and war seemed imminent. Roosevelt then went into action and swiftly convinced the French to allow the Kaiser to save face. A conference was convened, the Kaiser face saved and France took Morocco. The world's eyes were wide and focused on Roosevelt. An English historian commented *The two things in America which seem to me the most extraordinary are Niagara Falls and President Roosevelt.*

During this period Saint-Gaudens received an official, cautious letter from Director Roberts of the United States Mint. It was in regard to new coinage, but there was no commitment, nothing definite. Roberts suggested Saint-Gaudens, when in Washington drop around as the Mint was seeking the council of artists. But T.R., having decided that existing American coinage was not up to America's new image, had already picked Saint-Gaudens to redesign the coins with him. There would be no interference from outsiders like the director of the Mint. Saint-Gaudens wrote the President in mid-November: *You have hit the nail on the head . . . of course the great coins, you might say the only coins, are Greek.* Later, in an-

interest in the Philippines and was reassured there was none. Taft agreed, secretly, that Japan could assume a protectorate over Korea. Japan, and then Russia, agreed to send delegates to a peace conference in the United States.

France and England breathed a sigh of relief. The Kaiser had been acting up, claiming his nation had not been given its place in the sun. If war broke out with the Kaiser, the French and the English would need Russia as an ally. In August plenipotentiaries from Russia and Japan were greeted by President Roosevelt aboard the U.S.S. *Mayflower*, an-

No. 10. The Roosevelt Bears at Niagara Falls
" They dressed themselves in rubber suits,
With rubber hoods and rubber boots.''

swer to a suggestion of T.R.'s, he wrote again: *I remember you spoke of the head of an Indian, of course that is always a superb thing to do, but would it be a sufficiently clear emblem of Liberty as required by law?* Then Saint-Gaudens had an inspiration that he relayed to the President: *I can perfectly well use the Indian headdress on the figure of Liberty.* The model he selected was pretty, square-jawed Alice Butler of Windsor, Vermont. But by the following March, pain caused him to seek further medical treatment and he underwent a second cancer operation. Augusta was informed the tumor would return in a few years but further surgery was futile. While recovering, Saint-Gaudens received a letter from Stanford White saying he and Charles McKim would like to come up to New Hampshire. Saint-Gaudens replied: *For God's sake, I have been trying to get you up here for twenty years and no sign of you and Charles and now that we are having the worst Spring that ever occurred, you want to come up in five minutes. Now you hold off a little while and I will let you know, perhaps in a couple of weeks from now. But, come to think of it, our friend Ethel Barrymore is coming up here. Perhaps that's the reason you old suckers want to come.*

But the trip never came off. Instead Saint-Gaudens had to travel to New York for X-ray treatments and stayed at the Players Club. He was able to go over plans with White for the Whistler Memorial bas-relief planned for West Point. As in the old days, White was designing the base for the sculpture. Years before, the press had joked about Madison Square Garden being White's largest base for a Saint-Gaudens sculpture, the Diana.

Back in 1890, when actor Edwin Booth gave his residence for the Players Clubhouse, White had offered his services free of charge. He then took off the front stoop and added columns and a porch. At a New Year's dinner in 1893 President Cleveland presented a loving cup to Booth and the *Metropolis* published a list of famous "actors" who attended, including Chauncey Depew, Louis Tiffany, Saint-Gaudens and Stanford White. White had also designed the Tile Club, the Lambs, the Century, the Metropolitan, the Harmonie and the Brook clubs. Now, in 1906, he was completing, a few blocks from the Players Club, the Colony. This club was different. Backed by Morgan, Harriman and others, it was a club for women. A place where they could swim, exercise or smoke if they cared to. Its design by White was delicate, with narrow columns supporting a porch with wrought-iron railings, arched windows whose curves softened and complimented the delicate brickwork. But White also influenced his patrons to allow a novice to decorate the interiors instead of himself or Louis Tiffany. He had chosen the former

Dr. Parkhurst, owner of a "Byzantine jewel."

actress, Elsie de Wolfe, whose simplicity and good taste he admired, for the job. She had been successful on the stage, then invested all her money in a show starring herself and gone broke. After she did the interiors of Stanford White's new club, the super-rich sought her out, and one of the first was Henry Clay Frick. Frick, now out to show up his ex-partner, was constructing a palace on Fifth Avenue that, he said, would make Carnegie's mansion look like a miner's shack. Frick offered Elsie de Wolfe ten percent of the cost of whatever art objects she found for him, but she would not be allowed to accept anything from the dealer. On her first trip to Paris with Frick in search of objects, she learned part of the collection of Sir Richard Wallace was for sale. Frick had a lunch date but said if she insisted he would have a look. As he walked through the collection followed by Elsie, he pointed at an object and said simply: *I'll take this, and this and that, and this. The objects were three hundred thousand francs and up.* Miss de Wolfe later put down her reactions in her diary: *I followed at his heels, aghast, and I realized that in one short half-hour I had become a rich woman.*

"I realized that in one short half hour I had become a rich woman."—Elsie de Wolfe's realization after following Henry Clay Frick on an acquisition hunt.

At the same time he was involved in all these constructions, White was supervising the finishing of the Madison Square Presbyterian Church for the Reverend Dr. Parkhurst. You could stand in Madison Square Park, one of the loveliest sections of residential New York, and see the Farragut statue by Saint-Gaudens with its art nouveau base by White, the new Madison Square Church by White and Madison Square Garden by White directly across the street from the house Jennie Jerome Churchill was raised in. But the church was the jewel of the square despite the twenty-two story Flatiron Building, which still caused neck-stretching on the south end of the park. The Frick Collection still exists and brings pleasure to those who enter the building. But when the Advertising Club of New York took over Stanford White's Robb House, Dr. Percy Grant of

In the shadow of the Diana, Dr. Parkhurst's "jewel."

Stanford White's flowing art nouveau base supporting Saint-Gaudens' Farragut.

the Church of the Ascension told them: *You have purchased for your new clubhouse one of the finest in New York—a work of art. . . . Don't let any other architect tear it apart and remove the touches of White's genius. Save as much of White as possible. He had a wonderful sense of proportion. There is something about a house where he had a free hand that gives you a special feeling of comfort. That's why I say I would rather have a Stanford White house than a painting by Rembrandt.*

The Madison Square Presbyterian Church was torn down a little over ten years after its completion to make way for an office building. The British architect Gilbert Fraser was shocked: *How do you expect to have a beau-*

Frick's Diana by Houdon.

tiful city if you have no regard for your old buildings? In Stanford White you had one of the greatest architects of modern times. He was an artist; and this church was one of his masterpieces. It was exquisite, as fine as anything I have ever seen. And you tear it down, and build one of your hideous, if useful skyscrapers. It is as if we in England were to tear down one of Sir Christopher Wren's churches. John Champman added in Vanity Fair: The demolition of the Madison Square Presbyterian Church makes one feel as if our very monuments and triumphal arches were merely the decorations of a parade or scaffolding dressed for a holiday. Lath and plaster they were, and to lath and plaster they must return. There is no room in America for a past. This particular church was like a Byzantine jewel, so concentrated, well-built and polished, so correct, ornate and lavish that a clever Empress might have had it built. It represented wealth and genius, and was one of the few buildings left by Stanford White in which every stone had been weighed, every effect unified.

Yet, though they tore down this church, it lives. It was reproduced, even retaining the crosses designed in the bricks, as a synagogue in California.

At the same time, White's partner, Charles McKim, was putting the finishing touches to the stone mausoleum that was to house J. Pierpont Morgan's collection. Morgan had purchased the property adjacent to his home on Madison Avenue and Thirty-sixth Street. His son lived on the adjacent corner at Thirty-seventh Street. The building would be called the Morgan Library and would have underground passageways to both Morgan homes. McKim fought for a Renaissance palazzo constructed of white

The East Room of Morgan's Library.

marble, but with a difference: he wished to build without mortar. This meant using perfectly fitted blocks of marble in the classical Greek manner. It meant more time and more money, but Morgan agreed to it and the result was a monumental, flawless work of art for New York and its visitors. Proud of his work, McKim put his profile on the sphinx guarding the steps of the building. Two of the main rooms in the library were the West Room, to which Morgan would repair each morning when at home, and the three-story mural-ceilinged East Room.

On May 18, 1906, Alexander Berkman walked out of prison a free man. He was twenty-one when he was committed, he was thirty-five when he was released. During his imprisonment his unselfish "deed" had been condemned not only by the workers of the Homestead Mills, for whom he had acted, but also by socialists and his fellow anarchists led by Johann Most. His victim had not only survived his attack, he had gone on to become one of the richest men in the world and the Frick Collection ensured he would be remembered as a benefactor of mankind. Now, while Emma Goldman supported herself against the columns of the Detroit railroad station, her friends went to bring Sasha to her from the train. *My friends returned, a stranger walking between them, with swaying step. . . . That strange looking man, was that Sasha? . . . his face deathly white, eyes covered with large, ungainly glasses; his hat too big for him, too deep over his head—he looked pathetic, forlorn. I felt his gaze upon me and saw the outstretched hand. I was seized by terror and pity, an irresistible desire upon me to strain him to my heart. I put the roses I had brought into his hand, threw my arms around him, and pressed my lips to his.*

Frick in stone by Malvina Hoffman.

Stanford White's son Lawrence came down from Harvard.

"That strange looking man, was that Sasha . . ."
—Emma Goldman.

On reaching the restaurant, they ordered food and wine. *We drank to Sasha. He sat with his hat on, silent, a haunted look in his eyes. Once or twice he smiled, a painful, joy-less grin. I took off his hat. He shrank back embarrassed, looked about furtively, and silently put his hat on again. His head was shaved! Tears welled up into my eyes; they had shaved his head and dressed him in hideous clothes to make him smart at the gaping of the outside world.*

On June 25, 1906, Hattie Forsythe and another showgirl dropped by the Madison Square Garden tower apartment of Stanford White to say good-by to him. The girls were part of Anna Held's company leaving for Europe. When they found White was out, they joshed the elevator operator into telling White that Mrs. Harry Thaw had called. On receiving this message, White sent roses to Mrs. Thaw with his regrets that he had not been in. The night before, White had presented his wife with an amber necklace which she had refused because that type of amber brought bad luck. Lawrence White had come down from Harvard to be with his family, and a friend of his, seventeen-year-old Laura Chanler, had come from upstate New York with her parents to join them. White offered the necklace to Mrs. Chanler for Laura, but Mrs. Chanler too thought that

128

particular amber cursed. The following day Stanford White left for Virginia on business while Lawrence, Laura Chanler and another couple dined in New York before Laura took the train back to Geneseo, New York. But Stanford White never reached Virginia. Instead he dined at the Café Martin on Madison Square. Harry Thaw and his wife were in the café at the same time but never saw White as he was on the terrace and left without entering the main dining room. When Thaw left the table for a few moments, an actor stopped by to chat with Evelyn. She warned him that her husband was insanely jealous and not to let him find them chatting. The day before Thaw had stopped a

man on the street and threatened his life if he found him with Evelyn. The man thought he was crazy. Stanford White left the Café Martin and crossed the park to Madison Square Garden. He had stayed in town to attend the opening of Eddy Foy's new musical, *Mamzelle Champagne*. Later, during the performance, White failed to notice the entrance of a foursome which included Harry Thaw and his beautiful wife, Evelyn. The musical, like *Florodora*, had a sextette and they were singing "I Could Love a Million Girls" when Thaw got up and walked away from his party. He paced about and passed the seated figure of Stanford White who was too preoccupied to notice him. Thaw sat

The Roof Garden beneath the Diana.

ABOVE: *Harry Thaw in The Tombs shortly after his arrest.*

RIGHT: *Stanford White was preoccupied with* Mamzelle Champagne *and failed to see Harry Thaw.*

down with a stranger and discussed shipping and travel. When he returned to his table, the others said they were bored with the show and wanted to leave. Although it was a warm night, Thaw put on a straw hat and an oversize overcoat. Chatting away, Evelyn and the other couple neared the exit door before they realized Harry wasn't with them. He had dropped back, circled around the tables and approached White. He then pulled a pistol from his coat and fired a shot into White's head inches away, then pulled the trigger twice again as White, unrecognizable now, slumped onto the table, then slid beneath it. It was over in seconds and while women screamed, the manager motioned with his arms for the band to play, the chorus to sing. Thaw danced around holding the pistol above his head to show it was all over. When Evelyn heard the shots she cried: *Good God Harry! What have you done?*

He answered: *All right, dearie, I have probably saved your life.* He was disarmed by a fireman who held him until a policeman arrived. Thaw told the policeman: *He deserved it, I can prove it. . . . He ruined my wife and then deserted the girl.* Thaw then said to the man: *Here's a bill, officer. Get Carnegie on the telephone and tell him I'm in trouble.*

Although the murder of Stanford White took place on the night of June 25, the July issue of *Cosmopolitan* had gone to press weeks before and was already on the stands It contained a long article on the stage as training school for millionaires' wives. The elegant article described the *Florodora* "sestet" and their advent into wealth. There was a full-length photograph of one of then with the caption: *Mrs. Harry Kendall Thaw of Pittsburg, who was Florence Evelyn Nes*

*"...the face of an angel, the heart of a snake."—
Saint-Gaudens' description of Evelyn Nesbit.*

bit, a famous artist's model and chorus girl.
The article explained: *The struggle for social
position which Florence Evelyn Nesbit is
still making in the home of her millionaire
husband, Mr. Harry Kendall Thaw, brother
of Alice, the Countess of Yarmouth, is a cu-
rious commentary upon the ways of democracy. Born in Pittsburg, she came in the first
flush of girlhood to New York to make her
fortune. Her face was her talisman, and when
not behind the footlights in "thinking parts,"
she was employed as a model by illustrators
for trade and fashion journals at a wage that
would not keep the average chorus girl in
violets. Her beauty was supplemented by
good manners and innate tact, which are
serving her well in the trying position in
which her marriage has placed her in Pittsburg's snobbish world.*

Evelyn Nesbit Thaw's mother-in-law
had left for London aboard the liner *Minne-
apolis* three days before the murder. She had
been looking forward to this visit with her
daughter Alice, the Countess of Yarmouth,
for several months. Now, her friends and
relatives were afraid the elderly grande dame
might have a stroke when she learned from
the shipboard news that her son had killed a
man. Cables were hastily sent to the Captain,
warning him to use great tact in notifying
Mrs. Thaw of the incident.

Mrs. Stanford White was notified by telephone of the death of her husband and left
immediately for New York. At the Players
Club members worried about the effect on
the ailing Saint-Gaudens and felt forced to
tell him as gently as possible before he read
it in the papers. When he found out, he went
into a depression and couldn't face the
Whistler memorial with White's plans for
the base for many months. After he pulled

himself together, Saint-Gaudens wrote to a friend, referring to Thaw as *an idiot who had shot a man of great genius for a woman with the face of an angel and the heart of a snake.*

Thorstein Veblen wrote: *The first duty of a newspaper editor is to gauge the sentiments of his readers, and then tell them what they like to believe. By this he increases circulation.*

The morning papers began with factual reports on the tragedy. *The New York Times* caption read: **THAW MURDERS STANFORD WHITE.** In one part of its story, under the caption: *White Aided Mrs. Thaw,* the *Times* had a special from the theatrical manager, George Lederer, dated June 25, the night of the murder. Lederer said: *When Evelyn Nesbit was fifteen or sixteen years old she met Mr. White and subsequently he became a close friend of hers and of her mother's. I think that throughout, his friendship for the girl was entirely platonic. He was a persistent firstnighter and liked pretty girls. He took a strong personal interest in the Nesbits, assisted them financially and made them comfortable in every way. Subsequently the girl went on the stage, first appearing in "Florodora" in the Casino. Mr. White remained her very good friend and she in turn was grateful to him. She is of a frivolous disposition and no doubt refused to break off her friendship for him after marrying young Thaw, who is a cigarette fiend.* The *Times* article went on to say that White had persuaded Miss Nesbit's mother to let Evelyn try out on the stage and she then entered the *Florodora* company. White later persuaded George Lederer to engage her for his new show, *The Wild Rose,* in which she appeared as a gypsy dancer. Mr. Lederer then boomed her as a new beauty.

The article failed to mention that George Lederer's wife sued for divorce and named as corespondent Evelyn Nesbit.

In one of the articles on White's career, the *Times* spoke of his churches, clubhouses, architectural features for sculptors, interior designs, Madison Square Garden, Washington Arch, New York University, the University of Virginia, and then mentioned some of his famous residences: *a work by which he will always be remembered and which is considered by many of his friends as the best specimen of his genius is the Marble House, which he built at Newport for Mrs. William K. Vanderbilt. Its construction marked the zenith of his fame. He received carte blanche as to material and decoration. His bust now stands on a pedestal in the hall as a recognition of the success he achieved.* There was no mention of Alva and her daughter Consuelo's imprisonment in Marble House.

Hearst's *Evening Journal,* the night after the murder, had new interest for its readers. A headline screamed: **ALIENISTS DECLARE THAW SANE.** In smaller type the subhead declared: *Millionaire Assassin of Stanford White Hurried to the Tombs Where Two Noted Physicians Examine Him. Beautiful Wife of the Prisoner at the Hotel Lorraine.* The next day the *Evening Journal* carried three photographs of Mrs. Harry Thaw. One pose showed her as the Winter Maid, another as a Spanish dancer and the third as Mary Magdalen. The trials of Harry Thaw would continue to hold readers for two continuous years. Harry Thaw's defense would be that he had done the country a good turn by killing a ravisher of innocent young women.

President Roosevelt, once the trial got under way, would try to bar from the mail

Congressman Longworth and his bride, Alice. On their honeymoon they dined with the Kaiser.

President Roosevelt in the midst of his Panama Canal.

newspapers that carried the full, "disgusting" particulars. But at the moment he was preparing a trip and announced that he would soon visit the Republic of Panama and personally inspect the construction of the canal. He was immediately taken to task by the *Times: There is an unbroken usage that the President shall not leave the territory of the United States during his term of office.* The editorial went on to suggest that if he remained aboard a United States vessel, technically the President would still be on U.S. territory. But then, the *Times* couldn't really imagine T.R. visiting the isthmus without going ashore and getting into everything.

These days T.R. had more free time to run the country; Alice had married Congressman Longworth, with whom she had traveled to Japan along with the Taft party the previous year. Roosevelt had once declared he could do one of two things: *I can be President of the United States, or I can control Alice. I cannot possibly do both.* Now Alice was Longworth's problem. The day before White's death, the Longworths were still honeymooning in Europe and had dinner with Kaiser Wilhelm in Germany.

In November of 1906 President and Mrs. Roosevelt visited the Canal Zone. T.R. did

Harry Thaw and his fast-aging mother.

not stay aboard a U.S. vessel but explored the complex rail network being set up and the early construction of housing for the forty-five thousand workers who would be employed in the vast undertaking. Roosevelt had to decide whether to go with the Canal Commission or General Gorgas in eradicating yellow fever. The disease had been the cause of the failure of the French De Lesseps Company in its attempt before in the same area. Gorgas wanted to eradicate the Stegomyia mosquito, which he believed was the cause of yellow fever, while the Canal Commission believed cleanliness and fresh paint was the cure. T.R. gave Gorgas the go-ahead to begin war on the mosquito, with the result that the dread disease was eradicated. Another decision forced the President to circumvent Congress' edict of a multi-headed Canal Commission. Roosevelt felt the administrative policies too complex for more than one decisive leader and appointed as chairman of the commission Lieutenant Colonel George Goethals, a recognized expert in canal construction. To the other members of the commission Roosevelt stated simply: *If at any time you do not agree with Colonel Goethals' policies do not bother to tell me about it—your disagreement with him will constitute your resignation.*

While District Attorney Jerome was hard at work preparing the state's case against Harry K. Thaw, Mrs. William Thaw, returned from Europe, was preparing to throw a million dollars into her son's defense. The lawyers' plan was to show that White had been a monster deserving of such a tragic end, and that Harry Thaw carried a pistol because he feared for his own safety from said monster.

At the same time, Alexander Berkman

once again secured a pistol, but this time concealed the fact from Emma Goldman. *I understood his suffering, and my heart bled for my dear one, so bound by the past. In his depleted physical condition Sasha could find no work to do, and the atmosphere surrounding me appeared strange and alien to him. When we were alone in the flat, or in the company of Max, he breathed a little freer, and he was not unhappy with Becky Edelson, a young comrade who often came to visit us. All my other friends irritated and disturbed him; he could not bear their presence and he always looked for some excuse to leave. Generally it was dawn before he returned. I would hear his weary steps as he went to his room, hear him fling himself dressed upon his bed and fall into restless sleep, always disturbed by frightful nightmares of his prison life. Repeatedly, he would awaken with fearful shrieks that chilled my blood with terror. Entire nights I would pace the floor in anguish of heart, racking my brain for some means to help Sasha find his way back to life.* She finally came up with the idea of his going on a tour, lecturing on prison and its brutality. Suddenly, when he was due to speak in Cleveland, Sasha disappeared.

He had decided to take his own life, and because no one knew him in Buffalo, he had gone there to commit the act. But after two days, he was drawn to return to New York for a last look at his old love. It was young Becky Edelson who came running to Emma with the news that Sasha was alive. Later, after listening to his outpouring, Emma convinced him to return with her.

I held out my hand to him and begged him to come home with me. 'Only Stella is there, my dearest,' I pleaded, 'and I will see that no one intrudes upon you.' At the flat I found Stella, Max and Becky waiting anxiously for our return. I took Sasha through the corrido into my room and put him to bed. Sasha remained in bed for several days, asleep mos of the time and only half-aware of his surroundings during his waking hours. Max, Stella and Becky relieved me in taking care of him.

For the first time, the Nobel Peace Prize was awarded to an American statesman, Theodore Roosevelt, for his efforts during the Russo-Japanese conflict.

One of Broadway's most successful song-and-dance men, George M. Cohan, publishe his new song, "You're a Grand Old Rag," just as T.R. won the peace prize. The title for the song was a quote from a veteran of Pickett's memorable charge at Gettysburg. The show was *George Washington Jr.*, starring Cohan and including his father, mother and wife in the cast. Patriotic organizations thundered complaints against terming the flag a rag and George M. change the last word to *flag*. It then became a millior copy smash hit. Another play, not a musica opened at the Amphion Theatre. The villai of the piece, Stanford Black, knocks down a blind man and then kicks him. The blind man had asked what had become of his beautiful young daughter. The climax show Black seated at a performance on a roof garden when a young man shoots him. The close of the play is an impassioned speech b the murderer from his cell: *No jury on eart will send me to the chair, no matter what I have done or what I have been, for killing the man who defamed my wife. That is the unwritten law made by men themselves an upon its virtue I will stake my life. This wa* the opening salvo by Thaw's mother to wir public opinion to her son's side. She had engaged writer–P.R. man Ben Atwell to portray her son to the public in the role he was to play in his own defense as Thaw had refused to plead insanity. Instead, he would use the best defense, an offense. His side would attack the reputation of Stanford White. The newspapers had already led the way, and circulation proved it was what the readers wished to read. Even Ochs' *New York Times* declared in large caps on June 29: **COMSTOCK WANTS TO TELL ABOUT WHITE AND OTHERS. HE WAS INVESTIGATING REVELRY IN MADISON SQUARE TOWER.**

In the same edition the *Times* quoted Rockefeller's pastor, Dr. Eaton: *The murder of Stanford White by Harry Thaw reveals an absolutely rotten situation socially in New York. It strikes me that if there was a little more shooting in cases like that in which Harry Thaw shot Stanford White, if we are to believe the newspaper accounts, men would be more careful about their relations with other men's wives.*

A few weeks after the murder, attorney Joseph Shay reported to the district attorney's office that the suit against Thaw by Ethel Thomas was still pending. Miss Thomas charged that Thaw had beaten her with a dog whip. *The New York Times* reported: *Ida Vera Simonton, who was regarded as a possible witness in the Thaw case, is no longer in this country. It was Miss Simonton who declared that Stanford White sent her to Europe to bring Evelyn Nesbit and her mother back to this country. She said she found Mrs. Nesbit abandoned and practically penniless in London, while her daughter was touring the Continent with Thaw in an automobile.*

The *Times* also reported: *Thaw is evidently determined to convince everybody that there is no truth in the reported settlement of the twenty-thousand-dollar damage suit brought against him by Ethel Thomas.*

Also in the *Times*: *An important witness was discovered yesterday in Miss Rose Marston, formerly an artist's model and now a showgirl, who was one of Evelyn Nesbit's intimate friends when Miss Nesbit herself was posing in New York studios. Miss Marston said that she knew all about her engagements, dinners, and acquaintances with men. At that time, according to Miss Marston, Miss Nesbit did not know Stanford White. It was only when she went on the stage that she met the architect. She gave Assistant District Attorney Garvan the names of several men with whom the present Mrs. Thaw was on friendly terms during her studio life and it was understood that these men would be subpoenaed in the case.*

Again in the *Times*, the headline: **EMOTIONAL INSANITY THE THAW DEFENSE,** and the subheads: *To Say White Drugged, Ruined and Insulted Mrs. Thaw.* And: *Thaw Sought Comstock's Aid but Comstock Declares He Couldn't Quite Get White on Other Charges.* The article continued: *The defense will endeavor to show that Evelyn Nesbit, when a mere child, was drugged and ruined by White, and that after her marriage to Thaw, White took advantage of every opportunity to thrust himself upon her notice. It will offer evidence that he was wont to talk insultingly of the relations he had had with her, and that Thaw, learning of White's remarks, was worked up to a high pitch of resentment. That Thaw bought a revolver to kill White, or that the killing was premeditated, will be denied. . . . The Times*

Dress-up dinner in the home White built for Charles Barney. White in feather cap is third from left in second row.

also reported action by D.A. Jerome's office: *Every acquaintance of White, Thaw or Mrs. Thaw who is in a position to tell of their habits and the happenings in their lives will be subpoenaed and examined.*

The scandal was too big for most of White's friends and admirers. Only the clean-cut Gibson man, writer Richard Harding Davis, dared to speak out, and did so in *Collier's* in August. His defense of White's character was based on fifteen years of friendship: *... Since his death White has been described as a satyr. To answer this by saying that he was a great architect is not to answer it at all. ... What is more important is that he was a most kind-hearted, most considerate, gentle and manly man, who could no more have done the things attributed to him than he could have roasted a baby on the spit. Big in mind and body, he was incapable of little meannesses. He admired a beautiful woman as he admired every other beautiful thing that God had given us; and his delight over one was as keen, as boyish, as grateful as over any of the others. Described as a voluptuary, his greatest pleasure was to stand all day waist deep in the rapids of a Canadian river and fight it out with the salmon.*

President Roosevelt himself secured a three-year leave of absence for Robert Peary, but with the fitting of new boilers for the *Roosevelt*, delay piled on delay and now departure was put off to July. Peary would have liked to have had his former surgeon, Dr. Frederick Cook, aboard again, but the doctor had gained national acclaim by scaling Mount McKinley and was planning his own Arctic exploration backed by millionaire sportsman John Bradley. The captain of Cook's ship was named Bartlett just as was the captain of Peary's ship. They were cousins. Doubts were put in Peary's mind about Cook. Charles Nichols informed Peary he doubted Dr. Cook reached the top of Mount McKinley. Vilhjalmur Stefansson, another explorer, returned from Alaska and said he had heard the report of Cook's ascent on McKinley was a hoax. The delays continued and Peary realized it would be another year before he could set off for the north. So Cook had a year's headstart. Morris Jesup had died just when Peary thought his financial problems were at an end, and the panic of 1907 threatened everyone and everything.

On Thirty-fourth Street and Fifth Avenue stood one of the most solid-looking banks in America. It belonged to the Knickerbocker Trust Company and was built on order of its president by Stanford White in 1904. The president, Charles Barney, had known White many years and his home at Sixty-seven Park Avenue was designed by White in 1894. The painter Thomas Dewing thought Barney and his wife the handsomest couple he had ever seen, and Dewing was a painter of women. At the time the panic seeds were being sown, J. Pierpont Morgan was attending an Episcopal Convention in Richmond. Roosevelt had admonished the malefactors of great wealth for continuing to bring about as much financial stress as possible. The contributors to this panic were bankers-financiers Charles W. Morse and F. Augustus Heinze. Because of their copper speculations and previous shaky bank manipulations, their banks were hard put for cash. Pyramiding their controlling interest in the Bank of North America, they had grabbed control of the Mercantile National Bank and partial control of Barney's Knickerbocker Trust. Using the bank money, they now made an attempt to corner the copper market

Three weeks later Charles Barney died of a self-inflicted bullet.

"They are in trouble in New York, they do not know what to do and I don't know what to do."
—J. Pierpont Morgan.

through their Union Copper Company, which they had kited to sixty dollars a share. The Standard Oil people, with James Stillman heading their National City Bank, saw their chance. They realized that the money holding the shares of Union Copper belonged to the Morse-Heinze banks. Union Copper nose-dived from sixty to ten. Those who knew the banks' funds were behind the shares rushed to the banks to withdraw their deposits. When Morse and Heinze ran to the Clearing House for more funds to satisfy customers' demands for cash, the Clearing House confirmed publicly that depositors' funds had been used in copper speculation and the run on the banks accelerated. Morgan hurried from Richmond: *They are in trouble in New York, they do not know what to do, and I don't know what to do...* Stillman, of National City, wanted Morgan to help shore up some of the trust companies. Veblen's theory was that disruption means pecuniary gain for someone. Morgan was that someone.

Charles Barney knew Morgan; Morgan owned stock in the Knickerbocker Trust and it became imperative to Barney that the two meet. On October 21 Morgan set up a command post in his new library and started meeting with various financiers and bankers but refused to see Barney. The following day, the Knickerbocker Trust went under. Three weeks later, Charles Barney died of a self-inflicted bullet.

And the panic spread to other banks, other companies. After George Perkins, one of the Morgan partners, gave reporters an interview, both the *Sun* and the *Times* pointed fingers at the Trust Company of America as "the sore point." Withdrawals leap-frogged from one and a half million dollars on Tuesday to thirteen million the following day. The assets of that company included the major competitor of U.S. Steel, the Tennessee Coal and Iron Company. After telling the president of the bank to bring over his assets, Morgan stated that this was the place to stop the trouble. The controlling interest in the Tennessee Coal and Iron Company stock had been posted with the Trust Company for loans by the investment banking firm of Moore and Schley. Although the price of the stock was one hundred and thirty dollars a share, the investment firm had offered it to Morgan at ninety dollars and been turned down. Its actual value was two hundred and fifty dollars a share, and it would be worth ten times that figure when Tennessee Coal was fully developed. Morgan would get control for less than seventy-five a share in U.S. Steel

Bonds. But first, Judge Gary and Henry Clay Frick had to rush to Washington to see if Roosevelt would permit the purchase to stave off the panic without bringing suit under the Sherman Antitrust Act. A subsequent congressional investigation was called to learn if Gary and Frick had tricked the President by misrepresenting the facts in allowing Tennessee Coal to be swallowed by U.S. Steel at a bargain price. But by then the panic was over and Morgan and partners had made many additional millions. Morgan already had control of a thousand million dollars.

Thorstein Veblen wrote: *In the nature of the case, the desire for wealth can scarcely be satiated in any individual instance, and evidently a satiation of the average or general desire for wealth is out of the question. However widely, or equally, or "fairly," it may be distributed, no general increase of the community's wealth can make any approach to satiating this need, the ground of which is the desire of every one to excel every one else in the accumulation of goods. If, as is sometimes assumed, the incentive to accumulation were the want of subsistence or of physical comfort, then the aggregate economic wants of a community might conceivably be satisfied at some point in the advance of industrial efficiency; but since the struggle is substantially a race for reputability on the basis of an invidious comparison, no approach to a definitive attainment is possible.*

The same year, 1907, Henry Ford put into operation his assembly-line technology. He produced ten thousand look-alike Fords. He had gone against the grain, defied the financiers who insisted on heavier, more expensive cars for the rich, and created a car for Everyman. He had one other even more

There were four thousand car-makers, but every other car sold was a Ford. George Gould family of cars, Lakewood, New Jersey.

radical concept: the workers should be able to afford the product they made, the Ford car.

Shortly after the murder of Stanford White, Thaw's lawyers held a lengthy meeting with his wife Evelyn. She dictated for over four hours the lurid details that would be used in her husband's defense. Certain of these "details" were leaked to the waiting press. The impression of one reporter was that Mrs. Nesbit had sold her daughter at the age of sixteen to White, who then supported daughter, mother and son. The *Evening Journal* asked its readers: *Was Thaw Justified in Killing Stanford White?* and the letters poured in, with almost seventy percent approving of Thaw's act and describing

White as a coward with unspeakable objectives. A clergyman named Peters visited Thaw in prison and wrote: *I think he will get out of it. No sane jury will convict the passion-enslaved youth for avenging what he thought a stain on his honor. He will be a free man next Christmas; I think he should be.*

Evelyn's mother, now married to Charles Holman, announced she would testify at the trial—in Stanford White's behalf. To vindicate his good name she was willing to turn over all White's letters to the district attorney. The following day she issued a statement: *Thaw never had any reason to be jealous of Mr. White, who treated Evelyn as he would have treated a daughter. . . . His*

Evelyn was the only guest at the dinner party and tour which led to the bedroom in the tower.

While Harry fans himself, his mother pays attention to the judge.

letters will show that Thaw never had any intention of marrying Evelyn, and only did so when he was forced to. Mrs. Holman went on: *Evelyn never posed in a single studio that I had not visited myself and found to be a fit place for her. And it was Evelyn herself who insisted on going on the stage. She was headstrong, self-willed and beautiful, and that led to all her trouble.*

Clifford Hartridge, Mrs. William Thaw's personal attorney, left immediately for Pittsburg to see Mrs. Holman. On January 5 he was able to announce that because of her delicate state of health, Mrs. Holman would not testify at the trial after all. On January 9 the Countess of Yarmouth set sail from England to be at her brother's side during his trial.

On the other side stood William Travers Jerome, who had readied himself in the previous months by studying up on abnormal psychology, especially paranoia. He took a personal pledge to see that Thaw would be placed where he could do no further harm to himself or anyone else. But Harry Thaw had fired his first counsel, who wanted him to plead insanity. His new defense was that he had slain White in a fit of "temporary insanity," in the hopes of getting off without a sentence or confinement. The defense put Evelyn on the stand to reveal what she had said to Thaw that had caused him to commit his "act." Since she had only testified as to what she had told Thaw, Jerome could not question the veracity of what she had told, only *whether* she had told it to Thaw. Jerome was boxed in and Evelyn poured out her heart. She revealed that an actress, Edna Goodrich, had taken her to lunch with White and another man. After lunch White took the girls to his room with the red-velvet

The Roof Garden, tower apartments, Diana.

swing. He pushed them for a while, then took them for a ride in his electric car and returned Evelyn to her mother. Later White paid for Evelyn's mother to take a trip to Pittsburg and invited her daughter to a dinner party. Evelyn testified that she was the only guest and that after they had dined, White took her on a tour of the house that led to a bedroom. He insisted she drink a glass of champagne, after which the room began to spin, resulting in Evelyn's downfall. *When I woke up all my clothes were pulled off me and I was in bed. I sat up in the bed and started to scream. Mr. White was there and got up and put on one of his kimonos. The kimono was lying in a chair, and then I sat up and pulled some covers over me. There were mirrors all around the bed; there were mirrors on the side of the wall and on the top. Then I screamed and screamed and screamed, and he came over and asked me to please keep quiet, that I must not make so much noise. He said, "It's all over now." Then I screamed, "Oh, no!"*

The defense attorney now solicited from Evelyn that she had been a virgin when she visited White's flat. District Attorney Jerome stated he could prove that Stanford White was not in this country at the time Evelyn Thaw claimed she had been drugged and seduced by him. The defense attorney objected. It was not relevant whether White had or had not done such and such an act, only whether Evelyn Nesbit had told Harry Thaw that it had happened. There was no way to defend Stanford White when the judge sustained this defense motion.

Canada banned from the mails newspapers with full details of the trial and President Roosevelt asked his Postmaster General if he could do the same. District Attorney Jerome was not shocked by the testimony but by the actions of the press in printing the lurid details, including illustrations when possible. As the protests poured in against the press, Pulitzer's *World* printed an editorial reply: *The Thaw trial will have done a permanently valuable service if it destroys the veil of secrecy with which public modesty has surrounded certain vices. There are certain matters which every boy or girl is sure to learn about. The alternative is not that of knowledge or ignorance, but whether they will acquire their knowledge from their parents, their school teachers, their physicians and their clergymen, or from the slime of the gutter.... The more frankly, baldly and repulsively these facts are taught, the more repellent to vice will be their effect....*

The trial continued, the testimony became more lurid and circulation climbed as the defense's star witness Evelyn Nesbit Thaw told her tale.

On cross-examination, Evelyn admitted that she had posed for a photographer and White on a polar-bear rug clad only in a kimono. After her seduction by White, she continued to receive his financial support for her education and her brother's, as well as medical and dental expenses for her family. Jerome wanted to know if this was the way she reacted to the "treacherous" act against her "maidenly decency." In answer to another question she replied she hated Stanford White. Jerome then had the young actor Jack Barrymore subpoenaed. He was appearing in *Captain Jinks of the Horse Marines* in Boston and was reluctant to appear. A detective finally brought him to the courtroom. Jerome was anxious to learn about a "criminal operation" performed on Evelyn Nesbit at the time she was going with Barrymore,

Evelyn was led to the top and touched Diana's foot.

Nothing under the kimono.

whom she knew before meeting White or Thaw. But at the first opportunity Barrymore slipped away and avoided future subpoena servers by the expedient of distance. The jurors reached two verdicts. Seven found Thaw guilty, five found him innocent. It was a mistrial. Jerome was relieved. He did not want to convict Thaw of murder in the first degree. Jerome had had several doctors observe Thaw during the trial and agreed with them that he was insane and would have to be confined for the rest of his life.

The defense changed tactics for the second trial. Now they decided to admit that Harry K. Thaw was insane. This trial took only three weeks, with the defense presenting medical opinion depicting Thaw as a manic-depressive who believed it his duty to punish people for their misbehavior. Thaw, in the meantime, had taken up Christian Science and was corresponding with its leader, Mary Baker Eddy. The verdict was finally reached: not guilty by reason of insanity.

Thaw rejoiced, not realizing he would now be hospitalized.

Mary Baker Eddy, now in her eighty-seventh year, moved to Boston, much to the surprise of her admirers and detractors. Six months after the trial of Harry Thaw, she announced the reason for her move by informing the Christian Science Publishing Society's Board of Directors in July of 1908 that she wished a daily newspaper to be started.

The reasons Mrs. Eddy desired a newspaper were pointed out in her article "A Timely Issue": *Looking over the newspaper of the day, one naturally reflects that it is dangerous to live, so loaded with disease seems the very air. These descriptions carry fears to many minds, to be depicted in some future time upon the body. A periodical of our own will counteract to some extent this public nuisance; for through our paper, at the price at which we shall issue it, we shall be able to reach many homes with healing, purifying thought. It will be the mission of the* Monitor *to publish the real news of the world in a clean, wholesome manner, devoid of the sensational methods employed by so many newspapers. There will be no exploitation or illustration of vice and crime, but the aim of the editors will be to issue a paper which will be welcomed in every home where purity and refinement are cherished ideals. Mrs. Eddy stated:* The object of the Monitor *is to injure no man, but to bless all mankind.*

Emma Goldman had traveled to Europe to take part in a congress in Amsterdam and various meetings with comrades in England and France. She was content to leave her paper, *Mother Earth*, in Sasha's hands and felt he was getting along fine now with new friends, including Becky Edelson. She thought his attitude toward her might improve, but on her return she found: *Sasha's critical attitude to me had not changed; if anything it had become more pronounced. At the same time his interest in young Becky had grown. I became aware that they were very close to each other, and it hurt me that Sasha did not feel the need of confiding in me. I knew that he was not communicative*

by nature, yet something within me felt both offended and injured at his apparent lack of trust. I had realized even before I left for Europe that my physical attraction for Sasha had died with his prison years. I had clung to the hope that my having loved others had not changed my love for him, his old passion would flame up again. It was painful that the new love that had come to Sasha completely excluded me. My heart rebelled against the cruel thing, but I knew that I had no right to complain. While I had experienced life in all its heights and depths, Sasha had been denied it. For fourteen years he had been starved for what youth and love could give. Now it had come to him from Becky, ardent and worshipful as only an eager girl of fifteen can be. Sasha was two years younger than I, thirty-six, but he had not lived for fourteen years, and in regard to women he had remained as young and naive as he had been at twenty-one.

A few weeks later Emma was on a lecture tour, again leading her through Philadelphia, Baltimore, Washington, D.C., and finally to Pittsburg. *Pittsburg brought back memories: Sasha's martyrdom and the pilgrimages I used to make to the prison, the hopes I had cherished and that had not been fulfilled. Yet gladness was in my soul; Sasha had escaped his prison grave and I had had a large share in bringing it about. No one could take that consolation away from me.*

At the time of Stanford White's trial (for that was what the Thaw case became) there was no defense against "yellow journalism." Journalism itself was held in low esteem, and although for many years Pulitzer tried to give two million dollars to Columbia University to raise the level of journalism, the university refused to recognize that trade

Mary Baker Eddy in her eighty-seventh year moved to Boston to start a newspaper. "There will be no exploitation or illustration of vice and crime."

as a profession. When Stanford White had been accused of having three "studios," the papers printed the addresses. Later, the retractions were also printed, in the back of the papers, in small print. Richard Harding Davis, White's only defender at the time of the tragedy, wrote: *To the truth which was sad enough the untrue has been added. Within three days the awful charges fell to pieces of their own rottenness; but that did not correct the wrong that had been committed. Over all the country, over Europe, had been sent broadcast the hideous misshapen image of a man we knew to be so different. . . . The private detectives who for two years were hired to spy upon his every movement were unable to obtain one item of evidence against him.*

But most of White's friends did not come to his defense; they were afraid of attacks in the "yellow press," and besides, they did not realize the seriousness of the damage being done to his name and image. Slowly their statements did appear and a composite portrait of White took shape.

The celebrated painter Edward Simmons called White a *very simple person* and a *child and artist.* He described him in the 1890s as: *. . . unlike big men, always in a hurry, dashing about here and there, his body bent slightly forward, taking very short steps, trotting along, intent and busy. Red hair is, of course, supposed to mean violence; but White never lost his temper. He was sensitive and tender, with a tenderness that ordinary mortals sometimes find it hard to believe in.* Simmons told of seeing White in the Players Club after White had been given the task of repairing the Rotunda at the University of Virginia, which had been destroyed by fire. The Rotunda and the university were

the work of the architect Thomas Jefferson White, head in hands, seemed to Simmons *puzzled, confused and silent. What's the matter?* I asked. *It's that job down South, I've seen his plans, they're wonderful and I'm scared to death.*

Simmons also related how White had helped him out of financial holes. Once when they were riding together White asked if he would show him in a certain studio building

the rooms of an artist Simmons refers to as "X." *It seemed strange that Stanny intended calling on a man he knew not to be at home, but I kept still. Kneeling down, he shoved under the door a roll of bills which looked big-figured to me, and we fled. In the cab outside, I inquired what it all meant. 'You know he needs it. I have it. Why shouldn't I give it to him? But he'd never accept it, so you musn't tell.' 'How much was it?' I asked. 'Oh, I don't know.' Next day I heard X telling a friend that he had gone home the night before ready to pack his things as he was to be kicked out of his studio in the morning, but a most miraculous thing happened. He'd found a roll of bills under his door! He died without ever knowing who had helped him.*

William Chase, painter and one of the first teachers of the Art Students League, was in France at the time of White's death and gave an interview to the *Paris Herald*: *In my opinion Stanford White did more to beautify New York and to encourage architectural beauty everywhere in America than any other ten men. The Washington Arch, Madison Square Garden and Dr. Parkhurst's church, to go no further, established standards of taste that have proved of incalculable benefit. Yet now that his life has ended in a shocking tragedy, America seems likely to forget the debt we all owe him. Personally*

William Chase and his class for ladies. "White was one of the most loveable of men, full of spirit, bubbling with enthusiasm, always ready to encourage strugglers."

Pulitzer's monarchy at sea with crew of seventy-five. He named it the Liberty.

As he could not tolerate noise, doors near the royal suite were marked "not to be opened when Mr. Pulitzer is asleep."

White was one of the most lovable of men, full of spirit, bubbling over with enthusiasm, always ready to encourage strugglers. He was a man thoroughly alive, an artist to his finger tips; and he enjoyed life. If it be a fault to admire beautiful women, he possessed that fault, for never have I known a man more responsive or more appreciative of the beauty of women. And he did not conceal his admiration. He did not seem to regard it as anything to conceal. Why should he? His instincts were normal.

Pulitzer's new steam yacht was completed in December of 1907. It was almost a third longer than Morgan's *Corsair II* and carried a ship's crew of sixty as well as Pulitzer's personal staff, which brought the total crew to seventy-five. Whereas Morgan had his yacht deadheaded overseas, Pulitzer was now free of Morgan's White Star Line and could sail the ocean since his yacht had a capacity of six thousand miles without refueling. Aboard ship life was monarchial, with one ruling head and seventy-five loyal,

quiet subjects. Doors near the royal suite were marked "Not to be opened when Mr. Pulitzer is asleep." The yacht was named *Liberty*.

Pulitzer was the watchdog of liberty. It had been Pulitzer and his *World* that had come to the rescue of the French gift when there was no financing for a pedestal for "Liberty Enlightening the World." The arm of Liberty had then been set up in Madison Square and the *World* helped raise the funds that gave the statue a resting place. The rest of Bartholdi's lady had then been shipped over.

Now, as election time approached, Pulitzer learned that the Taft campaign had been given fifty thousand dollars by lobbyist-lawyer William Cromwell. Pulitzer had sailed to Amsterdam and was in Europe when he heard about the contribution. He cabled the *World*: *Who is he? Examine his record, especially his Panama record and his relations with corporations and trusts. Is it true he gave fifty thousand to the campaign fund? If so, why?*

In 1907 a young lady took a studio on Eighth Street and MacDougal Alley. She was a serious sculptor with two handicaps: one, she was a woman; two, she was wealthy. Ordinary wealth perhaps would not have been difficult, but this sculptor had been married in her summer home, The Breakers. Her winter home was the palatial Vanderbilt manse on Grand Army Plaza, Fifth Avenue and Fifty-eighth Street. She was the daughter and an heiress of Cornelius Vanderbilt and had married Harry Payne Whitney, heir to the Whitney fortune. Stanford White was the architect of their residence at Nine-seventy-two Fifth Avenue. At one exhibition

Almost singlehandedly, Pulitzer and his World *raised the funds for the pedestal for the Statue of Liberty. Here, in the heart of Madison Square, the arm of Liberty solicits aid in 1876.*

"*Mr. Luks, why do you keep following me this way?*"
"*Mrs. Whitney,*" Luks replied, "*because you are so God damn rich.*"

George Luks, one of the painters of the unbeautiful in urban life nicknamed the Ashcan School, followed the sculptor, Gertrude Vanderbilt, wherever she went. She turned to him suddenly and demanded: *Mr. Luks, why do you keep following me this way? Mrs. Whitney*, Luks replied, *because you are so God damn rich!*

Alva's ex, William K. Vanderbilt, complained of his wealth: *My life was never destined to be quite happy. It was laid out along lines which I could not foresee, almost from earliest childhood. It has left me with nothing to hope for, with nothing definite to seek or strive for. Inherited wealth is a real handicap to happiness.* His wife Alva had been the first person to bring an automobile to America. Their son, Willie K., offered a prize called the Vanderbilt Cup to the winner of an auto race on Long Island in 1904. Willie later married Virginia Fair, daughter of James Fair, one of the Comstock Lode partners. They had one son. At twenty-four he died in an auto accident.

James Stillman, the Rockefellers' banker who headed the National City Bank for many years, separated from his wife and traveled through France giving pieces of wrapped candy to small children. He collected the paintings of Mary Cassatt and dogged her footsteps as she viewed the Paris collections. One of the wealthiest men of his or any other generation, he described his life in a minor key: *I have never in all my life done anything I wanted and cannot now.*

Late in August of 1908 the Lloyd liner *George Washington* docked in New York after an uneventful crossing. One morning paper gave a list of the passengers, which included "Professor Freund of Vienna." The

W. K. Vanderbilt, Jr., in his ninety-horsepower Mercedes.

misspelling was noted without anger by the calm, cigar-smoking Professor Sigmund Freud. He had come to America at the invitation of the president of Clark University, Stanley Hall, to give a series of lectures. Before traveling to Massachusetts, Freud visited New York. He went through the beautiful Central Park created by Frederick Law Olmsted, toured the Chinese section for lunch, later examined the Jewish section of the Lower East Side and studied that "magnified Prater" Coney Island. He also visited Columbia University, but the visit that most interested him was to the Grecian collection at the Metropolitan Museum.

Emma Goldman was then lecturing in Vermont and Massachusetts. *The most important event of our Worcester visit was an address given by Sigmund Freud on the twentieth anniversary of Clark University. I was deeply impressed by the lucidity of his mind and the simplicity of his delivery. Among the array of professors, looking stiff and important in their university caps and gowns, Sigmund Freud, in ordinary attire,* *unassuming, almost shrinking, stood out like a giant among pygmies. He had aged somewhat since I had heard him in Vienna in 1896. He had been reviled then as a Jew and irresponsible innovator; now he was a world figure; but neither obloquy nor fame had influenced the great man.*

The psychoanalyst Ernest Jones reported that Freud lectured in German, without notes. At one point Dr. Jones passed on a request from a lady in the audience eager to hear Freud talk on sexual subjects. Emma Goldman???

The dean of the University of Toronto reported on the lectures: *An ordinary reader would gather that Freud advocates free love, removal of all restraints, and a relapse into savagery.*

In the Victorian age Freud wished to remove the fig leaf and examine our desires, which are unconscious. It was his contention that man, unable to satisfy unknown desires, becomes hostile to life and willing to destroy

"He had aged somewhat since I had heard him in Vienna in 1896. He had been reviled then as a Jew and irresponsible innovator."—Emma Goldman on seeing Freud at Clark University. The president of Clark University, Dr. Hall, is seated between Freud and Carl Jung. Behind Freud (with cigar) stand A. A. Brill, Ernest Jones (Freud's biographer) and Sándor Ferenczi.

it. Freud suggested a death instinct. *We either come to terms with our drives and desires, or we die.*

Shortly after Freud's lectures David Belasco opened his adaptation of the French play *The Lily*, which concerns a tyrannical father who prevents his two daughters from marrying. When one of them becomes the mistress of an artist, she is defended by her sister: *any fate for woman is preferable to that of an enforced celibacy.*

This was the first open recognition in the theater of the sexual needs of a woman. The *Nation* declared the play *pernicious from the moral and silly from the social point of view.* However, *The Lily* interested audiences and ran for over one hundred and sixty performances.

The presidential election neared in 1908 and Teddy Roosevelt lived up to his pledge not to run for a third term. *The New York Times* took a survey of newspaper editors across the country and found that T.R. was stronger than ever with the people. The *Times* announced, *tradition counts for nothing: will not in the slightest degree avail against the wave of popular favor that now promises to make Mr. Roosevelt the candidate.*

However, Roosevelt stuck to his promise and hand-picked his friend William Howard Taft as his successor. Although Taft preferred the Supreme Court Bench, his ambitious wife convinced him he should be President.

There was ill will between Japan and the United States ever since the settlement of the Russo-Japanese War. The

President Roosevelt and the next President, Taft.

Japanese people blamed Roosevelt and the Americans for their failure to secure indemnity payments from their vanquished Russian foe. When Japanese seal hunters were driven from the Pribilof Islands off Alaska, five Japanese fishermen lost their lives. In California, as Orientals cheapened the labor market, the "yellow journals" started fomenting hate with warnings of the "yellow peril." Finally, in 1906, the San Francisco Board of Education banned Japanese pupils from the public schools. The Japanese government protested and Roosevelt assured them *steps were being taken to remedy the matter thru the courts.*

Roosevelt was now afraid Japan would substitute America as her traditional enemy instead of Russia, if the U.S. continued to humiliate her. To his son Kermit he wrote: *I am perfectly willing that this Nation should fight any nation if it has got to, but I would loathe to see it forced into a war in which it was wrong.* To Cabot Lodge he wrote: *The Japanese seem to have about the same proportion of prize jingo fools that we have.* Roosevelt no longer considered himself a jingo.

T.R. announced he had enough funds to get the fleet to the Pacific on its trip around the world and if Congress would not appropriate additional funds, the fleet would be left in the Pacific.

However, he was receiving alarming reports that Japan was ready to strike against the United States, and the Kaiser warned him that ten thousand Japanese soldiers had infiltrated Mexico disguised as workers. Roosevelt decided that a conciliatory attitude on his part should be accompanied by a show of strength. He therefore ordered the fleet to circle the world. This was an immense undertaking foreign naval experts believed impossible. The chairman of the Senate Committee on Naval Affairs said there would be no funds appropriated for such an undertaking. Roosevelt replied he had enough funds to get the fleet to the Pacific, and if Congress would not appropriate additional funds, the fleet would be left there: *I will tolerate no assault upon the Navy or upon the honor of the country nor will I permit anything so fraught with menace as the usurpation by any clique of Wall Street Senators of my function as Commander-in-Chief.* The fleet, twelve thousand officers and men, sixteen battleships and smaller vessels, pulled anchor at Hampton Roads in mid-December, 1907. The Japanese instead of attacking, invited the officers and men to visit their islands. There were two major reasons why Roosevelt pushed the White Fleet's trip around the world: one, he wanted to arouse interest and enthusiasm for the Navy so he could obtain more funds for it; and two, he wanted foreign nations to accept the fleet's presence in the Pacific as well as in the Atlantic.

When Emma Goldman reached San Francisco on her lecture tour, the fleet was anchored there. *The meetings in San Francisco were being looked after by my friend Alexander Horr; not expecting any trouble where I had never been interfered with before, I felt at ease.* But the police chief and a retinue of detectives were at the station when she arrived and left four detectives on guard at her hotel. Emma asked Horr for an explanation: *Don't you know rumors have gone abroad that you are coming to San Francisco to blow up the American fleet now in the harbor?* Emma was shocked. *Stop your ridiculous invention, you do not expect me to believe that.* But Horr insisted Police Chief Biggey had boasted that he would *protect the fleet against the whole bunch of Emma Goldman and her gang.* With the fleet in the harbor, patriotism filled the air with hostile vibrations toward the Japanese nation. Emma then chose "patriotism" as the subject of her next lecture: *Leo Tolstoy, the greatest anti-patriot of our times, defined patriotism as the principle that justifies the training of wholesale murderers; a trade that requires better equipment for the exercise of man-killing than the making of such necessities as shoes, clothing and houses; a trade that guarantees better returns and greater glory than that of the honest workingman.*

Captain Bob Bartlett was once again at the helm of the *Roosevelt* when she finally steamed out of her berth on Twenty-fourth Street and the East River after her year-long delay. Matt Henson, who had been with Peary since their exploration for the proposed Nicaragua Canal, was also aboard. The steamer passed Blackwell's Island and continued on to Oyster Bay. President Roosevelt in his white duck suit swung aboard and did his own exploring, poking into every space, including the engine room. He then grasped Peary's hand: *I believe in you, Peary, and I believe in your success, if it is within the possibility of man.* He shook hands with all the other members of the expedition before debarking.

Under way, Peary worried about reports that had reached him from the ship *John R.*

T.R. aboard the Roosevelt *wishes Peary luck on his next attempt at the North Pole.*

Bradley. After dropping Dr. Cook and his supplies in Greenland, the ship had returned with the news that Cook was off for the Pole. Peary, the consummate planner, had never thought of this happening.

But almost everything else Peary did was well thought out. Studying books on conditions in Arctic regions enabled him to set down his thoughts in his diary before his first exploration of the North: *The physical makeup of the party should in all respects take pattern after the physical structure of a tough, hardy man. There should be one head ... one intelligent white man would represent the head, two other white men selected solely for their courage, determination, physical strength, and devotion to the leader would represent the arms, and the driver and natives the body and legs. The presence of women is an absolute necessity to render the men contented.... Finally the head should be absolutely free and independent, free to risk his own life and his companions, in the dark of some supreme moment, which holds within its short grasp utter success.... It is asking too much of masculine human nature to expect it to remain in an Arctic climate enduring constant hardship without one relieving feature. Feminine companionship not only causes greater contentment, but as a matter of both mental and physical health and the retention of the top notch of manhood, it is a necessity.... If colonization is to be a success in polar regions let white men take with them native wives, then from that union may spring a race combining the hardiness of the mothers with the intelligence and energy of the fathers. Such a race would surely reach the Pole if their fathers did not succeed in doing it.*

When the *Roosevelt* steamed across the Arctic Circle, finally approaching Cape York, where Peary usually secured the services of natives and their dogs, excited Eskimos paddled out in their kayaks to greet him. *Peary,* they shouted, *you are the setting sun, you always come back.*

When Henry Ford found a tough lightweight steel alloy being made in Europe, it enabled him to turn out a seven-foot-high monster with false doors and a hand crank known as the Model T. It soon became known as the "Tin Lizzie." Although there were over four thousand makes of cars, one out of every two cars sold would soon be a Ford. The T originally sold for eight hundred and fifty dollars; Ford eventually got it down as low as two hundred and sixty. It no longer cost as much as a house, and Ford's

Elite Steamers aim for St. Louis from the Cornelius Vanderbilt mansion at Fifty-eighth Street in 1904.

dream of the worker affording a car came true. Also part of Ford's dream was the neighborliness the inexpensive T would encourage, not only in America but among all the peoples of the world, a new neighborliness that would end wars. Ford figured, correctly, the new model would force road improvements by the increase in travel, and he placed the steering wheel on the left-hand side in anticipation of oncoming traffic. Soon he began experimenting with the assembly of the car while it was pulled along skids by men with rope. The model T came off the line at the rate of one every two minutes. When profits became, in Ford's mind, *awful*, he took a pencil and chopped twenty percent off the price to bring the profits *down*. When profits became *awful* again, Ford called a meeting and asked to have all the figures of overhead, materials and labor chalked up on a blackboard. The wage at that time was two dollars a day. Ford said, *try two-fifty*. The profits were still *awful. Try three dollars.* Then: *Try three-fifty.* Henry Ford finally found the profits acceptable when the wage reached five dollars a day minimum. He then reduced the work day to eight hours. Ochs of *The New York Times* said to his editors: *He's crazy, he's gone crazy.* And everyone knew to whom he referred.

The reaction was immediate. Unemployed men, some with wives, poured into Detroit by the thousands. The morning following the news report of Ford's new high wage, ten thousand persons pushed against the gates of the plant in the near-zero dawn. Ford wanted to turn out more than just cars, he wanted to turn out better men: *We want to make men in this factory as well as automobiles. I believe that I can do the world no greater service than to create more work for more men at larger pay. I can foresee the*

With model T's swinging off the assembly line at the rate of one every two minutes, profits became "awful" and Ford decided to do something about them.

time when we will have a hundred thousand men and more employed in this industry and I want the whole organization dominated by a just, generous and humane policy. But inside the plant panic, fear, thoughtlessness, moved the men to turn fire hoses on the eager mob and the icy water drove them back and froze against their ill-clad bodies.

On November 2nd, the day before the election, Pulitzer was aboard his yacht *Liberty* sailing from Havana. No one aboa knew of the editorial that appeared that da in the *Indianapolis News*. It asked embarra ing questions regarding wheeling and deali on the Panama Canal now under constru tion: *The campaign is over and the people will have to vote tomorrow without any official knowledge concerning the Panama Canal deal. It has been charged that the United States bought from American citizens for forty million dollars property that cost those citizens only twelve million.* (Actually, they had only paid three and a half million.) *Mr. Taft was Secretary of War at the time the negotiation was closed. There is no doubt that the government paid forty million for the property. But who got the money? We are not to know. The administration and Mr. Taft do not think it right that the people should know. The President's brother-in-law is involved in the scandal, but he has nothing to say. The candidate's brother has been charged with being a member of the syndicate. He has, it is true, denied it. But he refuses to appeal to the evidence, all of which is in the possession of the administration, and wholly inaccessible to outsiders. For weeks this scandal has been before the people. The records are in Washington, and they are public records. But the people are not to see them . . . till after the election, if then.*

On the 7th of December the *Liberty* docked at Charleston harbor. Joseph Pulitzer Jr. hurried aboard carrying a local paper, the *News & Courier*. In it was President Roosevelt's torrid reply to the *Indianapolis News* Panama editorial. T.R. called it a libel, a slander, an abominable falsehood. He also attacked the editor of the *News*, Delavan Smith. Pulitzer listened quietly as his son read him T.R.'s denunciation and the response to it given by Smith in Indianapolis. His editorial, he stated, was based on an account of the Panama deal in a "prominent New York newspaper." Pulitzer sat up. Cromwell, the original lobbyist for the Panama "deal," had sent an agent to the *World* a month before the election. The

agent warned the *World* against printing lies against Cromwell. He cautioned that he had already been to see District Attorney Jerome to warn him blackmailers were going to make political use of false charges regarding the Panama deal in the political campaign. He revealed the charges to the *World*'s editor, who checked them out with Cromwell himself. The *World* then printed the charges, including the reference to Jerome being informed that the Democratic party *was considering making public a statement that William Cromwell, in connection with Bunau-Varilla, a French speculator, had formed a syndicate at the time when it was quite evident that the United States would take over the rights of the French bond holders in the New Canal Company and that this syndicate included among others Charles P. Taft, brother of William H. Taft, and Douglas Robinson, brother-in-law of President Roosevelt.* The article also stated the syndicate had purchased the stocks and bonds of the defunct de Lesseps Company for about three and a half million dollars, with the full knowledge they would receive forty million from the U.S. government.

Unknown to Pulitzer, back at the *World* editorial offices, Bill Speer had prepared an attack on the President, calling him a liar. In bold caps the headlines read: **THE PANAMA SCANDAL—LET CONGRESS INVESTIGATE. WHO GOT THE MONEY?**

The *World* stated the forty million did not go to French citizens or to the French government, but to J. Pierpont Morgan and company—American citizens. The *World* then listed several statements made by President Roosevelt: *That the U.S. did not pay a cent of the forty million to any American citizen; that the U.S. government had no idea*

"It was the skill and unscrupulousness of Thomas Fortune Ryan [the taller man] to which many of the completed deals owe their success."

as to whom the money was distributed; that there was no syndicate in the U.S. that had any dealings with the government directly or indirectly. The *World* then stated: *each and all of these statements made by Mr. Roosevelt and quoted above are untrue, and Mr. Roosevelt must have known they were untrue when he made them.*

By now the election was over. Taft, Roosevelt's hand-picked successor, was to take office in March. In the meantime, President Roosevelt, before leaving on his African trip, went to Congress. In a special message addressed to the *libels,* he concluded with a direct attack on Pulitzer himself: *I do not believe we should concern ourselves with these particular individuals who wrote the lying and libelous articles . . . the real offender is Mr. Joseph Pulitzer, editor and proprietor of the* World. *While the criminal offense of which Mr. Pulitzer has been guilty is in form a libel upon individuals, the great injury done is in blackening the good name of the American people. It should not be left to a private citizen* [i.e., himself, now leaving office] *to sue Mr. Pulitzer for libel. He should be prosecuted for that by the governmental authorities. . . . It is a high national duty to bring to justice this vilifier of American people. . . . The Attorney General has under consideration the form in which the proceedings against Mr. Pulitzer shall be brought.*

Pulitzer listened as he was read T.R.'s address to Congress calling on the full might of the U.S. government to silence him. Suddenly he leaped up: *The* World *cannot be muzzled! That's your headline.* He then dictated the editorial response for the morning edition: *Mr. Roosevelt is mistaken. He cannot muzzle the* World. The editorial won-

"William C. Whitney [on the right] erected this monument of infamous graft."

dered why the President hadn't called for a congressional investigation of the Panama deal. *The American public had the right to know.* The editorial closed: *So far as the* World *is concerned, its proprietor may go to jail ... but even in jail the* World *will not cease to be a fearless champion of free speech, a free press and a free people. It cannot be muzzled.*

Pulitzer prepared to fight, but beneath his

tough exterior, he was afraid of imprisonment. Where would he be imprisoned, what were conditions like? Would he have anyone to talk to? When he learned Jerome had been asked to prosecute him, Pulitzer sent out spies to find out his intentions.

Less than a year before, Pulitzer's *World* had attacked Jerome: *Mr. Jerome is one of the tragedies of American politics.... By the manner in which he has conducted his office he has given stability to the Socialist charge that there is one kind of justice for the poor and another kind for the rich.* The paper's charges against Jerome had arisen over his failure to secure indictments against Thomas Fortune Ryan and the managers of the Metropolitan Street Railway. This company, whose stock had gone to two hundred and sixty-five dollars a share, was bilked dry and ended up in receivership. Seven years after the fact, and too late, the Public Service Commission began an investigation. The former secretary of the Metropolitan charged: *the Metropolitan Managers have engaged in a deliberate scheme of stealing trust funds, their own stockholders' money. Their crimes comprise of conspiracy, intimidation, bribery, corrupt court practices, subornation of perjury, false reporting, the payment of unearned dividends year after year, the persistent thefts of stockholders' money . . . result, the wreck and ruin of a great corporation . . . that a few men might become multimillionaires easily and quickly. . . . It was the genius of William C. Whitney that conceived the possibilities of the Metropolitan Railway, and erected this monument of infamous graft. It was the skill and unscrupulousness of Thomas Fortune Ryan to which many of the completed deals owe their success.*

When William C. Whitney had died a few years before, in 1904, he left a forty-million-dollar estate, but he had already dumped every share of his Metropolitan Street Railway Company. (The interiors of Whitney's Fifth Avenue residence had been described in many articles glorifying the triumph of architectural skills in the fitted old ceilings, the tapestries brought over from Europe, the ancient mantels of great beauty, the hangings and old canvases, done by Stanford

"Why go to Africa for big game?" T.R. tilting with Joseph Pulitzer.

". . . this isn't high finance; it's stealing."—William Travers Jerome.

White in 1900.) But there were no records, they had been burned and District Attorney Jerome had been unable to secure an indictment against Thomas Fortune Ryan, so the press, in frustration, turned on Jerome. But it wasn't chance that the laws created by the financiers protected them. Jerome had cried out against this during his Equitable Insurance investigations: *Within the past decade or so there has arisen a new class of crime, rather subtle crimes which do not come within the pale of the law. In the earlier days of American history when a man wanted to rob his neighbor, he did so by force, and there were laws provided which attended to his case. . . . There are no laws to cover 99 out of 100 cases of the crimes committed every day in this era in the name of high finance. . . . Up in Albany I found the assemblymen so busy attempting to carry off everything that wasn't nailed down that they had no time to listen. The trouble in this country is that the morality of a great many people is governed by what is on the statute books. Thousands of New Yorkers are entirely blind on the moral side and only know that an act is immoral when it is written into the law as a felony. The things that Equitable officials did were not criminal as defined in Section 528 in the Penal Code. . . . I contend, however, that in the moral sense they should come within the purview of this section and I defy them to distinguish their acts from the acts defined in it . . . this isn't high finance; it's stealing.*

Pulitzer sent a suggestion to his *World* editor: *Show how the machinery of justice is prostituted. For years we have asked Roosevelt to send somebody to jail; so he begins on the editors of the* World. *We pitched into Jerome because he did not do anything about wealthy law breakers; now he turns against*
the World. *Say frankly that neither he nor Roosevelt can muzzle the* World, *nor anybody. But make it dignified.*

Pulitzer's spies could learn nothing of Jerome's intentions. Finally, in desperation, Irwin S. Cobb of the *Evening World* (who had covered the Thaw trials) was asked to see what he could find out. Two hours later the laconic Cobb returned to the *World* offices. Pulitzer was at home in his "vault" bedroom. A call was put through to Pulitzer and he was informed that Jerome would not prosecute. Cobb was told to take the phone Pulitzer wanted to know how he did it! Cobb picked up the speaker in one hand, the receiver in the other: *I got on a surface car and went up to the Criminal Courts and sent in word to Mr. Jerome that a reporter from the* World *wanted to see him and when he came out I asked him and he told me.* For the only time in his life, Cobb heard Pulitzer's voice: *Well, I wish I might be God-damned!*

Pulitzer did not rejoice for long. The day before Roosevelt was to leave office, March 4, 1909, United States Attorney Henry L. Stimson secured an indictment in New York against the *World.* He had fallen back on the Harbor Defense Act of 1825, which protected the harbors from "malicious injury." There were almost three thousand government "reservations" in the States, and Stimson claimed each appearance of the *World* on a reservation constituted a separate offense.

Pulitzer realized *the mere threat of such a thing would stop any liberty of the press.* He urged his editors: *Another lesson I want to impress upon you all is that we shall not increase the power of the Executive any further; if this is to be a government of the people, for the people, by the people, it is a crime to put into the hands of the President such powers as no Monarch, no King, or Emperor ever possessed. . . . Congress has given this man too much power. I would rather have corruption than the power of one man.*

Pulitzer then decided to fight for the future of the free press. He not only put lawyers to work in New York and Paris, but also sent his own men to Panama and Colombia in search of evidence. Although Roosevelt had said: *Mr. Cromwell has sent on to me the complete list of the stockholders of the Panama Canal Companies,* no one ever saw that list, nor was a list found in supposed sealed records in a vault in France.

When the government's case against the *Indianapolis News* was presented before Federal Judge Albert Anderson, he stated: *There were a number of people who thought there was something not just exactly right about that* [Panama] *transaction and I will say for myself that I have a curiosity to know what the real truth was. . . .* When he dismissed the case, Roosevelt called Judge Anderson *a jackass and a crook.*

The government's case against the *World* was quashed in New York by Judge Charles Hough: *I am of the opinion that the construction of this act* [Harbor] *claimed by the prosecution is opposed to the spirit and tenor of legislation.* But Pulitzer still was not convinced of the future freedom of the press. He wanted victory in the Supreme Court. Since only the loser could appeal the verdict to the Court, Pulitzer kept insisting the government appeal until it finally did.

Two years later the *World* was able to

report: *The unanimous decision handed down by the United States Supreme Court yesterday in the Roosevelt-Panama libel case against the* World *is the most sweeping victory won for freedom of speech and of the press. . . . The decision is so sweeping that no other President will be tempted to follow in the footsteps of Theodore Roosevelt, no matter how greedy he may be for power. . . .*

But there was still no word on who got the forty million dollars.

On March 23, 1909, while the government was preparing its case against Pulitzer, T.R. set off on his great adventure in Africa. He was once again a private citizen, fifty years old, signed by *Scribner's* magazine to write about his African adventures for fifty thousand dollars. In England King Edward heard about the fee and mumbled: *President Roosevelt is coming out as a penny-a-liner.*

The estimated cost of the trip was seventy-five thousand dollars, which a group led by Andrew Carnegie and the Smithsonian Institution put up. Roosevelt hurried off for what he called *the joy of hunting the mighty and terrible lords of the wilderness, the cunning, the wary and the grim.* On Wall Street the cunning, the wary and the grim toasted the health of the lions and hoped the first one to see Teddy would see his duty and do it.

At that same time, in 1909, Houdini found a new love in Germany—a flying machine. He bought it, rented a hangar and hired a mechanic to show him how to fly it. He waited two weeks for proper wind conditions, then took to the air. He rose swiftly to a height of six feet and nose-dived, ruining the propeller and part of the body frame. When a four-week offer came from Aus-

Wall Streeters hoped the first lion to see Teddy
would see his duty and do it.

T.R. off for Africa. King Edward mumbled "President Roosevelt is coming out a penny-a-liner."

tralia, he had his biplane dismantled and shipped with him and his mechanic to that land. There Houdini had to learn to drive an automobile so that he could reach the airport in order to fly early in the morning when the wind permitted. He made over fifteen flights, once staying aloft for over six minutes. When he left Australia, he left his desire to drive and fly behind and never again drove a car or flew a plane.

In the elections of 1909 Pulitzer and the *World* backed Judge Gaynor for mayor. His opponent, campaigning on the "Civic Alliance" ticket, was William Randolph Hearst. Hearst's real ambitions were for the Executive Mansion in Washington. In 1904 he spent almost one and a half million dollars in his attempt to secure the Democratic nomination. His nomination was seconded by Clarence Darrow and he received two hundred and sixty three votes in the early balloting. Besides the President, Hearst was the only American quoted in full by newspapers in New York, Chicago, Los Angeles and

In 1909, Houdini rose six feet.

169

San Francisco. He owned them. If he had received the nomination and become the presidential candidate, all the opposition papers would also have had to quote him and his papers would have benefited. In 1905 Tammany, by now alarmed by his power, denied Hearst the mayoralty nomination. Hearst founded the Municipal Ownership League and ran on his own, attacking the Tammany "boodlers." Hearst received the most votes; he won. But Tammany dumped many ballot boxes in the river, threw in some new votes and Hearst lost.

A year later Hearst turned to Tammany for support. He offered half a million dollars for the gubernatorial nomination, an offer even his archenemy Boss Murphy could not refuse. Hearst's opponent was the insurance investigator Charles Evans Hughes. The *Bookman*, a literary journal, optimistically commented on Hearst's having received the gubernatorial nomination: *no case of moral destitution can now be regarded as altogether hopeless; nor need we discourage any aspiring young man by telling him he must have brains.* However, before Hearst could be given the Democratic nod, his opponents for that nomination had to be disposed of. One of them was District Attorney William Travers Jerome. The commissioner of credentials was state Senator Tom Grady, and his instruction from Boss Murphy was to secure the nomination for Hearst. Hearst delegates were bribed, picked up in saloons and upstate brothels. After Hearst got his nomination, Senator Grady admitted, *Boys, this is the dirtiest day's work I have ever done in my life.* But he needn't have worried. Boss Murphy saw to it that the entire Democratic ticket was elected, with one exception. When Hearst had been denied the mayoralty nomination by Boss Murphy the year before, he had run

illustrations of Murphy in his New York papers picturing him as a common crook in prison stripes. On election day Murphy sent out instructions that on no account was Hearst to be elected.

Now, in 1909, Gaynor was Murphy's choice and Hearst the main opponent. Hearst was defeated despite the vitriolic attacks by his papers on Gaynor. Even after his election loss, Hearst kept up his mass of invective against Gaynor. A few months after taking office the new mayor was shot by an unemployed dock worker. In his pocket was a Hearst editorial against the mayor, a sanctimonious attack on Gaynor for allowing the Jeffries-Johnson prize-fight films to be shown in theaters against the wishes of the citizenry. In other articles Hearst papers stated that an officer of the Christian Endeavor Society had called on Mayor Gaynor to stop the sordid films and was told he was a fool sent by fools. This was denied by that society. Mayor Gaynor lived and was able to point out that he did not have the power to stop the showing of the fight films. He also noted that Hearst's *American* and *Journal* had purchased exclusive rights to the still photographs and ringside stories of the fight. The attack on Gaynor had simply been exploitation for Hearst's own paper.

But Hearst seemed to have clout with the politicians, and in 1908 it was revealed why. The beginnings, however, went back four years. In 1904 revelations concerning the illegal operations of Standard Oil had given a couple of the company's employees the idea that the correspondence of John Archbold, the directing officer, might be of value to the press. The two, one the doorman, the other a porter at Standard Oil, approached the

Mayor Gaynor behind the former President, Vanderbilt in front.

Hearst's mass invective against Mayor Gaynor was effective. Gaynor was shot.

World with their proposition and were turned down. They then called on Hearst's *Journal* and were received with golden glee. The letters, stolen, photographed and returned to Archbold's desk, revealed that Standard Oil was corrupting the democratic system by giving substantial sums of money to congressmen, senators and other politicians. These were important men on important committees, including Senator McLaurin of South Carolina, Senator Penrose of Pennsylvania, Senator Bailey of Texas and the powerful Senator Foraker of Ohio. Two years before, Roosevelt, through the Hepburn bill, had pushed for rail reforms, including an end to rebates. Standard Oil was at that time accused of receiving over a million dollars a year in rebates. Senator Foraker attacked the Hepburn bill eighty-six times on the floor of the Senate.

Dr. Cook's expedition to the North Pole.

Had Hearst published all the letters received in 1904, he could have so shocked the nation that the corporate takeover his papers purported to battle against could have been prevented. Hearst campaigned as the champion of the common man and had the support of the liberal thinkers of the era, including Judge Seabury, Lincoln Steffens and Clarence Darrow. The reason he did not publish all the letters for four years was that he preferred to "use" the powerful individuals mentioned in the letters. In order to perpetuate this usage, when he finally published a letter about Senator Foraker in 1908, he used a forgery of the real letter. In this way he could not be forced to produce all the other letters, but if need be he had the photographic copy of the real thing in his vault. Shortly after the first letter appeared, the Rockefellers saw the light and began to advertise in Hearst papers.

In an investigation Hearst stated he did not pay for the letters. If he had, he would have been guilty of theft. But the two men who took the letters stated they were paid twelve thousand dollars for them.

Collier's Magazine asked why, when Hearst had had the real letters for four years, he had leaked only one, and why he had made a forgery when he possessed the real thing. It answered its own rhetorical question: *In order to exploit that secret accurate information!*

Roosevelt won against Standard Oil when the company was fined twenty-nine million dollars. This fine was set aside by the Supreme Court. Standard Oil paid nothing.

When the letter about Foraker and his payments from Standard Oil was published, Roosevelt attacked the Ohio Senator. But before the President did so, he sent for William Randolph Hearst. After much hemming and hawing, the President wanted to know if the Standard Oil letters referred to him. He was assured, with a high-pitched laugh, that if there were any such references they would never be published.

On reaching Etah in North Greenland, Peary learned that his former surgeon had indeed left the impression he was going to try for the North Pole. However, neither Peary nor his men could believe Cook was serious because he had departed with only two Eskimos. Cook had started from Etah for the Pole a year ago and had not yet returned. Peary thought he was not dead and would return when the Kane Basin filled in with winter ice. But he was concerned that Cook would be returning while he himself was heading north. Before he started, Peary wrote letters to his supporters warning them to be on guard and alert in regards to Dr. Cook. He also added in his note to President Roosevelt who had not yet left office: *John R.*

Bradley, Dr. Cook's backer in this enterprise . . . is a well known gambler, known in certain circles as "Gambler Jim" . . . he runs a gambling hell at Palm Beach, where both men and women gamble.

With T.R. on his eleven-month African hunt was his Pigskin Library. It consisted of some Shakespeare, Homer, Carlyle, Mahan's *Sea Power*, of course, a Bible, some Shelley, Keats and Dante, *Huckleberry Finn* and *Tom Sawyer*, among others. Roosevelt wrote of these books: *I almost always had some volume with me either in my saddle-pocket or in the cartridge-bag which one of my gun-bearers carried to hold odds and ends. Often my reading would be done while resting under a tree at noon, perhaps beside the carcass of a beast I had killed. . . .* T.R.'s game list included nine lions, eight elephants, six buffaloes, twenty-eight gazelles, thirteen rhinoceroses. Altogether two hundred and ninety-six animals were shot by T.R. and an additional two hundred and fifteen by Kermit.

"The institution of a leisure class has emerged gradually during the transition from primitive savagery to barbarism."—Veblen.

"Or more precisely, during the transition from a peaceable to a consistently warlike habit of life . . ."

"... the community must be of a predatory habit of life (war or the hunting of large game or both)."—*Veblen.*

But instead of returning home after his safari, Roosevelt accepted speaking invitations from Oxford University in England and the Sorbonne in Paris. The Kaiser insisted he also speak in Germany. As for protocol at the court functions he attended, T.R. stated he was not entitled to any special precedence: *To me there is something fine in the American theory that a private citizen can be chosen by the people to occupy a position as great as that of the mightiest monarch and to exercise a power which may surpass that of Czar, Kaiser, or Pope, and that then, after having filled this position, the man shall leave it an unpensioned private citizen, who goes back into the ranks of his fellow-citizens with entire self-respect, claiming nothing save what on his own individual merits he is entitled to receive.*

Toward the end of December, midnight slipped away, imperceptibly at first, and the sun reemerged in the Arctic regions. On February 22nd Peary left the ship and six days later stood at the edge of land at Cape Columbia. The ocean, as far as his eyes could travel, was a mass of packed, crushed ice. For the first time he could see no open water. Bartlett, in the pioneer group, left first with the heavy sledge loads. His instructions were to travel no more than ten miles a day over the rugged ice packs. He was to proceed at that rate until overtaken by the rest of the party. On the morning of his own departure Peary discovered a vicious wind from the east, a direction he had never encountered wind from before. The Eskimos felt it the work of the devil; already six dogs had died of distemper. Some of the Eskimos were in trouble from the weather; two could not go on, leaving twenty-four in the party. It was fifty below zero without the wind. Henson left with his Eskimos and was followed in

turn by the other groups; Peary's was the last party to go. At the end of the first day Peary and his group and Ross Marvin with a second group found the igloos left by Bartlett and his men. Bartlett was ahead, preparing the next camp in accordance with the plan. Two days later Peary, with the last group, came upon open water, a quarter-mile wide. The others had made it across before the wind had whipped the opening, destroying the ice connecting other bodies of ice. As he slept on the edge of the lead, Peary was awakened by the sound of grinding ice. The lead was closing. He quickly awakened his men and they shoved onto the shifting packs of crushed ice, floating, shifting with the movement of the frozen water.

As they progressed, they were delayed by opening leads. They progressed again after days of delay, until one by one the other teams were sent back. The final team to return, leaving only Peary and Henson as a team with their Eskimos and dogs, was Captain Bartlett's. Before heading back, Bartlett took sightings and made his observations, concluding that Commander Peary should reach the Pole in eight days. He wrote: *I return from here in command of the fourth supporting party. I leave Commander Peary with five men, five sledges with full loads, and forty picked dogs.*

Peary planned to kill some of the dogs to feed the others. In his own diary Peary noted: *Bartlett has done good work and been a great help to me. I have given him this post of honor because he was fit for it, because of his handling of the* Roosevelt, *because of his saving me hundreds of petty annoyances, and because I felt it appropriate, in view of England's magnificent Arctic work . . . that it should be a British subject who could boast*

that next to an American he had been neare[r] to the Pole.

At that moment Peary was a hundred an[d] thirty-three miles from the Pole. Six days later, having made excellent time (the dogs were often able to gallop), Peary and his party made their last and most northerly camp on earth. This, he told Henson, is to b[e] Camp Morris K. Jesup. He then proceeded to make, that day and the following, a serie[s] of observations. First, he traveled ten miles ahead and took readings that showed he ha[d] passed the Pole. Then he wrote down: *I ha[d] now taken thirteen single, or six and one-ha[lf] double altitudes of the sun, at two different stations in three different directions at four different times. . . . I had allowed approximately ten miles for possible errors in my observations, and at some moment during these marches and countermarches I had passed over or very near the point where north and south and east and west blend int[o] one.* The date Peary reached the Pole and planted the flag of the United States was April 6, 1909.

Harry Houdini told his audiences to ask him the exact date of Caracalla's birth, or th[e] day of the year heretic clergymen were hun[g] in Scotland or, later, the day the United States jumped into the World War. It was a[trick he was willing to explain and usually di[d]. The events all occurred on April 6th, coincidentally the same day he was born. He claimed his ability to escape was made possible by his ability to twist his body and dislocate his joints, along with abnormal powe[r] of expansion and contraction that enabled him to free himself from the tightest of bonds. To those wishing to follow in his footsteps, he advised bending over backwar[d] and picking up a pin with the teeth. In this

It was harder for Houdini to get publicity.

manner he eliminated his future competition before it could get started.

But now, Houdini had returned to America and was trying once more to secure publicity from the New York papers. The press and thousands of onlookers lined the dock of an East River pier. When the police arrived and found Houdini about to be handcuffed, sealed inside a nailed box and dropped into the river, they cried: "Not on my beat!" A waiting tug, "just happening by," picked up the press and Houdini's crew and paraphernalia. They steamed to deeper waters. The newsmen themselves were then able to put the cuffs on Harry and nail him into the wooden box. He was lowered away, escaped quickly when out of sight, stayed under as long as his breath would allow, then bobbed to the surface to the delight of all. That night he opened at Hammerstein's Roof Garden, where they still had the huge water tank built a few years earlier for the "sensational" act of swimmer Annette Kellerman. She had appeared in a one-piece bathing suit.

Harry's pay was more than a Barrymore received for a leading role on Broadway: one thousand dollars a week. The first week he insisted on being paid in gold pieces. He persisted until Hammerstein complied, then took the coins to his two aides in his dressing room where the three of them polished the golden double eagles until they glistened. Then Houdini put his hoard into a canvas bag and headed for One hundred and thirteenth Street: *Mamma, do you remember before Father died, he made me promise to always take care of you?* He poured the contents of the canvas bag into her lap. Years later, when asked what was his greatest moment, he answered his happiest was when he poured the gold into his mother's lap and watched her face.

Publicity worked, and the public looked up to Houdini.

In describing their return struggle from the North Pole, Henson said after two marches Peary was almost a dead weight but that they could not have gone on without him as *he was still the head and heart of the party*. By the time they had reached the solid ice of Grant Land, the Eskimos were overjoyed with their good luck. One threw himself on his sledge and cried in delight that the devil was asleep or having trouble with

his wife or they never would have gotten back so easily.

At this point, they still did not know the leader of one of the divisions, Ross Marvin, had been crossing a lead of new ice when it gave way, dragging him to his death. When they reached Crane City and Peary could write in his diary in the comfort of an igloo, he wrote that his life work was accomplished. After twenty-three years of effort and hard work, privations and hardships, risks and suffering, he had done it: *I have won the last great geographical prize, the North Pole, for the credit of the United States, the service to which I belong, myself, and my family . . . I am content.*

When Peary finally boarded the *Roosevelt* twenty days after reaching the Pole, he heard about Ross Marvin's death: *The news staggered me, killing all the joy I had felt at the sight of the ship. . . . Nearly every member of the party had been into the water and narrowly escaped the death which claimed Ross Marvin.* Now he was getting more news as the *Roosevelt* started its journey from the frozen north. Dr. Cook had told some Eskimos he had been to the North Pole. At Etah Peary had his Eskimos question Ettookashoo and Ahpelah, Cook's two Eskimos. They told them that Dr. Cook said he had gone a long way on the sea ice but that he lied. He had never gone out of sight of land. Peary relaxed, and according to his tradition, staged a walrus hunt to provide meat for the Eskimos' winter supply.

When the *Roosevelt* steamed into Indian Harbor, Labrador, Peary sent his famous message: *Stars and Stripes nailed to the Pole.* A letter was waiting for him from Jo, telling him that if he had failed once again, to try to

Peary and Captain Bartlett aboard the Roosevelt *the day they returned to civilization. Success after twenty-three years.*

content himself with his family: *My nerves are all gone. You must, you must come home.* At this same time, Dr. Frederick Cook, Peary's former surgeon, was being feted by the King of Denmark. Five days before Peary had sent his message from Indian Harbor, Cook had sent his, claiming discovery of the North Pole, from the Shetland Islands on his way from Greenland to Denmark. Based on knowledge from Cook's two Eskimos that they had never been out of sight of land and that the trip of over four hundred miles each way could not have been made by one team consisting of Cook and two Eskimos, Peary denounced Cook's claim. He sent wires to the press stating Cook had lied. Meanwhile,

Cook, learning of Peary's having reached the Pole, congratulated him and said he was happy to share the honors; two reaching the Pole was better than one. Soft-spoken, gentle, he added that he had instructed his Eskimos not to reveal the details of their trip. The public reaction was immediate. In a poll of seventy-five thousand persons in Pittsburgh, seventy-three thousand sided with Dr. Cook. Fifty-eight thousand did not believe Peary had ever reached the Pole.

On the front page of *The New York*

Five days before Peary's return, Dr. Cook claimed he had reached the North Pole and was fêted from Denmark to New York.

Peary sent wires to the press denouncing Dr. Cook as a liar and a fraud. Cook announced humbly, "There is enough honor in it for the both of us."

Times of November 14, 1909, were the following items: **TO EXAMINE COOK'S RECORDS. PROF. ELLIS STROMGREN CHOSEN AS HEAD OF DANISH COMMITTEE.** Another item: **PERRY TO BE A CAPTAIN. PROMOTION ON THE WAY TO COME THROUGH THE REGULAR CHANNEL.** And another: **NOBEL PRIZE FOR EDISON.** And finally **NOTHING WRONG—ROOSEVELT. WORD RECEIVED FROM HIM AT MOMBASA.**

As Roosevelt traveled about Europe on his lecture tour, he began to receive complaints about the policies of President Taft. Although he enjoyed his role as a private American citizen, he began to give policy suggestions to several nations. In London he warned the British of their menace to the civilized world: . . . *if you do not wish to establish and keep order there . . . get out of Egypt.*

T.R. in Egypt.

After leaving England, where George V was now the ruler, Roosevelt was greeted in Germany by Kaiser Wilhelm. The Kaiser and George V were cousins: their grandmother had been Queen Victoria. Another cousin of the Kaiser was Czar Nicholas of Russia. Roosevelt spent many hours with the Kaiser, and one day, while reviewing the troops, the two spent five hours together on horseback. The following day T.R. received a set of photographs of himself and the Kaiser on their horses, with humorous remarks written in English by the Kaiser. One read: *The Colonel of the Rough Riders lecturing the Chief of the German Army.* Roosevelt had gone to great lengths to explain the suggestions of Andrew Carnegie on setting up a council of nations to arbitrate international conflicts that in the past had been settled on the battlefields. Carnegie donated the financing for a Peace Palace in The Hague to house a Permanent Court of International Justice and a Permanent Court of Arbitration. The Peace Palace opened in 1913 and held two successful conferences. The third conference called for 1916 was canceled due to war.

President Taft suggested the principles of arbitration be used in reference to France

"The Colonel of the Rough Riders lecturing the Chief of the German Army."—Kaiser Wilhelm II.

and England, wishing that all questions determinable by the principles of law and equity be submitted to The Hague Tribunal. This was less than a year after T.R. had explained the working of The Hague Tribunal to the Kaiser. Now Roosevelt assailed the idea and in effect attacked his old friend Taft. T.R. stated he could accept a treaty with England, since the British would never commit an act that could not be arbitrated, but he did not trust France in the same way. Later, in October, Taft's government, under the Sherman Antitrust Act, brought suit against the United States Steel Company. The action cast reflections upon T.R. for allowing the Tennessee Coal and Iron Company to be swallowed by Morgan, for allowing, in effect, the Morganization of that industry. Roose-

velt felt the action implied that he had eithe been the tool of industry or a fool who had been used by big business. The presidential election was the following year, and T.R., furious now, threw his hat in the ring. He would fight Taft for the nomination.

After being severely buffeted about by Hearst's *Journal* and *American*, as well as b the *World*, William Travers Jerome was defeated in his bid for a third term as distric attorney. He left the office in 1909. However, he never lost interest in the Harry Tha case nor his belief that Thaw, for his own protection as well as the public's, should never regain his freedom. Now in private practice, he followed all attempts of Thaw' mother to have her son freed and volunteer his services as a friend of the court to prevent her success. Alienists examining Thaw listed one of the conditions he was suffering from as paranoia. Thaw persisted in claiming that Jerome was his personal enemy and should be locked up instead of himself, that the former D.A. was "erratic and probably a menace. . . . "

One of J. Pierpont Morgan's unsuccessful Morganizations was the International Maritime Marine Company. This gigantic combination had been in the works at the same time Morgan was working out the U.S. Steel combination. There was an intense competition on the high seas, often with dire results for all lines involved. Morgan, with his love of order, proposed to do away with this disorderliness by creating one huge combination of shipping companies including German, British and American lines. He acquired two American lines, and then the British Leland Lines. The English and Germans balked at the prospect of Americans controlling the seas. England began to give subsidies to defend the Cunard Lines and the German government supported the Hamburg-American Line.

Edward Steichen's portrait of J. Pierpont Morgan.

But Morgan succeeded in pulling together the Atlantic Transport, American, Leland, Dominion and Red Star Lines. Finally he got the White Star also. In true Morgan tradition, the company was deeply overcapitalized at one hundred and seventy million dollars. Morgan and Company received six hundred and fifty thousand for expenses, and the Morgan syndicate fifty million in bonds as well as twenty seven and a half million in stock in I.M.M., plus control of the company for putting up the fifty million in cash to accomplish the syndication. George Perkins, Morgan's partner, was able to sell four million

The Titanic *on her*
maiden and final voyage.

dollars' worth of stock to the New York Life Insurance Company. Perkins was also an officer of New York Life. During the insurance investigations he had explained how he had "bargained" and got a good deal on some stocks for New York Life. When pressed to learn with whom he had "bargained," he admitted it was with the seller—himself.

The pride of Morgan's International Mercantile Marine was a new ship, the largest steamship ever launched, the *Titanic*. When she left her Southampton pier on her maiden voyage in April of 1912, *The New York Times* commented on her tremendous suction in comparison to other ships: *The bigger vessel's extraordinary powers of suction were exemplified when she left her Southampton pier and jerked the steamer* New York *from her moorings*. Aboard the *Titanic* on her maiden voyage was John Jacob Astor and his recent bride, Madelaine Talmadge Force.

A few years before, Ava and John Jacob had agreed on a divorce, with Ava having custody of seven-year-old Alice while eighteen-year-old Vincent remained with his father. Father and son had made two long voyages together on the family yacht, *Nourmahal*. When John met Madelaine and fell in love with her, his son realized his step-mother-to-be was one year his junior. When his bride became pregnant in Europe, John Jacob decided to hurry home so that his offspring would be born in America. Unlike his cousin Waldorf, who had become an English citizen, John Jacob was proud to be an American. He had graduated from Harvard and his son was now a student there.

Ava, still a beauty, moved to England and conducted her love life in an open manner.

LEFT: *Vincent Astor with his father, John Jacob Astor.*

BELOW: *John Jacob Astor and his new wife, Madelaine Talmadge Force, slightly younger than Vincent.*

One of the most eligible bachelors, who had once courted Nancy Langhorne before her betrothal to William Astor, was Lord Ribblesdale. Nancy had found him a social butterfly and snob. She rejected him. Ava married him and became Lady Ribblesdale. He then settled down, tired of the social life, and Ava hated him forever after.

When Peary on the maiden voyage of the steamer *Roosevelt* ordered Captain Bartlett to hit the ice at full speed, he was testing his own design to be sure the vessel would be safe in the frozen Arctic seas. Captain Smith, commander of the *Titanic*, with its fifteen separate watertight bulkheads, was convinced his ship was unsinkable. This

On the New York American's *bulletin board, word that Mrs. John Jacob Astor had been rescued.*

was also the belief of the Morgan group that owned this pride of the White Star Line. Therefore, although warned he would be passing through an ice field, the captain ordered full speed ahead in the hopes of securing a new speed record for the International Maritime Marine Company and the White Star Lines.

A lad who had just turned twenty-one and lived in the slum section of Brownsville was operating the wireless for the English Marconi Company's Wanamaker station. Marconi, an Italian who had been unable to convince his government of the importance of his wireless device, had taken it to England. In New York crowds had flocked to watch the operator atop Wanamaker's, one of the city's busiest department stores. Because the signals radiated in all directions, the Navy called it *radio* and the Great White Fleet had a number of radiotelegraphy machines on twenty of their ships.

On April 14th the young operator of the Wanamaker station was casually listening to the flow of dots and dashes crowding his receiver. Suddenly he received a dim, distant signal, distorted by static. He fell to deciphering the code. It was from the S.S. *Olympic: Titanic ran into iceberg. Sinking fast.* The young operator notified the press, then stayed at his key for the next seventy-two hours. President Taft ordered all other wireless stations on the East Coast closed down so as not to interfere with the incoming messages. David Sarnoff, the young operator, said: *Much of the time I sat there with nothing coming in. It seemed that the whole anxious world was attached to my earphones during the seventy-two hours....* Sarnoff finally left his station after the name of the last survivor was received. Although Astor's young

A bullet in his chest a few months before.

T.R. was unhappy with President Taft and Taft shook his head and cried, "If I only knew what the President wanted!"

bride had been safely lowered away into a lifeboat, Astor had remained aboard and drowned with fifteen hundred and sixteen other passengers and crew members. In New York his son Vincent had spent most of Monday and Tuesday at the White Star offices on lower Broadway, finally leaving in tears.

The progressives fought dramatically for the delegate majority for their preferred candidate, Teddy Roosevelt. Taft won out. Under the leadership of Morgan's long-time partner, George Perkins, Roosevelt and the progressives bolted the Republican party. Now T.R.'s sanity was seriously questioned. In Chicago a real estate man put up five thousand dollars for anyone who could prove Roosevelt was not insane. Dr. Allen Hamilton posed questions of T.R.'s sanity in *The New York Times*, while a prominent psychologist, Morton Price, stated *T.R. would go down in history as one of the most illustrious psychological examples of the distortion of the conscious mental processes*

J. Pierpont Morgan stopped in England to tell Victoria Sackville-West he loved her. She invited him back for a week and noted that after a few moments she forgot about his nose.

is a physical marvel that he was not dangerously wounded. He is one of the most powerful men I have ever seen laid on an operating table. The bullet lodged in the massive muscles of the chest instead of penetrating the lung.

The Republicans were a house divided in 1912. For the forty years up to 1901, only one Democrat, Cleveland, had taken the presidency from them. But the power did not rest with the elected Republicans, but with their financiers, men like Morgan, Vanderbilt, Rockefeller and Carnegie. Now Roosevelt and Taft had divided the party so severely that the Democratic candidate, Woodrow Wilson, former governor of New Jersey, was elected. When T.R. had first returned from his African-European trip and the progressive Republicans had flocked to his side, President Taft had shaken his head and cried: *If I only knew what the President wanted!* T.R., during the heat of his battle with Taft, had said: *We stand at Armageddon and we battle for the Lord. . . .* Now T.R. relaxed, admitted defeat and announced: *The fight is over. We are beaten. There is only one thing to do and that is to go back to the Republican party.* He was already thinking of 1916.

through the forces of subconscious wishes. T.R., in turn, called Taft a "fathead" and a "puzzlewit." But on October 14th, on his way to give a campaign speech in Milwaukee, T.R. was shot by a man later identified as John Crank. The bullet pierced the manuscript of his speech before lodging itself in his chest. Bloodied, Roosevelt insisted on being taken to the platform where he was to speak, refusing to see a doctor until after the talk: *I will make this speech or die. It is one thing or the other.* In a whisper he addressed the audience: *I am going to ask you to be very quiet and please excuse me from making a long speech. I'll do the best I can, but there is a bullet in my body.*

After the operation the surgeon said of Roosevelt: *It is largely due to the fact that he*

In 1912 J. Pierpont Morgan had hurried through the capitals of Europe in search of soon-to-be-forbidden treasures. In England the seventy-four-year-old financier stopped to see the fifty-year-old Victoria Sackville-West and confess his love for her, which would never change. He apologized for being so old. She recorded in her diary that after a few moments of his attractive personality, she forgot all about his nose. But Morgan had competition from both William Waldorf Astor, who longed for the touch of her body,

BIRTHPLACE OF WOODROW WILSON.   STAUNTON, VA.

and the infatuated artist busy immortalizing her in marble, Auguste Rodin. On his return to the States, Morgan was summoned before the Pujo Committee, which was investigating the money trust. Morgan insisted a man could not get a monopoly on money: *No, sir, he cannot. He may have all the money in Christendom, but he cannot do it.* When asked if commercial credit was based primarily upon money or property, Morgan said: *No, sir, the first thing is character.* Before money or property? *Before money or anything else.*

On January 7, 1913, the seventy-five-year-old Morgan left for another trip to the Mediterranean. Once again, he climbed aboard the Thomas Cook steamer, *Khargeh,* for a trip up the Nile to Khartoum. But he

was irritable and the chef and waiter were replaced by the Thomas Cook representativ He was ailing now and the trip was stopped near Aswan so that he could be returned to Alexandria. Feeling recovered, he traveled on to Rome, to the apartments usually reserved for his staff at the Grand Hotel. The he muttered, *I've got to go up the hill,* and died.

In March Woodrow Wilson was sworn into office. His father had been a printer, then a Presbyterian minister. His mother's father had also been a Presbyterian minister. His wife, Ellen Louise Axson, was the daug ter of a Presbyterian minister. Wilson never attended Harvard. He had graduated from Princeton and the University of Virginia Law School. In his inaugural address he stated: *The great government we love has too often been made use of for private and selfish purposes and those who used it have forgotten the people. There had been something crude, heartless and unfeeling in our effort to succeed and be great; our thought has been, let every man look out for himself; let every generation look out for itself. . . . I summon all honest men, all patriotic, all forward-looking men to my side. God helping me, I will not fail them if they will but counsel and sustain me.*

Roosevelt announced: *I'm going to South America.* The expedition included his son Kermit and set off on October 4, 1913. Roosevelt confessed: *I had to go, it was my last chance to be a boy.* Before he left, he found time to write a quick note of advice to his niece Eleanor's husband, Franklin D. Roosevelt, who was now Assistant Secretary of the Navy, following in T.R.'s footsteps: *It is not my place to advise, but there is one matter so vital that I want to call your attention to it. I do not anticipate trouble with Japan, but it may come, and if it does, it will come suddenly. In that case we shall be in an unpardonable position if we permit ourselves to be caught with our fleet separated. There ought not to be a battleship or any formidable fighting craft in the Pacific unless our entire fleet is in the Pacific. Russia's fate ought to be a warning for all time as to the criminal folly of dividing the fleet if there is even the remotest chance of war.*

In South America Roosevelt was struck down with jungle fever. Even when his temperature reached a hundred and five degrees, he continued to write articles for *Scribner's Magazine.* Then after injuring his leg in a canoe accident, the abscesses caused unbearable pain and he called his son Kermit to his side: *We have reached a point where some of us must stop. I feel I am only a burden to the party.*

But Kermit refused his father's suggestion that they abandon him and they continued on through the uncharted regions of Brazil, down the River of Doubt, mapping this unexplored region. (Later, the river was renamed Rio Téodoro.) The food supply ran out, they were caught in torrential downpours for days on end. One man drowned, another killed a member of the party and fled into the dense underbrush. T.R. lost thirty-five pounds before they emerged from the jungle and had to be assisted by a cane and two men as he toiled down the gangway. Ten days later he was off for Europe; Kermit was getting married in Spain.

Periodically from New York shipments of vanilla éclairs in lots of two hundred were sent to Matteawan State Hospital for the Criminal Insane. They were ordered for Harry K. Thaw, who then shared the sweets with certain inmates and guards. He was soon given the run of the grounds. Thaw's mother spared no expense in her continuing crusade to free her son. The superintendent of Matteawan, John Russell, was forced to resign after an investigation showed he was involved in a twenty-thousand-dollar bribe conspiracy to free Harry. A few years before, while in France, Evelyn gave birth to a baby boy whom she named Russell Thaw. She claimed Harry was the father, the child the result of a visit to his private quarters at Matteawan. Harry denied it. Now, in 1913, the boy was three and living in New York with Evelyn. In August, on a sunny Sunday morning, Harry escaped in a taxicab and a black Packard touring car rented at fifty dollars a day for the occasion. The escape

Evelyn Nesbit Thaw in France. She gave birth to a baby boy conceived, she said, in Harry's quarters at Matteawan.

was arranged by a Hearst editor, Alfred Lewis, who paid the drivers twenty thousand dollars for participating in the escape. At first Thaw, who had slipped out the Matteawan gates as a milk truck entered, w driven in a taxicab, then he was transferred to the fast Packard touring sedan. Thaw k looking behind to see if Jerome was in pursuit and asked if there were car tools to fig him off with if he came after him. He was also bothered by his sweet tooth so his rescuers had to stop for a double-dip chocolat soda. He then sent a postcard to his mom i Pittsburg and another to the Associated Pr threatening them with a law suit if they did treat his escape with "dignity." Heading f Canada, the car broke down in Rochester and the escape party changed to a rented horse and buggy. Later they caught a train headed for Quebec. A deputy sheriff who boarded the train in New Hampshire read about the escape in the latest paper and noticed the boisterous Harry seated behin him. When Harry asked him if he could guess who he was, the deputy sheriff repli *Harry K. Thaw.* Harry said quietly: *Don tell anyone.*

In Canada, which was the next stop, the deputy sheriff placed Thaw and his companions under arrest and insisted the Canadian authorities hold them until American authorities could reach them.

William Travers Jerome, acting as a frie of the court, had been at most of the hearin to release Harry, and through his interroga tions had prevented his release. Thaw's mother, according to the *World*, had by now spent over a million dollars trying to free Harry. "The Secret Unveiled," writte by Mrs. Thaw, claimed Jerome planned to delay the second trial until Harry went cra in the Tombs.

Evelyn predicted Harry would soon be caught, saying he was sure to walk up to a stranger and proclaim: "I am the famous Harry Thaw." She also asked for police protection, in fear Harry would head for New York to kill her. Thaw had been put in a hospital ward by the Canadian authorities and began giving interviews to Canadian newsmen. Crowds gathered outside the hospital of the escaped "hero." *The New York Times* reported: *Men and women almost trampled upon each other in a mad rush to shake his hand. When he went to the courtroom he rode in an open carriage, acclaimed by the populace, lifting his hat and bowing right and left like an emperor.*

Clarence Shearn, Hearst's legal eagle for forty years, appeared in Canada with a battery of alienists who swore Harry was sane. William Travers Jerome conferred with the U.S. Attorney General on the extradition of Thaw and was appointed a Special Deputy Attorney General. He left almost immediately for Canada. To a *New York Times* reporter Jerome explained why New York State wanted Thaw back: *If Thaw were to remain free, everyone would say it was Thaw's millions which bought his freedom. . . . Why, the very fact that Thaw was at liberty would have a demoralizing effect on the people.* The *New York Journal* again printed stories supporting Thaw's right to kill Stanford White, claiming Thaw had *rendered a considerable service to the community.* The Canadians were threatening Jerome and he had to be given police protection. *Current Opinion* reported: *Lawyers opposed to Thaw are threatened with death. Waitresses in the village hotel, touched with the general idiocy, refused to serve them. . . . Every little while the crowd gathers and threatens to rush the jail in rescue of the maniac, who bows to it and addresses it*

through his cell window. When Jerome was told to leave the courtroom by the presiding judge, the courtroom cheered the judge.

The Canadian government finally became embarrassed by the publicity given their hero-worshiping citizens. Against the wishes of Thaw's lawyers, Harry was deported, ending up in New Hampshire, where his lawyers protected him from the ubiquitous Jerome by securing a writ of habeas corpus preventing Thaw's removal from the state. Thaw now became the celebrity of New Hampshire and was cheered as a hero whenever he appeared in public. Many months later Thaw was finally extradited and returned to the Tombs in New York. Jerome, who had spent almost ten years on Harry Thaw, lost interest and withdrew from the case. A new trial was held and Thaw, pronounced "sane," was released from custody. As he left the courthouse a free man, thousands cheered him. The *New York Sun* dedicated an editorial to Harry called: **HOW TO BE A HERO.** It read: *At length, the long ignominious drama is ended. The paranoiac walks forth free, delivered sane by a jury of his intelligent fellow citizens; and he becomes as he had previously become even in sober New Hampshire, a conquering hero, the idol of the populace. Cheering crowds crush around him. Women weep over him. Men esteem it an honor to shake the hand crimson with the blood of Stanford White. . . . In all this nauseous business we don't know which makes the gorge rise more, the pervert buying his way out, or the perverted idiots that hail him with wild huzzas.*

Harry's mother told reporters: *We, Harry and I, are going to live very quietly now. He will be home tonight. My happiness is complete.* But Harry announced he was busy and wouldn't have time to visit his mother

A group photograph of T.R. and his party, and by slight of hand, Houdini. Publicity for both.

right now. Harry K. Thaw was once again on his own. At least prison had cured him of whipping women; he was arrested for whipping a boy.

Teddy Roosevelt had sailed for Europe for Kermit's wedding ten days after his return from South America. After departing from Liverpool for the United States, he attended a séance on the second day at sea. It seems Houdini was aboard the same ship, and the passengers had requested that he conduc a séance. At first Houdini seemed reluctant t do so, then announced he would. He asked if anyone had any questions he or she wishec answered, then waited with a slate on his lap Teddy Roosevelt stood and asked if through his "medium," Houdini could trace T.R.'s recent explorations on the slate. The "spirit medium" who answered Houdini's call was a recent victim aboard the *Titanic*, William Stead. After a long period of silence when scarcely a breath was taken, Houdini's hand began to shake, then moved slowly across the slate. When he was finished, there was a perfect map of that part of Brazil with its River of Doubt and jungle areas explored by Roosevelt. T.R. jumped up in astonishment and told Houdini it was the most amazing thing he had ever witnessed.

The president of the British College of Psychic Science, J. Hewat McKenzie, wrote in his book *Spirit Intercourse:*

The last occasion on which the author, under strict test conditions, saw Houdini demonstrate his powers of dematerialization, was before thousands, upon the public stage of the Grand Theatre, Islington, London. Here a small iron tank, filled with water, was deposited upon the stage, and into it Houdini was placed, the water completely covering his body. Over this was placed an iron lid, with three hasps and staples, and this was securely locked. The body was then completely dematerialized within this tank within one and a half minutes while the author stood immediately over it. Without disturbing any of the locks Houdini was transferred from the tank directly to the back of the stage in a dematerialized state. . . . Dematerialization is performed by methods similar in operation to those in which psychoplastic essence is drawn from the medium. . . .

Houdini was credited with mediumistic powers. However, he fought those who preyed on others, taking advantage of the credulity of the naive. In his book he tore into the deductions of Mr. McKenzie crediting him with *dematerialization*. Houdini wrote: *Just as all Spiritualist believers do, so Mr. McKenzie relied on what he thought he saw, and therefore failed to affirm or negate his misguided and misdirected vision by rational application of his conscious intelligence.*

Houdini did not have miraculous powers; he had the ability to work hard as a professional. He hated sham, and revealed later how he had fooled T.R.: *I was about to sail from London for America and learned at the ticket office that Colonel Roosevelt was to be a fellow-passenger, although no public announcement had been made of the fact. Figuring things out in advance, I foresaw the customary request from an entertainment committee of passengers for a performance from me on board ship, and I also realized that Colonel Roosevelt would be the dominating presence in the audience. I therefore resolved to work up something which would involve some recent activity of his. It so happened at that time he was returning from his trip of exploration in South America with the announcement of the discovery of the River of Doubt. He had given, privately, a map of his explorations to a famous London newspaper and it was to be published three days after the steamer had sailed. No one, with the exception of Colonel Roosevelt and one or two others, knew the details of the map. I therefore determined to get a copy . . . it is always easy to get people to assist one in a trick.*

In 1914 the Scott Joplin Music Publishing Co. released the "Magnetic Rag." No publisher could be found for it; as with his two-hundred-and-thirty page opera *Tree-monisha*, Scott was forced to copyright and be his own publisher. For three years Joplin tried to have his opera performed and had dedicated himself to that task. The story of the opera concerned a Negro couple named Ned and Monisha who live on a plantation in Arkansas. They are surrounded by ignorance and superstition and belief in conjurers. They pray for a child and find one under a tree. They name her Tree-Monisha. It is a fable of a race held in the grip of superstition, with a folk-hero, Treemonisha, ready to lead them to enlightenment and full development. While Joplin was ignored, publicity went to the pseudo-rag men of Tin Pan Alley. The *New York Dramatic Mirror* reported: *[Irving] Berlin has one dream . . . I shall write an opera completely in ragtime. I have not yet fully developed my story but it will of course be laid in the South. . . . The opera will be following out my idea that beautiful thoughts can best be expressed by syncopation. It alone can catch the sorrow, the pathos of humanity. . . .*

News of Houdini's amazing feat with Roosevelt's mystery map of the South American trip had given additional fame to the escape artist when he opened at the Victoria Theatre in July. Often called the "man who walks through walls," he announced he would do just that. A rug was placed on the center of the stage, while to one side, bricklayers constructed an eight-foot-by-ten-foot wall, the audience watching as brick and mortar united in the construction. The wall was made atop a steel beam, which was on casters, raising the beam three inches above the floor. The wall and beam were then rolled to the middle of the stage, where Houdini had a committee standing on the rug at either end of the wall to be sure there was no trickery. The rug was there to prevent the use of a trapdoor. Threefold screens were now placed on both sides of the wall and Houdini entered one, raised his hands over his head so that the audience could see them above the screen. He lowered them and moments later raised his hands above the screen on the other side of the brick wall. Instead of applause, the audience sat dumbfounded. He had dematerialized and passed through the wall. Actually, Houdini had revealed just what he

T.R. coming into the harbor. Under the smokestack, the Assistant Secretary of the Navy and his wife, Eleanor.

Kaiser Wilhelm. His cousins were Czar Nicholas of Russia and George V of England.

was going to do before he did it. When he went behind the screen, a stagehand, at Houdini's signal, opened a trap door under the rug so Houdini could squeeze under the wall with the aid of the sagging carpet. The committee standing on the carpet prevented the sag from showing. Sensational as the act was, Houdini dropped it. The stagehands were in on it, and knowledge breeds contempt and unveils a secret.

But now, in 1914, humanity seemed to be enjoying itself, in ragtime. Ever since John Philip Sousa's smashing introduction of the beat at the Paris Exposition in 1900, ragtime had been sweeping Paris and all of Europe. One Saturday night, when part of the English fleet were guests of the German Emperor in Kiel, the ship's band played ragtime and sailors of both the German and English fleets reveled together, enjoying the generosity of the Kaiser's gift of free beer and tobacco along with the ragtime festivities. Early the following morning, Sunday, June 28th, the Kaiser took a visiting English admiral to see his new yacht, the *Meteor*, number five. The Kaiser explained to his English guest: *I am passionately fond of yachting . . . I race only with German crews now. Time was when I had to have British skippers and Brtish sailors. You see my aim is to breed a race of German yachtsmen.*

Although family ties united most of the royalty of Europe, their respective nations squabbled over colonial claims in Asia, Africa and the Middle East. France was at odds with Germany over certain claims, and Czar Nicky sided with France against his cousin Willy. George V also sided with France against his cousin Willy, while Wilhelm sided with the Austro-Hungarian Empire. Italy felt aligned to Germany, and to keep

the peace, everyone armed to the teeth. The Maxim gun could cut down a platoon in two seconds, so they all ordered the new machine gun by the thousands. European harbors began to fill with newly constructed destroyers and battleships that towered above the peaceful quays and belched ominous black clouds of smoke. To keep the peace and stem the rising tide of Slavic sentiment for union with Serbia, the Archduke Francis Ferdinand of Austria traveled to a corner of the Austro-Hungarian Empire to visit the Slavic city of Sarajevo. He then traveled in an open touring car with his wife, the Duchess of Hohenberg, beside him. Their three children remained in Vienna. Waiting for the royal couple in Sarajevo were seven Serbian assassins. While the Kaiser was showing his yacht to the English admiral on this sunny Sunday morning, one of the assassins armed with a bomb, stood on a bridge spanning the Miljacka River. When the heir to the Austro-Hungarian throne and his wife neared the bridge in their open touring car, the bomb was thrown and the assassin leaped from the bridge to make his escape. The bomb struck a corner of the car and bounced away from the couple. It exploded, slightly injuring some spectators lining the road. The Archduke made sure his wife was all right and ordered the car on to the City Hall, where he was to deliver his address to the citizenry. Later, still concerned about the victims, he ordered his driver and the Austrian general riding in front to take them to the hospital to see that the injured had been properly taken care of. On the way a wrong turn caused them to stop and back up. Another assassin stepped up and fired one shot each of the royal couple. The driver sped up and the Austrian general in the front thought another miracle had saved the lives of the couple. Later he wrote in his diary: *While*

"*Soferl . . . Soferl . . . don't die. Live for our children.*"
—*Last words of Archduke Francis Ferdinand.*

RIGHT: *Nicholas, Czar of all the Russias.*

LEFT: *George V sided with France against his cousin Willy.*

with one hand I drew out my handkerchief to wipe the blood from the Archduke's lips, Her Highness cried, For God's sake! What has happened to you? Then she sank down from her seat with her face between the Archduke's knees. I had no idea that she had been hit and thought that she had fainted from shock. Then His Royal Highness said: Soferl . . . Soferl . . . don't die. Live for our children. Moments later, both were dead.

The ruling head of the Austro-Hungarian Empire, Franz Josef, had to be notified of the tragedy. His nephew Archduke Francis Ferdinand was heir to the throne. Franz Josef had lost his wife, the Empress Elizabeth, to an assassin who stabbed her through the heart with a sharpened file. (He could not afford a knife.) His son, Crown Prince Rudolph, had committed suicide, and his brother, Maximilian, had died by firing squad in Mexico. The Emperor shut himself off from communication with the outside world and had the young couple buried quietly. For three weeks the world awaited his reaction. While Europe held its breath, hearts beat to the drums of war. Rumors of what action the Emperor would take were ominous. Three and a half weeks later Austria dictated ten odious demands to Serbia with an ultimatum of forty-eight hours for reply. Germans waited to hear the reply. So did Russians, Austrians, Italians and the French and English. Finally, a bulletin flashed to the capitals of the world: Serbia had rejected the Austrian demands. The German populace began to chant *WAR! WAR! Down with Serbia! Down with Russia!* In Russia crowd[s] chanted in the streets for *WAR! WAR! Down with Austria! Down with Germany!*

In desperation, Nicky of Russia cabled hi[s] German cousin Willy: *In this most serious moment, I appeal to you to help me. An ignoble war has been declared on a weak country. The indignation in Russia, shared fully by me, is enormous. I foresee that very soon I shall be overwhelmed by pressure brought upon me, and forced to take measures which will lead to war. I beg you in the name of ou[r] old friendship to do what you can to stop your allies from going too far.*

The Kaiser had felt the same way as his cousin in Russia and had already cabled him an urgent appeal for peace. But the Austrian troops had moved against Serbia and the Czar was forced to call three million young men into uniform to protect the Serbians. The Kaiser, in turn, placed his troops in com[bat readiness.

Years before, during arguments over Morocco, Germany had drawn up contingency war plans to attack France through Belgium. Now the German soldiers, singing hymns, marched in precision to the borders of neighboring Belgium. England announce[d] that if the Germans marched into Belgium, she would join the war on the side of the French. Unless events changed, England would go to war at midnight. The First Lord of the Admiralty, Winston Churchill wrote: *War would be declared at midnight. As far as we had been able to foresee the event, all our preparations were made. Mobilization was complete. Every ship was in it[s] station; every man at his post. The tumult of*

First Lord of the Admiralty Churchill wrote: "Every ship was in its station; every man at his post. The tumult of the struggle for life was over: It was succeeded by the silence of ruin and death."

the struggle for life was over: It was succeeded by the silence of ruin and death.

In America mothers thanked God the ocean separated them and their sons from the European madness. The official position of the United States, set by President Wilson, was one of neutrality, and he asked that every man and woman stay and act impartial in thought as well as action. T.R. said: *If I had been President, I should have acted on the thirtieth or thirty-first of July, as head of a signatory power to The Hague treaties, calling attention to the guaranty of Belgium's neutrality and saying that I accepted the treaties as imposing a serious obligation which I expected not only the United States but all other neutral nations to join in enforcing. Of course, I would not have made such a statement unless I was willing to back it up.* T.R. began to write articles and give addresses on America's duty and obligation to the weak. *The New York Times* editorial declared: *With Germany's declaration of war against Russia, the bloodiest war ever fought on earth and the least justified of all wars since man emerged from barbarism has apparently begun.*

One youth in Europe admitted: *Even as a boy I was not a "pacifist," and all attempts at an education in this direction came to naught. . . . As a boy and a young man I had often formed the wish that at least once I might be allowed to prove by deeds that my national enthusiasm was not an empty delusion. Often I considered it a sin to shout: 'Hurrah' without perhaps having the inner right to do so; for who may use this cry without having proved himself there where all play is at an end and where the inexorable hand of the Goddess of Fate begins to weigh*

nations and men according to the truth and the durability of their convictions? Thus my heart, like that of millions of others, was overflowing with proud happiness that at last I was able to free myself from this paralyzing feeling. . . . Therefore I am not ashamed today to say that, overwhelmed by impassionate enthusiasm, I had fallen on my knees and thanked Heaven out of my overflowing heart that it had granted me the good fortune of being allowed to live in these times . . . but even then one had no idea of the possible length and duration of the struggle now beginning. One dreamt of being home again in winter to continue work in renewed peace. On August 3rd the youth submitted a petition requesting permission to serve in a Bavarian regiment. The request was granted the following day and Adolf Hitler reported to his regiment a few days later.

The voice against the drumbeats of war in France in July of 1914 was the parliamentary leader and journalist Jean Jaurès. Forever outspoken in social causes, the founder of *L'Humanité* had been active in the Dreyfus case. He now turned his voice against the coming conflict sweeping the continent. On July 31st, on the street, in daylight, this spokesman for peace was silenced by a single bullet from an assassin's gun. Now the sons of France would join the sons of Serbia, Austria, Hungary, Germany, Italy, Turkey, Greece and England, with no voice raised against their senseless death.

At that moment President Wilson was sitting by his wife's bedside, cheering her up with all the good news he could muster. She was dying of Bright's disease. While Wilson tried to preserve peace in the nation and comfort his wife, T.R. was on the stump making pronouncements about what he would have done when the Germans marched into Belgium had he been President. On August 6th President Wilson burst into tears as his doctor informed him his wife had died.

During the summer rumors had been circulating that Anthony Comstock would not be reappointed special agent of the postal authorities and might also lose his post as head of the Society for the Suppression of Vice. *Harper's Weekly* dedicated the poem "The Passing of St. Anthony" to him with the closing verse: *For 'tis no more than fair to say: Each one of you has played his part— Each done his best in his own way—To popularize the Nude in Art.*

A few years earlier, Comstock had staged a raid on the famous Art Students League. He seized the League's magazine, *The American Student of Art*, and arrested the League's bookkeeper. The magazine had contained reproductions of nudes done by the students. Comstock's contention was that nudity was all right in its acknowledged place, the studio, but not all right prowling around in the public streets or in the home where it might suggest impure thoughts. Comstock argued: *Wild animals are all right in their cages, but when they break out they must be suppressed.* After this episode he had condemned the paintings, "Goose Girl" by Millet and "September Morning" by Chabas. He tried to prevent the publication of an official report on prostitution and arrested a child for selling postcards depicting couples dancing the tango that same year.

But he was not deposed, as *Harper's Weekly* had expected. He retained both his leadership of the Society for the Suppression of Vice and his office as agent of the Post Office. When the husband of Margaret Sanger gave a Comstock agent Mrs. Sanger's book on birth control, *Family Limitation*, he was immediately arrested. Comstock took the leading role in his conviction. With her husband in prison, Margaret Sanger, a former nurse, made plans to open a birth-control clinic. When it opened the following year, she, too, was arrested.

Emma Goldman immediately stepped into the gap and mixed frank and open birth-control discussion with her antiwar lectures. She also spoke on free love and the most tabooed subject of the day, homosexuality. Her own comrades tried to stop her from treading on such an unnatural theme, as anarchists were already considered depraved. But to Emma *it made me surer of myself and more determined to plead for every victim, be it one of social wrong or of moral prejudice. The men and women who used to come to see me after my lectures on homosexuality, and who confided to me their anguish and their isolation, were often of finer grain than those who had cast them out. Most of them had reached an adequate understanding of their differentiation only after years of struggle to stifle what they had considered a disease and a shameful affliction. One woman confessed to me . . . she had never met anyone who suffered from a similar affliction, nor had she ever read books dealing with the subject. My lecture had set her free; I had given her back her self-respect. In trying to cure her 'disease' she had nearly gone insane. This woman was only one of the many who sought me out. Their pitiful stories made the social ostracism of the invert seem more dreadful than I had ever realized before. To me anarchism was not a mere theory for a distant future; it was a living influence to free us from inhibitions, interna-*

The official position set by President Wilson was of neutrality.

no less than external, and from the destructive barriers that separate man from man.

Years later Freud wrote to a despairing mother in America: *I gather from your letter that your son is a homosexual. I am most impressed by the fact that you do not mention this term yourself in your information about him. May I question you, why you avoid it? Homosexuality is assuredly no advantage, but it is nothing to be ashamed of, no vice, no degradation, it cannot be classified as an illness; we consider it to be a variation of the sexual function produced by a certain arrest of sexual development.*

At the time he wrote that letter, Freud was seventy-nine years old. But now, in 1914, Freud was fifty-eight years of age and a pacifist, and his native Austria had just declared war on the Serbians. Instead of reacting with horror, Freud proved to have the boyish outlook of a T.R. He announced: *for the first time in thirty years I feel like an Austrian.* When Freud learned Germany was going to join Austria in the coming madness, he wrote: *I should be with it with all my heart if only I could think England would not be on the wrong side.* He wrote to his brother Alexander: *All my libido is given to Austro-Hungary.* Three weeks and a few crushing defeats of the Austrians by the Serbs in Galicia later, his enthusiasm waned. When German boots marched to Austria's aid, he

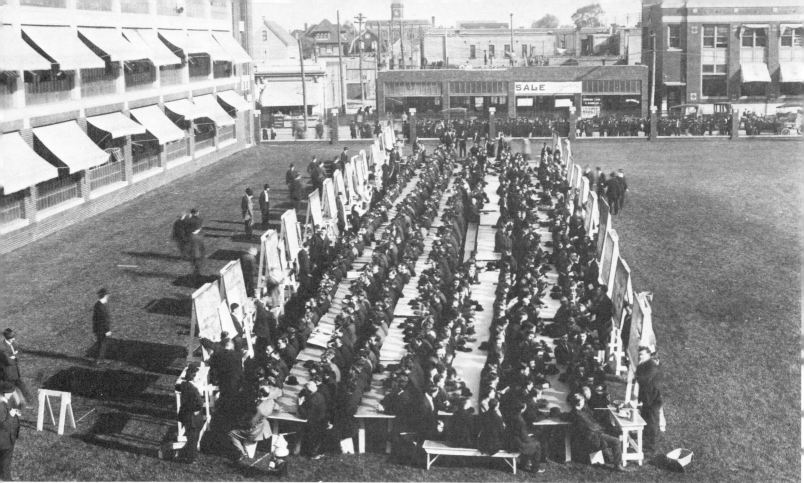

Equal opportunities for all.
Outdoor English lessons at
Ford's Highland Park plant.

commented: *Germany has already saved us.*

Freud seemed proud when his two sons were taken into the army. One advanced to lieutenant, the other was made a cadet. His favorite sister, Rosa, saw her son taken, too. That summer, on the Italian front, Rosa's only son was killed and Freud had reason to consider Lord Kitchener's prediction of a war of three years' duration. It was not to be a matter of weeks and a few men sacrificed. The Austria of fifteenth-century Ferdinand III and his son Maximilian had all but been forgotten. At that time, father and son had increased the holdings of their dynasty through a series of arranged marriages. Their motto: *Let others wage war; thou happy Austria, marry.*

The headline of the *Detroit News* an-

nounced: **WORKERS GET TEN MILLION OF FORD'S PROFITS THIS YEAR: 26,500 WILL SHARE.** A subhead ran: *Hours of labor shortened to provide work for thousands more in plant.*

In February of 1915, in celebration of the opening of the Panama Canal, the Panama-Pacific Exposition opened in San Francisco. The stellar attraction that had crowds lining up was a replica of Henry Ford's new Highland Park assembly lines. It was the public's introduction to mass production. Ford's ideas, inventions and developments were unpatented, to be shared for the asking. For nine months the Exposition assembly line operated three hours a day and turned out twenty newly assembled Model-Ts a day.

In Ford plants some employees wore

The 1912 model T with its creator at the wheel.

badges. There were no titles; Ford did not believe in them. The badges announced in some cases "light work only," or simply "blind." Ford had decided his employment gates would not be selective because "somebody had to do it." There was no color barrier; criminals, the lame and the halt were all given equal opportunities. Open-air English lessons were held for those who could not speak the language. After lowering the work day, he raised the pay of the workers and announced they would share in the profits. The basis of the sharing was not on work done in the plant but on need and good citizenship in the community. Ford insisted he was not just out to make cars and profits; he wanted to make men. To lower profits, he reduced the cost of the car. He then sold more cars and reduced the cost again, until he realized his dream of a work force able to afford his car. The price had come down from nine hundred dollars to three hundred and sixty dollars. Singlehanded, Ford had reduced the gap separating the lives of the wealthy from those of the worker. Now, in 1915, he refused to take part in the arms race.

Although President Wilson had called upon the American people to exercise the strictest neutrality of thought as well as deed, his government did not follow this advice. When England announced a blockade of Germany, the U.S. ceased all trade with that country and recognized the blockade without protest. America's actions toward its English-speaking cousins were different. The London *Times*, perhaps to provoke Germany, printed the following editorial: **AMERICA AND THE ALLIES:** *The American people as a whole have given the Allies an assistance which is recognized with gratitude by us and angrily resented by the enemy. They have lavishly supplied us with arms, with muni-*

"Neutral! When you are supplying enemies of ours with rifles, guns, ammunition, and selling none to us!"—Admiral von Tirpitz.

tions, with equipment, with stores, with provisions for our armies. . . .

In Vienna Freud was suffering from frostbite of the hands and had gone days without food. In Germany Mrs. William Bullitt, whose husband was an official in the American Embassy in Berlin, noted the suffering of the average German: *The rains continue. In some sections of the country the peasants are paddling around their potato fields in boats trying to save a portion of their crops . . . if the rain continued, there would be no food left. Yesterday, when I was coming home, my tram was halted by a marching regiment. The band at its head was playing; each soldier wore a bunch of flowers in his belt, and by this token one knew they were bound for the front. . . . Four women in my tram began to sob. . . . The men were not even of my people, but the hideous, tragic foolishness of the thing this swinging column symbolized, and the sorrow of the weeping women near me, brought the hot tears smarting to my eyes.*

The Germans, in desperation, decided to take a great risk: they would try to stop supplies from reaching Britain. Although France and England had flotillas of submarines by 1900, Admiral von Tirpitz had opposed them for the German Navy on the grounds they were defensive weapons. In 1905 the Krupp works produced the Karp class submarine and the gyroscopic compass had by then been perfected. But the Germans did not have the engine they were seeking until 1913. They then built ten submarines with Diesel engines. They soon ordered an additional seventeen. Churchill felt secure—the English had a fleet of fifty-five subs; the French had seventy-seven, although they were smaller boats. Once the war started, the Germans secretly fitted out their larger subs with surface guns. It was cheaper to sink a small freighter with guns than with the precious few torpedos carried on each sub. On the 4th of February, 1915, the Kaiser released an order to sink commercial vessels around the British Isles. The United States protested for some of its citizenry still wintered abroad.

Admiral von Tirpitz was interviewed by the former Senator from Indiana, Albert Beveridge, now a journalist. When Beveridge explained that Americans were impartial and neutral as President Wilson had requested, von Tirpitz exploded: *Neutral? When you are sending provisions to Eng-*

land, France, Russia and none to us! Neutral! When you are supplying enemies of ours with rifles, guns, ammunition, and selling none to us! When Beveridge mentioned the rumors of a submarine blockade of England, von Tirpitz rose to his full six feet and asked: *Why not? England is trying to starve us. She could not do that if we did not get a pound of provisions from other countries! But she is trying to do so. Are we not to retaliate? Why is it that whatever England does seems all right to Americans, while they object to anything Germany does of the same kind?*

Anthony Drexel had sailed from his home in England on the *Lusitania*, pride of the Cunard line. In America he spent time with his relative, Elizabeth Drexel Lehr, and her husband Harry. Suddenly, Elizabeth wanted to do something for the French war victims, perhaps help Anne Morgan, J. Pierpont's daughter, who had as a child announced she would never be a rich fool. She was now running the Comité Américain des Régions Dévastées in Paris. Or Elizabeth could help Mrs. W. K. Vanderbilt in her hospital of the American Ambulance. Mrs. Vanderbilt climbed the steep staircases six or seven times a day leaving the elevators for the wounded. To Elizabeth's surprise, Harry readily agreed it would be a good thing to help out. They would return with Anthony Drexel. But Harry refused to sail on a ship not under the United States flag. Drexel canceled his return booking on the *Lusitania*. They then sailed on the American liner, *New York*.

Before the return trip of the *Lusitania* for England, warnings were placed in New York papers advising passengers against sailing on ships belonging to enemies of Germany. Individuals proposing to sail on the *Lusitania* re-

Miss Anne Morgan, who once said she would not grow up to be a rich fool, headed the Committee on American Funds for French Wounded Soldiers.

Mrs. W. K. Vanderbilt, at work in her hospital of the American Ambulance in France.

ceived letters urging them not to do so from German officials. The Cunard people admitted that the *Lusitania* on one trip, when threatened, had raised the flag of the United States. They justified the use of the neutral flag under such circumstances. But this vessel was faster than any submarine the English knew of; it was capable of doing twenty-five knots for twenty-four hours at a time. The *Lusitania* had been built to wrest the transatlantic speed record from the Germans, and had done so on September 13th. But her triumph brought foreboding to seafaring men as September 13th had been a Friday.

As the *Lusitania* neared the coast of Ireland, Captain Walther Schwieger was scanning the horizon from the conning tower of his submarine with his powerful binoculars. He wrote in the ship's log: *Ahead and to starboard four funnels and two masts of a steamer with course perpendicular to us come into sight. Ship is made out to be a lar[ge] passenger steamer. We submerged to a dep[th] of eleven meters and went ahead at full spe[ed] taking a course converging with the one of the steamer hoping it might change its cour[se] to starboard, along the Irish coast.* Passenge[rs] on the deck of the *Lusitania* had crowded t[he] rail to look at the coast of the Emerald Isle, glistening and green in the midday sun. Th[e] Irish, struggling for their independence afte[r] seven hundred years of British rule, favore[d] the Germans in the war. Erskine Childers and his American wife had smuggled rifles from Germany on their yacht, the *Osgood,*

*"The steamer turns to starboard, takes course to
Queenstown, thus making possible an approach for
a shot."—From the log of Captain Schwieger's
submarine.*

to aid the Irish struggle. Roger Casement had been hung after returning to Ireland on a German submarine. But now the luncheon gong sounded and the passengers, including seven hundred Americans, filed into the vast dining room for the last meal of the voyage.

Captain Schwieger noted: *The steamer turns to starboard, takes course to Queenstown, thus making possible an approach for a shot.*

Many boats crowded come down head first, or stern first, in the water, and immediately fill and sink. Fewer lifeboats can be made clear on the port side, owing to the slant of the ship. The ship blows off. In the front appears the name Lusitania *in gold letters... It seems as if the vessel will be afloat only a short time, submerge to twenty-four meters and go to sea. I could not have fired a second torpedo into this throng of humanity attempting to save themselves.*

Cabinet trouble on either side of President Wilson. Secretary of State Bryan resigned because Wilson was too belligerent while Secretary of War Garrison, seated on the far side of Wilson, resigned because he thought the President too benign.

At three p.m., after running at top speed, the submerged craft was ahead of the *Lusitania* and in a position to fire a shot from seven hundred meters. Captain Schwieger described in his log the last moments of the liner: *The ship stops immediately and quickly heels to starboard, at the same time diving deeper at the bow. She had the appearance of being about to capsize. Great confusion aboard, boats being lowered to water....*

Theodore Roosevelt immediately called the sinking an act of piracy, but was contradicted from a New York pulpit by a minister who declared: *It is not piracy, for piracy had no government behind it. This is organized murder....* The minister reflected the distance Americans had traveled from neutrality when he closed with: *It is getting to be too much to ask America to keep out when Americans are drowned as part of a European war.* Three days later, in a speech in Philadelphia, Wilson announced America's intentions: *The example of America must be a special example. The example of America must be the example not merely of peace because it will not fight, but of peace because peace is the healing and elevating influence of the world and strife is not.*

Wilson's Secretary of State, William Jennings Bryan, believed Americans should not be permitted to travel on ships of the belligerent nations. When the President composed a strong note of protest over the sinking of the *Lusitania*, Bryan felt the tone was that of an ultimatum that could lead this country into the war. Rather than be a party to such an act, he resigned as Secretary of State. The Hearst papers lauded him for his act of conscience. Hearst's *American* declared: *Whether the* Lusitania *was armed or not, it was properly a spoil of war, subject to attack and destruction under the accepted rules of civilized warfare. . . . The* Lusitania *incident is, of course, no cause for a declaration of war.*

Teddy Roosevelt blasted out that America would earn *measureless scorn and contempt if we follow the lead of those who bleat to high heaven for peace when there is no peace.*

An editorial, signed by Hearst, declared the United States had no right to interfere or insist that Germany refrain from submarine warfare. On the surface it seemed that Hearst was on the same side as President Wilson, Emma Goldman, Eugene Debs and Henry Ford. Their motivations, however, were dissimilar.

Henry Ford, who had by now been called many things including "socialist" and "anarchist" because of his labor policies, announced he would dedicate his fortune and

T.R. in 1915 just as he cried, "Damn the mollycoddles!"

Ford announced he would dedicate his fortune and life to bring peace to the world. With him, Rosika Schwimmer and Louis Lochner.

life to securing peace in the world. Rosika Schwimmer, a lecturer on woman suffrage, birth control and peace, responded. She had already persuaded the International Congress of Women at The Hague to support her policy of mediation by neutrals and had gathered evidence showing the belligerents were open to mediation. However, Madame Schwimmer was a Hungarian and was considered an enemy by the Allies and an alien by Americans.

The woman who had presided over the International Congress of Women held at The Hague in 1915 was Jane Addams. A well-known pacifist, she had founded Hull House in Chicago and had been a pioneer in early welfare laws affecting labor, women and children. A few years before she had commented: *We may at last comprehend the truth of that which Ruskin had stated so many times, that we worship the soldier not because he goes forth to slay, but to be slain.* Now she was interested in Ford's efforts to secure peace in Europe.

Another respondent to Ford and his appeal for peace was the journalist Louis Lochner. An ardent pacifist, he had recently attended a meeting in Washington with President Wilson and the chairman of the Fifth International Peace Congress, David Jordan, who was also president of Stanford University.

Ford decided New York was the place to meet and sound out others on the concept of sending a neutral commission to Europe. On November 21st the group meeting in New York included Jane Addams, Ford, Rosika Schwimmer, Louis Lochner, Dean Kirchwey of Columbia University and Paul Kellogg of the Publication Survey. When Lochner suggested a special ship to take the peace commission to Europe, Ford jumped at it as something to arouse interest, something men could see and react to. For the same reasons Jane Addams objected: it was too flamboyant. But by that evening Ford had chartered the Scandinavian-American liner *Oscar II*. The next day they went to Washington and met with President Wilson. Ford offered to finance a

neutral peace commission if the President would appoint one. He explained their concept of a neutral commission of delegates from different countries involved in "continuous mediation." Wilson approved the idea but hedged—there might be a better idea. He must remain free and could not tie himself to one project. When they left, Ford remarked that the President had missed a great opportunity: *He's a small man.*

The group returned to New York and met with forty reporters at the Biltmore Hotel. Ford said, slightly abashed by the large turnout: *A man should always try to do the greatest good to the greatest number, shouldn't he? We're going to try to get the boys out of the trenches before Christmas. I've chartered a ship, and some of us are go-*

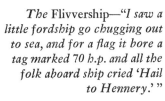

The Flivvership—*"I saw a little fordship go chugging out to sea, and for a flag it bore a tag marked 70 h.p. and all the folk aboard ship cried 'Hail to Hennery.'"*

Ford offered his friend Thomas Edison a million dollars to sail on his peace ship, but Edison turned a deaf ear to the offer.

ing to Europe. Ford went on to explain their weapon would be: *the longest gun in the world, the Marconi.* Aboard the Peace Ship would be Thomas Edison, Jane Addams, John Wanamaker, William Jennings Bryan and the biggest and most influential peace advocates in the country who could get away, Ford said.

The New York press went to work on Ford the next day. The *Tribune* announced: **FORD—EXPANSION AND CHALLENGE. GREAT WAR ENDS CHRISTMAS DAY. FORD TO STOP IT.** On the editorial page of the late Joseph Pulitzer's *World* appeared: **THE FLIVVERSHIP** ... *I saw a little ford-ship go chugging out to sea, and for a flag it bore a tag marked 70 h.p. and all the folk aboardship cried 'Hail to Hennery.' And so without a quiver the dreadful task they dare, of teaching peace to France and Greece and Teuron, Celt and Bear. Ho for the good ship*

Flivver, propelled by heated air! The *New York Herald* called the *Oscar* the cruelest joke of the century, and from the *Baltimore Sun* came the wish that William Jennings Bryan would captain the "ark" so that: *if a brutal German submarine should sink her nothing would be lost.*

One hundred and fifteen invitations went out from Ford to influential advocates of peace around the country. But there were now only nine days to sailing time, December 4th, and that must be departure time if Ford was to keep his promise to get the boys out of the trenches by Christmas, the birthdate of the Prince of Peace.

As the refusals began to pour in, Ford's own pastor, Dean Marquis, tried to dissuade him from going. Ford turned the tables on the earnest pastor: *It is right to try to stop war, isn't it?* Marquis could not deny it. *Well you have told me that what is right cannot fail.*

Thomas Edison informed Ford that he would not go and Ford replied to his old camping buddy: *you must, I'll give you a million dollars if you go.* But the founder of General Electric was partially deaf and could not hear the offer. It was repeated but Edison remained deaf to the entreaties of his friend. William Jennings Bryan came to the dock and informed Ford he would try to meet him at The Hague, but could not sail with him. Jane Addams became ill and remained at Hull House, but wired to Lochner to *keep the enterprise in hand.* She admired the motivations behind the Peace Ship venture, but was concerned by the reactions of the press to the slogans, the participants aboard ship and the attitudes of the entire group. Ford now appealed to former President Taft, and

Aboard ship, Ford was presented with two squirrels, Bryan and Ford, who would be happy amongst the "nuts."

to his camping friends John Burroughs and Luther Burbank, among other prominent Americans. Helen Keller wired she was with Ford in heart and soul, but she didn't go.

On the last night in New York Dean Marquis and Mrs. Ford argued well into the night trying to stop Henry from sailing. But in the morning, after withstanding every argument, he could not be deterred from his peace attempt. When asked by reporters on the shore for a last word to the public he said: *Tell the people to cry peace and fight preparedness.* Aboard ship, Ford was presented with two squirrels, Bryan and Ford, who would be happy among the "nuts."

As the *Oscar* pulled away from the dock, Lochner stood watching Ford while the crowds lining the pier cheered him on: *Again and again he bowed, his face wreathed in smiles that gave it a beatific expression. The magnitude of the demonstration, and many a strong man there was who struggled in vain against tears born of deep emotion, quite astonished and overwhelmed him. I felt then* *that he considered himself amply repaid for all the ridicule heaped upon him.*

At the same time, in 1915, the leader of the preparedness movement was T.R.'s old friend and former commanding officer at San Juan Hill, General Leonard Wood. Supported by private organizations, he conducted a training camp at Plattsburgh, New York. Businessmen, students and volunteers of all sorts received an abbreviated military preparedness course. Four of the first trainees were Roosevelts: Quentin, eighteen; Archibald, twenty-one; Kermit, twenty-six; and Theodore Jr., twenty-eight. It was during his visit at this time that Roosevelt announced that *the people should stand behind the President only when he was right!*

The shipboard list included sixty-seven delegates, thirty-six students, twenty-eight journalists, two photographers, twenty-three business staff and ten others. The press, whenever able, cornered Ford as their main quotable focal point. He was often baited: Don't you feel that this is a holy cause? *No. I don't*

Although President Wilson was still against the war or preparedness for war, T.R.'s old friend General Leonard Wood opened a preparedness camp and T.R.'s four sons attended. T.R. announced the people should stand behind the President—only when he was right!

know what you mean by "holy." Instead of a "holy" cause, I consider this expedition a people's affair. Are you not sailing with faith Yes. But it is faith in the people. I have absolute confidence in the better side of human nature. People never disappoint you if you trust them. Only three out of six hundred convicts in my factory have failed to make good.

Ford had hoped that his Peace Ship would drive preparedness from the front pages of the American mind. He now unlimbered his long gun, the Marconi, and sent peace exhortations to the leaders of all the belligerent nations. But on their third day at sea the peace people learned that President Wilson had delivered his message to Congress advocating preparedness with a plea that the standing army be increased.

The ship of peace was in troubled waters. The delegates, who had been about to sign a Declaration of Principles denouncing preparedness, now balked at going contrary to their President's wishes. Although all were ardent to see the war ended, most would not sign and the *Oscar* became a ship divided. Only the press was overjoyed; conflict meant news. The dove had flown the coop.

Mary Hopkins, one of the delegates, reappraised their position: *One-hundred-fifty everyday people have been brought face to face with a great idea, the thought of world disarmament. . . . A ship-of-fools crossed the Atlantic in 1492. A ship-of-fools reached Plymouth in 1620. Can it be that in this ship-of-common-fools, we bear the Holy Grail to the helping of a wounded world?* The entire delegation then repledged itself to peace by continuing mediation before the ship reached Norway.

When the *Oscar II* docked at an empty pier in Oslo, the temperature was twelve below zero. The weather and the reception were attuned. Ford, who had taken ill while at sea, went immediately from the boat to his hotel room and collapsed into bed. The Norwegian press praised Ford as a modern-day Tolstoy, but like the New York press, ridiculed the mission.

A few days later, as the delegates prepared to visit Sweden, Ford slipped away with Dean Marquis and sailed for home. There, Alton Parker, the 1904 Democratic candidate for the presidency, denounced Ford as: *a clown strutting on the stage for a little time.* Teddy Roosevelt, the Nobel Peace Prize winner, agreed with Parker and stuck in his own oar: *Mr. Ford's visit abroad will not be mischievous only because it is ridiculous.* T.R. continued to preach preparedness as the road to peace, while Emma Goldman continued to contradict him: *Ever since the beginning of the European conflagration, the whole human race almost has fallen into the deathly grip of the war anesthesis, overcome by the mad teeming fumes of a blood-soaked chloroform, which has obscured its vision and paralyzed its heart. Indeed, with the exception of some savage tribes, who know nothing of Christian religion or of brotherly love, and who also know nothing of dreadnaughts, submarines, munition manufacture and war loans, the rest of the race is under this terrible narcosis. The human mind seems to be conscious of but one thing, murderous speculation. Our whole civilization, our entire culture is concentrated in the mad demand for the most perfected weapons of slaughter. . . . Just like cattle, panic-stricken in the face of fire, throw themselves into the very flames, so all of the European people have fallen over each other into the devouring flames of the furies of war, and America, pushed to the very brink by unscrupulous politicians, by ranting demagogues and by military sharks, is preparing for the same terrible feat . . . the most dominant factor of military preparedness and the one which inevitably leads to war, is the creation of group interests, which consciously and deliberately work for the increase of armament whose purposes are furthered by creating the war hysteria. This group interest embraces all those engaged in the manufacture and sale of munitions and in military equipment for personal gain and profit. For instance, the family Krupp, which owns the largest cannon munition plant in the world; its sinister influence in Germany, and in fact in many other countries, extends to the press, the school, the church and to statesmen of highest rank. Shortly before the war, Karl Liebknecht, the one brave public man in Germany now, brought to the attention of the Reichstag that the family Krupp had in its employ officials of the highest military position, not only in Germany, but in France and in other countries. Everywhere its emissaries have been at work, systematically inciting national hatreds and antagonisms. The same investigation brought to light an international war supply trust who cares not a hang for patriotism, or for love of the people, but who uses both to incite war and to pocket millions of profits out of the terrible bargain. Militarism swallows the largest part of the national revenue. Almost nothing is spent on education, art, literature and science compared with the amount devoted to militarism in times of peace, while in times of war everything else is set at naught. . . . If for no other reason, it is out of surplus energy that militarism must act to remain alive; therefore, it will seek an enemy or create one artificially. In this civilized purpose and methods, militarism as sustained by the state, protected*

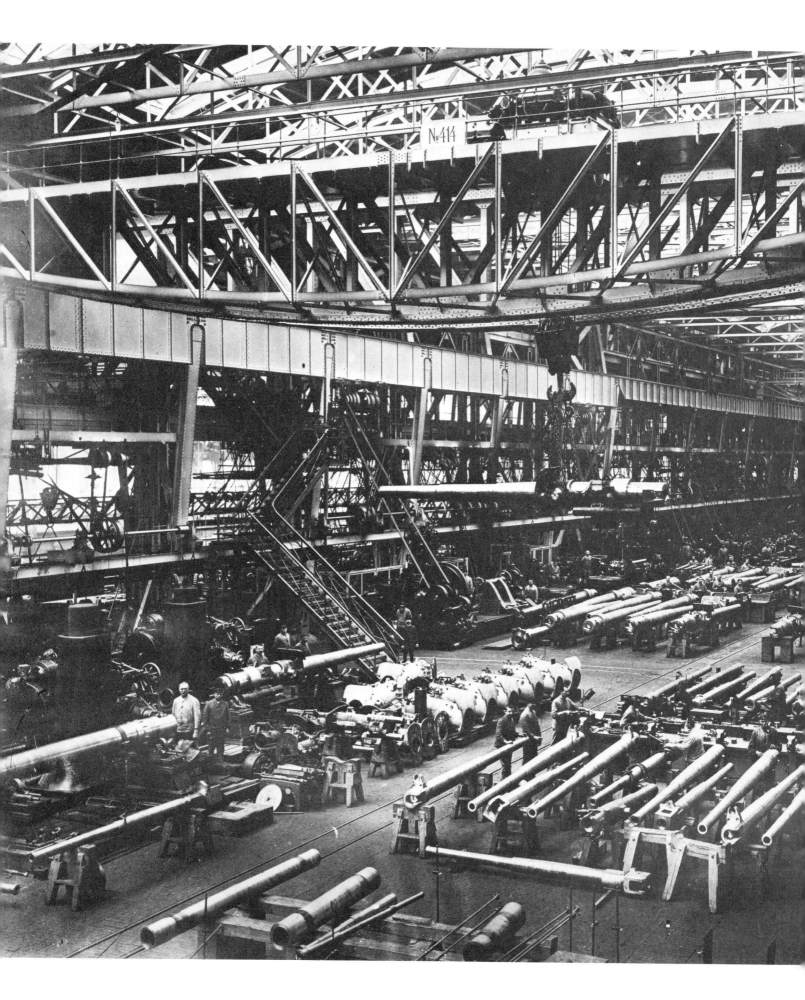

Krupp Works, Germany. "The human mind seems to be conscious of but one thing, murderous speculation."—Emma Goldman.

*Krupp Works 2. "Our whole civilization, our entire culture is concentrated in the mad demand for the most perfected weapons of slaughter."
—Emma Goldman.*

by the laws of the land, is fostered by the home and the school, and glorified by public opinion. In other words, the function of militarism is to kill. It cannot live except through murder.... Is America to follow suit, is it to be turned over to the American Krupps, the American military cliques? It almost seems so when one hears the jingo howls of the press, the blood and thunder tirades of bully Roosevelt....

At one of the meetings Henry Ford had attended in Norway he had tried to appease the munition makers Emma Goldman attacked as one of the major causes of war. Ford had invented a new tractor and announced to his astonished Norwegian audience that this revolutionary tractor would take the terrible drudgery out of farming.

The machine would be the drudge, instead of the man. He offered it to the armament manufacturers as a substitute for arms, suggesting they could make an even greater fortune from the tractor. He informed his spellbound listeners that the tractor was not patented. It was free to any manufacturer who wanted to copy it. Under Ford's continuing financial support, the emissaries of his Peace Ship traveled from neutral country to neutral country, securing delegates for "continuous mediation." With the new delegates, principles for a lasting peace were arrived at which included the right of self-determination, guarantees of freedom of the seas, parliamentary control of foreign policy and a league of nations to promote peaceful cooperation between nations and the peaceful settlement of disputes. They then issued an appeal to all belligerent nations for a peace conference. Only the Germans responded that they would be willing to negotiate. The Allies refused.

In December of 1916 President Wilson sent a message to each of the belligerents asking on what terms they would consider peace. The Germans agreed to confer; the Allies refused. When Wilson made his "Peace without Victory" speech, Ford felt the President was doing all that was possible to secure peace and terminated his support of the peace crusade.

Houdini's favorite actress, Bernhardt, the Divine Sarah, was performing in Ottawa at the time of her seventy-second birthday, October 23, 1916. When she arrived in New York for a month's engagement at the Knickerbocker Theatre in November, she was celebrated at the Metropolitan Opera House and presented with a bronze likeness by actor John Drew. In his presentation speech he handed her the statuette from "the actors and actresses of America." However,

when the Gorham Company could find no one to pay the three-hundred-fifty-dollar cost of the bronze, they sent the Divine Sarah the bill. Bernhardt then returned the statuette with a bristling note in French. Houdini learned of this and quickly sent his own three-hundred-and-fifty-dollar check to Gorham and asked that Mme. Bernhardt accept the bronze as a gift of the vaudeville artists of America. Her stay in New York was a success. Once again, she had captured the hearts of Gotham theater audiences, although she was now seventy-two and had had one leg amputated.

One of the most vociferous voices raised against the war was that of William Jennings Bryan. At a peace rally in New York he declared: *Some nation must lift the world out of the black night of war into the light of that day when peace can be made enduring by being built on love and brotherhood, and ours is the nation to perform the task.*

But in Europe death hung heavily over the

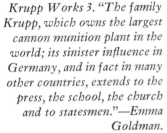

Krupp Works 3. "The family Krupp, which owns the largest cannon munition plant in the world; its sinister influence in Germany, and in fact in many other countries, extends to the press, the school, the church and to statesmen."—Emma Goldman.

Ford offered his new tractor to the munition-makers. More profits through peaceful endeavors.

land, shrouding the battlefields in a deep, dank mist. No man could live upon the fields, so both sides had dug beneath the ground and the lines of trenches went from the North Sea to the English Channel. Some were five hundred miles long, with no end. There was no flank to attack. Men and rats lived together until the shells whistled overhead. The shells announced an attack. First they would shell the guns behind the trench that was the target, then the trench itself. Then the men would come pouring out of their trenches five hundred yards away, bayonets fixed, and try to reach the enemy trench. The machine guns chattered at them and they fell and died and piled one atop the other until the burial of them produced trenches and mounds as long as those they had attacked. And if they reached the enemy trench and captured it, a counterattack launched similar to their attack gave it back to the enemy. No ground was gained, nor lost. Just the lives of men. At Verdun five hundred thousand French lay beside four hundred thousand Germans, strangers in a common death. In one day sixty thousand British lives were lost.

In America there were many who wanted to join the fun. Alan Seeger, Harvard 1910, got in. In a poem he wrote: *I have a rendezvous with Death . . . at some disputed barricade, When Spring comes back with rustling shade . . . And apple-blossoms fill the air . . . I have a rendezvous with Death.*

Although Seeger survived that Spring of 1916, Death found him on the 4th of July. He fell in a minor support attack for the coming Somme offensive. E.E. Cummings, John Dos Passos and Ernest Hemingway hurried over, joined the ambulance corps to drive the corpses in their race with death; Dos Passos watching troops moving up: *des-*

The Kaiser, speaking to von Hindenburg and Ludendorff, agreed to confer; the Allies said no.

peration in their eyes. But Dos Passos, the pacifist, also wrote: *the winey thought of death sings in the spring blood.* Now as they watched the officers of the ancient orders, they began to hate the pot-bellied middle-aged planned butcheries of the generals so full of suspicion that e.e. cummings was arrested, put in detention for three months because a friend had written to the notorious Emma Goldman, a threat to the livelihood of generals everywhere.

And when Wilson sent messages asking the belligerents the aim of their fighting, no one answered. Yet America wanted to join the fun, if you listened to the loudest voices. But now in St. Louis, at the national Democratic convention, there was hope. The name William Jennings Bryan brought the thousands of delegates to their feet, cheering. Bryan smiled, through tears, happy they were cheering not the man, but the ideal of peace. Wilson had kept them out so far, and they chose him again. And when the nation had to decide between Charles Evans Hughes and Wilson, the Democrats ran ads to show

*Ambulance driver
E. E. Cummings.*

what the choice meant:

> You Are Working—Not Fighting!
>   Alive and Happy—Not Cannon
>   Fodder!
> Wilson and Peace with Honor?
>   or Hughes with Roosevelt and
>   War?
> The people chose Wilson and peace.

The Kaiser had given assurances to President Wilson that commercial vessels would not be sunk without warning, and because of the American protests had cut down the number of submarines on order. But even with the rules requiring that all hands of a doomed ship be transferred safely to lifeboats before sinking of the ship, the German subs had taken a heavy toll. In five months the average number of ships sunk was thirty-seven. Then, in March, more than a hundred British ships went down. Even Winston Churchill worried: *I watched with a fear*

that I never felt at any other moment of tha. struggle, the deadly upward movement of the curve of sinkings over the arrival of new construction.

But by September of 1916 the situation fo the Germans was also becoming desperate. The American Ambassador in Berlin, Jame Gerard, noted: *As these people get desperat the submarine question gets deeper and deeper under the skin. I really think that it i only a question of time. . . . The hate of America grows daily, if indeed it is possible to be greater. . . .*

Freud wrote to a friend referring to the tobacco which he loved: *for my part it is th only excuse I know for Columbus' misdeed. In another letter, he expressed his depression over events: since we can only regard the highest civilization of the present as disfigur. by a gigantic hypocrisy, it follows that we are organically unfitted for it. We have to abdicate, and the Great Unknown, He or It lurking behind Fate, will sometime repeat*

John Dos Passos.

Ernest Hemingway.

such an experiment with another race. In another note: *I know for certain that I and my contemporaries will never again see a joyous world.*

The one time Freud had felt encouraged was when Wilson had requested that the belligerents state their essential war aims. Now he wrote to a friend: *I believe that if the submarines do not dominate the situation by September, there will be in Germany an awakening from illusions that will lead to frightful consequences.* He also wrote: *My Mother will be eighty-three this year and is no longer very strong. I sometimes think I shall feel a little freer when she dies, for the idea that she might have to be told that I have died is a terrifying thought.* By now he had completely turned around in his thoughts on the war: *I suppose we have to wish for a German victory and that is (1) a displeasing idea, and (2) still improbable.* He began to feel there would be no peace until the Americans arrived.

In January of 1917 Count von Bernstorff notified the United States that zones had been established around the British Isles and in the Mediterranean Sea within which all ships carrying contraband for the enemy would be destroyed. One American vessel would be permitted to sail weekly in each direction. Ambassador von Bernstorff was handed his passport and diplomatic relations with Germany terminated on February 3rd. Wilson had not yet been inaugurated and still hoped for peace through "armed neutrality." Roosevelt said bluntly: *There is no question of "going to war." Germany is already at war with us.* Try as he might, everything including the Germans was stacked against Wilson. Only Hearst seemed to be for peace and nonintervention. Hearst attacked the Allies seventy-four times, defended the Ger-

mans seventeen times, and printed sixty-th..
antiwar pieces, according to a count by the
New York Tribune.

When in mid-March the Czar was over-
thrown in Russia, two thoughts struck Pres
ident Wilson. The Russian people, under
starvation conditions, had rebelled and wou
possibly force the withdrawal of Russia fro
the war. This would permit the Germans to
withdraw her troops from the east and
strengthen her struggle in the west. Althou
in the past he had been repelled when he
thought of joining the Allies because of the
autocracy of the Czar (which was even wo..
than his German cousin's), now America
would be fighting alongside democratic Be
gium, France and England. The opponents
would be imperial Austria-Hungary and ir
perial Germany. Although the President h
finally decided the only protection for Am
ican honor, safety and ideals was war, he
asked encouragement of his friend Colonel
House, who wrote in his diary: *I said it wa..
not as difficult a situation as many he had
already successfully met, but that it was on
for which he was not well fitted. . . . I
thought he was too refined, too civilized, to
intellectual, too cultivated not to see the in
congruity and absurdity of war. . . .*

By now the Germans had sunk eight
American ships. When President Wilson
finally asked Congress to recognize the rec
course of Germany to be an act of war
against the United States, he also said: *It is
fearful thing to lead this great peaceful peo
ple into war, into the most terrible and disastrous of all wars; civilization itself seems
be hanging in the balance. But the right is
more precious than the peace, and we shall
fight for the things which we have always
carried nearest our hearts—for democracy*

*Under starvation conditions, the Russians overthrew
the Czar, and Russia withdrew from the war.*

for the right of those who submit to authority to have a voice in their governments, for the right by such a concert of free peoples as shall bring peace and safety to all nations, and make the world itself at last free. To such a task we can dedicate our lives and our fortunes, everything that we are and everything that we have, with the pride of those who know that the day has come when America is privileged to spend her blood and her might for the principles that gave her birth and happiness and the peace which she has treasured. God help her, she can do no other.

Congress and the gallery stood and applauded the President, and as he left the capital, crowds on the street stood in the rain and applauded him. To one of his aides Wilson said quietly, his eyes filled with tears: *My message today was a message of death for our young men. How strange it seems to applaud that.*

EPILOGUE

On April 6, 1917, President Woodrow Wilson signed a Declaration of War against Germany, and before the ink was dry, Theodore Roosevelt was in the President's office. He pleaded with Wilson to permit him to lead a volunteer division in France against the Germans. Wilson was charmed by Teddy but refused his request on the grounds that T.R. was sixty years of age and intolerant of discipline. When nine weeks later General John J. "Blackjack" Pershing sailed for Europe with the First American Expeditionary Force, Roosevelt's four sons sailed with him. T.R. was challenged while speaking at a war rally as to why he wasn't "over there." At first he hesitated, then said softly: *I did my level best.* The crowd then cheered him and T.R., getting up steam, declared: *I have sent over my four boys, for each of whose lives I care a thousand times more than I care for my own. . . .* T.R.'s youngest son, Quentin, now twenty, became a fighter pilot and soon wrote home of the excitement of his first kill of a Boche: *All of a sudden his tail came up and he went into a spin.* A few months later, a headline said simply: **QUENTIN KILLED.** A heartbroken Teddy Roosevelt died six months later.

Houdini, who could escape anything, rushed to enlist, but failed to escape his age, forty-three. He was rejected and then threw himself into bond rallies and shows for servicemen. A new act was the pulling of five-dollar gold pieces from the air with a new twist: he tossed the coins to the dough boys about to ship overseas. He tossed out over fourteen hundred of the coins and for the first time refused publicity for a new "act."

Henry Ford could not believe Wilson would let America be drawn into the war. When she was, Ford announced: *I am a pacifist but perhaps militarism can be crushed only with militarism.* When he offered to produce whatever the government needed without a penny of profit, the press chided him, reminding the public of his recent pacifist "notions." In a few years Ford started a series of vicious anti-Semitic articles in his new publishing venture, the *Dearborn Independent.* He became a despot, hired gangsters to beat up union men and fought his son Edsel into his grave.

Emma Goldman formed the No-Conscription League with Alexander Berkman to inform the public of the menace of the Conscription Bill pending before Congress. Although they would not advise against registering for conscription, Emma Goldman and her League would defend and inform those who did as to their rights. At one meet

LEFT: *"I did my level best. I have sent over my four boys, for each of whose lives I care a thousand times more than I care for my own." Quentin became a boy again, excited over his first "kill." When he fell from the air, Teddy died six months later.*

Eugene Debs was also imprisoned for antiwar work and is shown at the Atlanta penitentiary on receiving notification of his nomination for President on the Socialist ticket, 1920. He received over a million votes.

ing over ten thousand persons attended, including policemen and soldiers, but Emma kept the peace. Both Emma Goldman and Alexander Berkman were arrested for their activities and sentenced to two years in prison and fined ten thousand dollars each. On their release, they were deported to Russia. There they found the "new" Russia as tyrannical as the Czarist regime they had originally escaped. Refused reentry into the United States, they lived in Nice, where Sasha finally took his life.

Woodrow Wilson went to Europe after the Allied victory to fight for the "Peace without Victory" he had pledged. He brought with him his Fourteen Point peace plan, which was ignored by Lloyd George and Clemenceau. His fight to get the United States into a League of Nations was defeated under the leadership of T.R.'s follower, Henry Cabot Lodge. Wilson finally suffered a breakdown, but continued on, feeling he had to work for acceptance of the League as *the only hope for mankind.* Even after suffering a stroke, he continued his fight! But in the 1920 elections Wilson and his dream of America in the League were defeated and Warren Harding became the new President.

Eugene Debs, the conservative union leader who had been arrested during the Pullman strike in Chicago, was arrested for his opposition to the war. He was convicted of violating the new Espionage Act and sentenced to ten years' imprisonment. From prison Debs ran for President in 1920 against Wilson and Harding and received over a million votes. Wilson said he would never let Debs out of jail, but Harding, after he was elected, released Debs and asked to meet him.

Rosika Schwimmer, the force behind Ford's Peace Ship, became Hungary's min-

First Lord of the Admiralty.

ister to Switzerland in 1918. In 1921 she moved to the United States and in 1927 applied for citizenship. When she replied she would not bear arms, her application was rejected. On reaching the Supreme Court, she again lost, although Justices Holmes and Brandeis dissented. When asked if she would kill a man, she had answered: *If it is a question of fighting, as much as I desire American citizenship, I would not seek the citizenship.*

Evelyn Nesbit tried to take her own life, unsuccessfully. She then moved to the West Coast and took up sculpture. In her memoirs she said Harry always meant to "get" Stanford White because of an incident that had taken place before he met her. She also confessed she had always loved Stanford White.

William Travers Jerome died in 1934 and was buried in the Jerome family vault at Greenwood Cemetery in Brooklyn. One large wreath bore a card reading: *Though we have been enemies I have always respected you.* The card was signed: *Harry K. Thaw.*

When Sigmund Freud received an invitation from Albert Einstein for an exchange of views on the question "Why war?" he replied: *I expected you to choose a problem lying on the borderland of the knowable....* Although Freud always advocated more freedom in love, he remained very much a prude with his colleagues, remonstrating with the irrepressible psychoanalyst Sándor Ferenczi: *I see that the differences between us come to a head in a technical detail which is well worth discussing. You have not made a secret of the fact that you kiss your patients....* Freud suffered through thirty-three operations on his jaw for cancer. At the age of seventy-nine, he was rescued from Austria, now in Nazi hands, by Ernest Jones, an English psychoanalyst and later Freud's biographer. His four elderly sisters, Paula, Rosa, Dolfi and Marie, were refused entry into France and were incinerated by the Nazis.

Franklin Delano Roosevelt, fifth cousin of Teddy R., tried to follow in his illustrious cousin's footsteps. While serving as Assistant Secretary of the Navy, a managerial job, F.D.R. tried for active duty or just to get into uniform. When he was finally permitted to visit naval bases and witness shellfire, he claimed he had seen action. Although at first he fought Tammany, he saw the light, made up and was soon their candidate.

Winston Churchill proved to be inadequate as Lord of the Admiralty and was removed from the job, although he protested that he lived for it. The one important thing he did do was go over some heads and give the go-ahead on an armed tractor idea. He gave the money and naval guns to be mounted on the tractors. When four hundred and fifty of these "tanks" led an attack at Amiens, General Ludendorff declared: *it was the black day of the German army in the history of the war*. Four hundred guns and twenty-eight thousand Germans were captured and the trench stalemate was over. The Kaiser, the man behind the European madness, escaped to Holland from Germany with the aid of the British Royal Family. He was invited back to Germany twenty years later by Adolf Hitler.

In the 1940s it was still possible to say: not even the names have changed.

Suffering, according to Freud, is nothing more than sensation. Therefore, suffering or

The British royal family helped the Kaiser escape to Holland. Twenty years later he was invited back, by Adolf Hitler.

pain only exists so far as we feel it. One of the most effective ways of bringing on pleasure and relief from suffering is through chemistry. Perhaps there is more to du Pont's slogan "Better Living Through Chemistry," than intended. Intoxication, drugs bring on pleasant sensations and cut off unpleasurable impulses.

The readiest safeguard from the suffering caused by human relationships is isolation, keeping oneself apart from other people. One has the option of withdrawal from society as addict or hermit. These are negative means and are useful in the alleviation of unpleasure. The better and more positive method, according to Freud, was to become a member of the human community and work for the common good with techniques provided by science. At the same time there were advocates of mystical means of achieving the same ends. By mastering the internal source of our needs, Yoga and the wisdom of the East built

a defense against suffering by killing off the instincts. Mary Baker Eddy announced there was no sensation in matter. Both religion and the negative defenses of the East were proscribed by Freud for killing the joy of the instincts and the higher civilization possible only by all men working for the human community. External suffering caused by nature is dealt with as best we are able. Internal suffering is also being dealt with. But where we have fallen down in our struggle for the alleviation of suffering is in the field of human relations. Perhaps when this negative aspect is dealt with, we will find joy not only in the ends but in the means as well. There is hope for mankind as long as man has not lost the ability to love.

GENERAL BOOKS

Brome, Vincent. *Freud and His Early Circle.* New York: William Morrow & Co., 1967.

Brown, Norman O. *Life Against Death.* Middletown, Conn.: Wesleyan University Press, 1959.

Costigan, Giovanni. *Sigmund Freud.* New York: The Macmillan Company, 1965.

Dobriansky, Lev E. *Veblenism.* Washington, D.C.: Public Affairs Press, 1967.

Dorfman, Joseph. *Thorstein Veblen and His America.* New York: The Viking Press, 1934.

Dowd, Douglas F. *Thorstein Veblen.* New York: Washington Square Press, Inc., 1964.

Eddy, Mary Baker. *Prose Works: Other than Science and Health with Key to the Scriptures.* Boston: Trustees under the Will of Mary Baker G. Eddy, 1925.

Ellis, Havelock. *Studies in the Psychology of Sex.* New York: Random House, 1936.

Glover, Mary Baker. *Science and Health with Key to the Scriptures.* Renewed by Mary Baker G. Eddy. Boston: 1903.

Heilbroner, Robert L. *The Worldly Philosophers.* New York: Simon and Schuster, 1972.

Hitler, Adolf. *Mein Kampf.* New York: Reynal & Hitchcock, 1939.

Jones, Ernest. *The Life and Work of Sigmund Freud.* New York: Basic Books, Inc., 1961.

Peary, R. E., U.S.N. *Nearest the Pole.* New York: Doubleday, Page & Company, 1907.

Riesman, David. *Thorstein Veblen.* New York: Charles Scribner's Sons, 1953.

Sievers, W. David. *Freud on Broadway.* New York: Hermitage House, 1955.

Veblen, Thorstein. *The Theory of Business Enterprise.* New York: Charles Scribner's Sons, 1904.

SOURCES

———. *The Theory of the Leisure Class*. New York: The Viking Press, 1899; Macmillan & Company, 1912.

Weinberg, Arthur, and Weinberg, Lila, eds. *Instead of Violence*. New York: Grossman Publishing, 1963.

Wilbur, Sibyl. *The Life of Mary Baker Eddy*. Boston: Christian Science Publishing Society, 1908, 1960.

POLITICS

Adams, James Truslow. *The March of Democracy*. Vol. 11. New York: Charles Scribner's Sons, 1933.

Brodie, Bernard, and Brodie, Fawn M. *From Crossbow to H-Bomb*. Bloomington: Indiana University Press, 1962.

Charnwood, Lord. *Theodore Roosevelt*. Boston: The Atlantic Monthly Press, 1923.

Corey, Lewis. *The House of Morgan*. New York: Grosset & Dunlap, Inc., 1930.

Garraty, John A. *Right-Hand Man*. New York: Harper & Brothers, 1960.

*Goldman, Emma. *Living My Life*. 2 vols. New York: Alfred Knopf; Dover ed., 1931.

Halstead, Murray. *Illustrious Life of William McKinley: Our Martyred President*. Chicago: The Memorial Publishing House, 1901.

Jantzen, Steven. *Hurrah for Peace, Hooray for War*. New York: Alfred Knopf, 1971.

* Lorant, Stefan. *The Life and Times of Theodore Roosevelt*. Garden City, N.Y.: Doubleday and Company, 1959.

Morison, Samuel Eliot. *The Oxford History of the American People*. New York: Oxford University Press, 1965.

Regier, C. C., and Smith, Peter. *The Era of the Muckrakers*. Chapel Hill: The University of North Carolina Press, 1932.

Tolstoy, L. *Tolstoy's Writings on Civil Disobedience and Non-Violence*. New York: Bergman Publishers, 1967.

Tuchman, Barbara W. *The Proud Tower*. New York: The Macmillan Company, 1966.

Wasserman, Harvey. *Harvey Wasserman's History of the United States*. New York: Harper & Row Publishers, 1972.

Wheeler, George. *Pierpont Morgan and Friends*. Englewood Cliffs, N.J.: Prentice-Hall, Inc., 1973.

SOCIETY

Amory, Cleveland. *The Last Resorts*. New York: Harper & Brothers, 1952.

———, and Bradlee, Frederic, eds. *Vanity Fair*. New York: The Viking Press, 1960.

Beard, Charles, and Beard, Mary. *A Basic History of the United States*. Garden City, N.Y.: Doubleday, Doran & Co., 1944.

———. *The Rise of American Civilization*. New York: The Macmillan Company, 1927.

Blesh, Rudi, and Janis, Harriet. *They All Played Ragtime*. New York: Oak Publishing, 1971.

Bok, E. *The Americanization of Edward Bok*. New York: Charles Scribner's Sons, 1923.

Brough, James. *Princess Alice*. Boston: Little, Brown and Company, 1975.

Churchill, Allen. *The Upper Crust*. Englewood Cliffs, N.J.: Prentice-Hall, Inc., 1970.

Comstock, Anthony. *Traps for the Young*. Cambridge, Mass.: The Belknap Press of Harvard University Press, 1967.

Galbraith, John Kenneth. *The Affluent Society*. Boston: Houghton Mifflin Company, 1958.

Gammond, Peter. *Scott Joplin and the Rag-

* Major contribution to research.

time Era. London: Angus & Robertson Ltd., 1975.

Gresham, William Lindsay. *Houdini: The Man Who Walked Through Walls*. New York: Henry Holt and Company, 1959.

Harvey, George. *Henry Clay Frick, the Man*. New York: Charles Scribner's Sons, 1928.

Kavaler, Lucy. *The Astors*. New York: Dodd, Mead & Company, 1966.

Langhorne, Elizabeth. *Nancy Astor and Her Friends*. New York: Praeger Publishers, 1974.

Lehr, Elizabeth Drexel. *King Lehr and the Gilded Age*. London: J. B. Lippincott Company, 1935.

Lerner, Max. *America as a Civilization*. New York: Simon and Schuster, Inc., 1957.

Lord, Walter. *The Good Years*. New York: Harper & Brothers, 1960.

Lundberg, Ferdinand. *Imperial Hearst*. New York: Equinox Cooperative Press, 1936.

Lynes, Russell. *The Art-Makers*. New York: Atheneum, 1970.

————. *The Tastemakers*. New York: Harper & Brothers, 1949.

Lyons, Eugene. *David Sarnoff*. New York: Harper & Row, 1966.

Morris, Lloyd. *Postscript to Yesterday*. New York: Harper & Row, 1947.

Nicolson, Nigel. *Portrait of a Marriage*. New York: Atheneum, 1974.

O'Connor, Richard. *The Golden Summers*. New York: G. P. Putnam's Sons, 1974.

Raph, Theodore. *The Songs We Sang*. New York: Castle Books, 1964.

Rheims, Maurice. *Flowering of Art Nouveau*. New York: Harry N. Abrams, Inc., 1961.

Steffens, Lincoln. *The Autobiography of Lincoln Steffens*. New York: Harcourt Brace Jovanovich, 1931.

Steinway, Theodore. *People and Pianos*. New York: Steinway & Sons, 1953.

Sullivan, Mark. *Our Times*. New York: Charles Scribner's Sons, 1935.

* Swanberg, W. A. *Pulitzer*. New York: Charles Scribner's Sons, 1967.

This Fabulous Century. New York: Time-Life Books, 1962.

* Weems, John Edward. *Peary: The Explorer and the Man*. Boston: Houghton Mifflin Company, 1967.

PREDOMINANTLY STANFORD WHITE

Andrews, Wayne. *Architecture in New York*. New York: Harper & Row, 1969.

* Baldwin, Charles C. *Stanford White*. New York: Dodd, Mead & Company, 1931.

Black, Mary. *Old New York in Early Photographs*. New York: Dover Publications–New-York Historical Society, 1973.

Goldstone, Harmon H., and Dalrymple, Martha. *History Preserved*. New York: Simon and Schuster, 1974.

Kouwenhoven, John A. *The Columbia Historical Portrait of New York*. New York: Doubleday & Company, Inc., 1953.

Langford, Gerald. *The Murder of Stanford White*. Indianapolis: The Bobbs-Merrill Company, 1962.

Nesbit, Evelyn. *Prodigal Days: The Untold Story*. New York: Julian Messner, 1934.

O'Connor, Richard. *Courtroom Warrior*. Boston-Toronto: Little, Brown and Company, 1963.

Tharp, Louise Hall. *Saint-Gaudens and the Gilded Era*. Boston: Little, Brown and Company, 1969.

PREDOMINANTLY PHILOSOPHY AND CONCEPT OF THAT ERA

Cowley, Malcolm. *A Second Flowering*. New York: The Viking Press, 1973.

Filler, Louis. *A Dictionary of American Social Reform*. New York: Philosophical Library, Inc., 1963.

Freud, Sigmund. *Civilization and Its Discontents*. James Strachey, ed. New York: W. W. Norton & Company, Inc., 1961. Originally published 1930.

Herndon, Booton. *Ford: An Unconventional Biography of the Men and Their Times*. New York: Weybright and Talley, Inc., 1969.

Mumford, Lewis. *The Condition of Man*. New York: Harcourt Brace Jovanovich, 1944.

* Nevins, Allan, and Hill, Frank Ernest. *Ford: Expansion and Challenge*. New York: Charles Scribner's Sons, 1957.

Rae, John B., ed. *Henry Ford*. Englewood Cliffs, N.J.: Prentice-Hall, 1960.

NEWSPAPERS, MAGAZINES, PERIODICALS

American Journal of Sociology
Baltimore Sun
Century Magazine
Chicago Tribune
Cincinnati Enquirer
Collier's
Cosmopolitan Magazine
Harper's Weekly
Indianapolis News
Ladies' Home Journal
Munsey's Magazine
The Nation
New York Evening Journal
New York Herald
New York Sun
The New York Times
New York Tribune
New York World (Morning)
Paris Herald
Pittsburgh Herald
Sears Roebuck Catalogues
Theatre Playbills
Vanity Fair
Washington Post
World Work

* Major contribution to research.

PICTURE CREDITS

The photographs in the book, which add so much to the work as a whole, appear through the kindness, interest and courtesy of the following sources:

The Bettmann Archive, New York City (BA)
Mrs. Cary Bok, Camden, Maine (CB)
Brown Brothers, Sterling, Pennsylvania (BB)
Clark University Archives, Worcester, Massachusetts (CU)
Culver Pictures, New York City (CP)
The Ford Archives, Dearborn, Michigan (FA)
The Frick Collection, New York City (FC)
The Metropolitan Museum of Art, New York City (MMA)
The Morgan Library, New York City (ML)
Museum of the City of New York (MCNY)
New-York Historical Society, New York City (NYHS)
The Theodore Roosevelt Collection, Harvard College Library, Cambridge, Massachusetts (TRC)
Saint-Gaudens National Historic Site, Cornish, New Hampshire (SG)
The Waldorf-Astoria, New York City (WA)
Mrs. Lawrence White, St. James, New York (LW)
The Whitney Museum of American Art (Flora Irving), New York City (WM)

All others are from the collection of the author—(WF).

ii: WF; iv: left BB, right BA; v: left WF, top SG, bottom CP; x–1: CP; 2–3: MCNY; 4–5: CP; 8: NYHS; 9: left NYHS, right SG; 10: upper CP, lower J. Clarence Davies Collection/MCNY; 11: left NYHS, center MCNY, upper right LW, lower right LW; 12: upper left LW, lower left SG, upper right SG, lower right CP; 13: BB; 14: upper BB, lower CP; 15: upper left WF, center BA, right WF; 16: BB; 17: MCNY; 18: WF; 21: MCNY; 22: BB; 23: BB; 24: BA; 25: Byron Collection/MCNY; 26: Music and Theatre Collection/MCNY; 27: Byron Collection/MCNY; 28: top BB, bottom MCNY; 29: upper and center by Jacob A. Riis, Jacob A. Riis Collection/MCNY, lower right MCNY; 30: TRC; 31: TRC; 32: MCNY; 32–33: centerfold MCNY; 33: NYHS; 35: by Jacob A. Riis, Jacob A. Riis Collection/MCNY; 36: BB; 37: BB; 38: MCNY; 39: BB; 40: CB; 41: BB; 42: BB; 43: upper CP, left CP, right BB; 44: left TRC, upper right WF, lower right TRC; 45: MCNY; 46: left Jacob A. Riis Collection/MCNY, right MCNY; 47: BB; 50: MCNY; 51: CP; 52: WA; 53: CP; 54: left CP, upper right BB, lower right CP; 55: BB; 56: BB; 57: TRC; 58: TRC; 59: TRC; 60: BB; 62–63: MCNY; 65: MCNY; 67: lower left TRC, upper right BB; 68: upper left TRC, lower right MCNY; 69: TRC; 71: BB; 72: BB; 73: BB; 74: CP; 75: BB; 77: TRC; 78: lower left TRC, upper MCNY, right MCNY; 79: BB; 80: BA; 81: WF; 82: upper left BB, lower right CP; 85: upper left BB, upper right SG, lower right SG, lower left MCNY; 87: BB; 88: MCNY; 89: upper BA, lower BB; 90: upper TRC, lower SG; 91: BB; 92: WF; 95: left WF, right TRC; 96: TRC; 97: MMA; 98: TRC; 99: WF; 100: upper Byron Collection/MCNY, lower CP; 101: lower CP, upper BB; 102: BB; 104: CP; 105: upper Alfred Stieglitz Collection, 1933/MMA, lower BB; 106: MCNY; 108: CP; 109: CP; 110: WA; 111: BB; 112: MCNY; 114: upper left and right ML, lower right BB; 115: upper MCNY, lower TRC; 116: MCNY; 117: MCNY; 119: WF; 121: TRC; 122: BB; 123: WF; 124: upper right BB, lower left MCNY; 125: left NYHS, upper right and lower right MCNY; 126: FC; 127: upper ML, lower FC; 128: left BB, right LW; 129: BB; 130: left BA, right NYHS; 131: BA; 133: MCNY; 134: BB; 135: BB; 138: LW; 140: BB; 142: CP; 143: upper CP, lower BB; 144: NYHS; 145: BB; 146: CP; 147: BA; 149: upper MCNY, lower BB; 150: left MCNY, right WF; 151: NYHS; 152: WM; 153: CP; 154: CU; 155: TRC; 156: TRC and Moffett Studio–Chicago; 157: BB; 158–59: MCNY; 160: FA; 162: BB; 163: BB; 165: upper BA, lower BB; 168: TRC; 169: upper TRC, lower MCNY; 171: upper TRC, lower MCNY; 172: BB; 173: TRC; 174: BA; 176: CP; 177: MCNY; 178: BB; 179: BB; 180: BB; 181: TRC; 182: TRC; 183: ML; 184–85: BB; 186: left BB, right CP; 187: BB; 188: left MCNY, right BA; 189: MCNY; 190: WF; 192: MCNY; 194: TRC; 196–97: TRC; 198: WF; 199: BB; 200: BB; 201: BB; 202: BB; 205: BB; 206: FA; 207: BA; 208: BB; 209: BB; 210: BB; 211: CP; 212: BB; 213: TRC; 214: FA; 215: FA; 216: BA; 217: FA; 218: TRC; 220–21: BB; 222: BB; 223: BB; 224: FA; 225: BB; 226: BB; 227: BB; 228: BB; 229: BB; 230: MCNY; 231: BB; 232: BB; 233: BB; 234: TRC.